Essential law for information professionals

Paul Pedley

facet publishing

© Paul Pedley 2003, 2006

Published by
Facet Publishing
7 Ridgmount Street
London WC1E 7AE

Facet Publishing is wholly owned by CILIP: the Chartered Institute of Library and Information Professionals.

Paul Pedley has asserted his right under the Copyright Designs and Patents Act 1988 to be identified as the author of this work.

First published 2003
This second edition 2006

British Library Cataloguing in Publication Data
A catalogue record for this book is available from the British Library.

ISBN-13: 978-1-85604-552-0
ISBN-10: 1-85604-552-8

Typeset in Aldine 401 and Humanist 521 by Facet Publishing.
Printed and made in Great Britain by MPG Books Ltd, Bodmin, Cornwall.

Dedication

This book is dedicated to the memory of Justin Arundale. During what was then The Library Association's Members' Day 2001, Justin approached me about jointly authoring a book on essential law for information professionals, and so this was very much his idea. Tragically Justin died on 12 September 2002. I would very much like to record my thanks to him for his help, advice and encouragement in the early stages of working on the book, and I missed the opportunity that we would otherwise have had of being able to continue that exchange of ideas and thoughts about a topic that both of us found to be so interesting.

Disclaimer

Paul Pedley is not a lawyer and is not able to give legal advice. The contents of this book are intended to raise awareness of key legal issues affecting information professionals, but the book does not constitute legal advice and should not be relied upon in that way.

Copyright notice

Contents

List of figures and tables

Copyright

Table

Data protection

Freedom of information

The Information Commissioner

Re-use of public sector information

Breach of confidence and privacy

Contracts and licensing agreements

Cybercrime and computer misuse

Disability discrimination

Human rights

Legal deposit

Table of statutes, etc.

Acts of Parliament

Statutory Instruments

International treaties and conventions

European directives

European regulations

European decisions

COM DOCS (COM Documents are working documents of the European Commission)

*At the time of writing, not yet published in *Official Journal* and therefore had no directive number.

Table of cases

Abbreviations

ALCS	Authors Licensing and Collecting Society
APIG	All Party Internet Group
APPSI	Advisory Panel on Public Sector Information
ASA	Advertising Standards Authority
BAILII	British and Irish Legal Information Institute
BBC	British Broadcasting Corporation
CA	Court of Appeal
CAP	Committee of Advertising Practice
CAUCE	Coalition Against Unsolicited Commercial E-mail
CCTV	Closed Circuit Television
CDPA	Copyright Designs and Patents Act 1988
CEHR	Commission for Equality and Human Rights
CILIP	Chartered Institute of Library and Information Professionals
CIPD	Chartered Institute of Personnel and Development
CIQM	Centre for Information Quality Management
CLA	Copyright Licensing Agency
CMA	Computer Misuse Act
CMLR	Common Market Law Reports
CPS	Crown Prosecution Service
CPU	Central Processing Unit
DACS	Design Artists Copyright Society
DCMS	Department for Culture, Media and Sport
DDA 1995	Disability Discrimination Act 1995
DDA 2005	Disability Discrimination Act 2005
DoS	Denial of Service
DPA	Data Protection Act 1998
DPP	Director of Public Prosecutions
DRC	Disability Rights Commission
DSA	Direct Selling Association
EBLIDA	European Bureau of Library, Information and Documentation Associations
EBLR	European Business Law Review
ECDR	European Copyright and Design Reports
ECHR	European Convention on Human Rights
ECJ	European Court of Justice

ECMS	Electronic Copyright Management Systems
ECR	European Court Reports
ECUP	European Copyright Users Platform
EEA	European Economic Area
EIIA	European Information Industry Association
EIPR	European Intellectual Property Review
EIR	Environmental Information Regulations
EIRENE	European Information Researchers Network
ERO	Electoral Registration Officer
EU	European Union
EuroCAUCE	European Coalition Against Unsolicited Commercial E-mail
FAQs	Frequently Asked Questions
FOIA	Freedom of Information Act 2000
FOI(S)A	Freedom of Information (Scotland) Act 2002
FSR	Fleet Street Reports
GCHQ	Government Communications Headquarters
HMSO	Her Majesty's Stationery Office
HRA	Human Rights Act 1998
HREOC	(Australia's) Human Rights and Equal Opportunities Commission
ICANN	Internet Corporation for Assigned Names and Numbers
ICO	Information Commissioner's Office
ICOLC	International Coalition of Library Consortia
ICSTIS	Independent Committee for the Supervision of Standards of Telephone Information Services
IFLA	International Federation of Library Associations
IFPI	International Federation of the Phonographic Industry
IFTS	Information Fair Trader Scheme
IPR	Intellectual Property Rights
ISP	Internet Service Provider
ITC	Independent Television Commission
JISC	Joint Information Systems Committee
LACA	Libraries and Archives Copyright Alliance
LCD	Lord Chancellor's Department
LDLA	Legal Deposit Libraries Act 2003
LISU	Library and Information Statistics Unit
MPA	Music Publishers Association
MPAA	Motion Picture Association of America
MSP	Member of the Scottish Parliament

NA	Narcotics Anonymous
NESLI	National Electronic Site Licence Initiative
NHS	National Health Service
NLA	Newspaper Licensing Agency
OECD	Organization for Economic Co-operation and Development
OFT	Office of Fair Trading
OPAC	Online Public Access Catalogue
OPSI	Office for Public Sector Information
PA	Publishers Association
PCA	Press Clippings Agency
PII	Professional Indemnity Insurance
PLS	Publishers Licensing Society
PRO	Public Record Office
PSIH	Public Sector Information Holder
RFID	Radio Frequency Identification
RIPA	Regulation of Investigatory Powers Act 2000
RPC	Reports of Patent Cases
RSS	Really Simple Syndication
RUSA	Reference and User Services Association
SCIP	Society of Competitive Intelligence Professionals
SENDA	Special Educational Needs and Disability Act 2001
SIS	Secret Intelligence Service
SMS	Short Message Service
SPO	Statutory Publications Office
TLR	Times Law Reports
TRIPS	Trade Related Aspects of Intellectual Property Rights
TSO	The Stationery Office
UCC	Universal Copyright Convention
UDRP	Uniform Domain Name Dispute Resolution Policy
UKOLUG	UK Online User Group
UKOP	United Kingdom Official Publications (a product published by TSO)
UNESCO	United Nations Educational, Scientific and Cultural Organization
URL	Uniform Resource Locator
VAT	Value Added Tax
VDU	Visual Display Unit
WIPO	World Intellectual Property Organization
WTO	World Trade Organization

Glossary

Acquis communitaire – the body of EU law (or Community legislation).

Civil law – has a number of different meanings. Civil law, in contrast to criminal law, deals with disputes between individuals or organizations. The state's role is simply to provide the means by which they can be resolved.

    The phrase 'civil law' is also used within the context of the legal system, when in contrast to the common law system. The civil law system is used by most of continental Europe and parts of Latin America, and in this system the law is written down in statutes in a very logical and organized (codified) way across all subject areas. In such systems, precedent (from judicial decisions) is not normally recognized as a source of law, although it can be used as a supplementary source.

Common law – English law is called common law because it aims to be the same, whichever court makes a decision. The common law system is based on the principle of deciding cases by reference to previous judicial decisions (known as 'precedent'), rather than by reference to written statutes drafted by legislative bodies.

Computer misuse – could be used to refer to a wide range of activities including: accessing inappropriate material on the internet, such as pornographic material; inappropriate use of e-mail, hacking, spreading viruses, fraud, theft, copyright abuse or the use of a computer to harass others.

Computer programs – includes programs in any form, including those which are incorporated into hardware, and also includes preparatory design work leading to the development of a computer program provided that the nature of the preparatory work is such that a computer program can result from it at a later stage.

Contract – an agreement between two or more parties. It creates a legally binding obligation upon the parties involved. It is a promise or set of promises which the law will enforce.

Criminal law – the branch of law which defines crimes and fixes punishments for them.

    A crime is an offence where the state acts against the individual in order to defend a collective interest. Punishments for crimes are fines, probation, community service or a prison sentence.

Cybercrime – defined by the British police as the use of any computer network for crime. In the Council of Europe's Convention on Cybercrime it is defined as 'criminal offences committed against or with the help of computer networks'.

Cybersquatting – the deliberate registration of a domain name knowing that it is a name used by an existing party.

Defamation – the act of damaging the reputation of another by means of false and malicious communications, whether written or spoken.

Delict – a wilful wrong, similar to the common-law concept of tort.

Denial of service attacks – occur when massive quantities of otherwise normal messages or page requests are sent to an internet host, with the result that the server is overloaded, is unable to deal with legitimate requests and in effect becomes unavailable.

Droit de suite ('Artists resale right') – a right which entitles authors and their successors in title to a percentage of the sale price, net of tax, whenever original works of art, in which copyright subsists, are re-sold in transactions involving art market professionals.

Interdict – a Scottish term for a temporary restraint.

Legal deposit – the legal requirement for publishers to deposit with the British Library and the five other legal deposit libraries.

Lending – making available for use for a limited period of time and not for direct or indirect economic or commercial advantage.

Libel – a written defamation.

Pharming – connecting to a PC with the intention of retrieving sensitive information and keystrokes, in order to trap login names and passwords.

Phishing – the fraudulent acquisition, through deception, of sensitive personal information such as passwords and credit card details, by masquerading as someone trustworthy with a genuine need for that information.

Precedent – the principle of deciding cases by reference to previous judicial decisions.

Prescribed library – the definition of prescribed library (as set out in Part A of Schedule 1 to The Copyright (Librarians and Archivists) (Copying of Copyright Material) Regulations 1989: SI 1989/1212) makes it clear that the library must be not for profit. The list set out in the Regulations includes:

- Public libraries
- National libraries
- Libraries of educational establishments
- Parliamentary or government libraries
- Local government libraries.

- 'Any other library conducted for the purpose of facilitating or encouraging the study of bibliography, education, fine arts, history, languages, law, literature, medicine, music, philosophy, religion, science (including natural and social science) or technology, or administered by any establishment or organization which is conducted wholly or mainly for such a purpose'.
- Any library outside the UK which exists wholly or mainly to encourage the study of the above subjects.

Rental – making available for use for a limited period of time and for direct or indirect economic or commercial advantage.

Slander – oral defamation, the use of the spoken word to injure another person's reputation.

Spoofed website – a website which is deliberately designed to look like a legitimate site, sometimes using components from the legitimate site.

Spyware – a category of malicious software which is designed to intercept or take over control of a PC's operation without the knowledge or consent of the computer user. The term is used to refer to software which subverts the computer's operation for the benefit of a third party.

Sui generis – a Latin term which literally means 'of its own kind or type', constituting a class of its own. In relation to database right it refers to the rights that were newly created in order to protect databases.

Tort – torts are essentially civil wrongs that provide individuals with a cause of action for damages in respect of the breach of a legal duty.

Walled gardens – internet portals where the operators guarantee the quality of the limited number of sites which can be accessed through them.

1 General law and background

1.1 Introduction

This chapter provides a brief introduction to the United Kingdom's legal system (1.2), contrasting the common law system (1.2.1) which operates in England and Wales with the civil law system (1.2.2) which is used in most of continental Europe. It then gives a brief overview of the civil and criminal courts (1.3) as well as other decision-making bodies such as tribunals (1.3.4). Sources of law are briefly outlined (1.4), including both primary sources – statutory material and law reports (1.4.2) – and secondary sources. There is an explanation of how laws are made, following the stages through which a bill goes before it becomes law (1.4.1). There is also a brief listing of key websites for legal information (1.4.4).

The chapter looks at the law of the European Union (1.5), and then concludes with a brief outline of key legal concepts – what is meant by criminal law (1.6.1), civil law (1.6.2), the law of tort/delict (1.6.3) and the law of contract (1.6.4).

1.2 Legal system

The United Kingdom consists of three distinct jurisdictions, each with its own court system and legal profession: England and Wales, Scotland, and Northern Ireland.

The UK joined the European Economic Community (now the European Union) in 1973, which means that we are required to incorporate European legislation into UK law, and to recognize the jurisdiction of the European Court of Justice (ECJ) in matters of EU law. The ECJ, broadly speaking, hears two types of case. One is disputes between member states or actions brought by the Commission against member states. The other is 'preliminary rulings', where a court in a member state refers a point of EU law – the case then returns to the court of origin for a decision in light of the ruling.

When the Labour Party came to power in 1997, it embarked on a number of constitutional reforms. These included a programme of devolved government. We now have a separate Scottish Parliament and Welsh Assembly. Northern Ireland already had its own Assembly.

The Scottish Parliament legislates in areas of domestic policy, but matters best dealt with at UK level remain reserved to the UK Parliament and government. These include defence, foreign affairs, economic and fiscal policy, social security, employment law and aspects of transport and energy policy.

The Government of Wales Act 1998 gave the Welsh Assembly powers to legislate in domestic areas, but this excludes foreign affairs, defence, taxation, overall economic policy, social security and broadcasting. It is only able to pass subordinate legislation – Statutory Instruments – not Acts. In June 2005, the government issued a consultation paper entitled 'Better governance for Wales' (Wales Office, Cm 6582 ISBN 010 165 8222) which aimed to review and improve the working of the Assembly.

The UK is a signatory of the European Convention on Human Rights[1] and this was incorporated into UK law through the Human Rights Act 1998.

There is no written constitution as such in the UK. The constitutional law of the UK consists of statute law and case law. In addition there are international treaties and conventions to which the UK is a signatory which have binding force.

There are two basic systems of law: the common law system, which is used in England and Wales; and the civil law system, which is used by most of continental Europe and parts of Latin America. The legal systems of England, Wales and Northern Ireland are very similar. Scotland has a hybrid system of civil and common law.

1.2.1   Common law system

English law is called common law because it aims to be always the same, whichever court makes the decision. It began soon after the Norman Conquest of 1066, when the king and court travelled around the country hearing grievances. The common law system is based on the principle of deciding cases by reference to previous judicial decisions (known as 'precedent'), rather than to written statutes drafted by legislative bodies. For example, the basic concepts of contract law are found in precedent. A body of English law has evolved from the 12th century onwards.

Reported cases present specific problems out of which a point of law is extracted. Formulation of the law is bottom-up, from a specific event to a general principle. Judicial decisions accumulate around a particular kind of dispute and general rules or precedents emerge. These precedents are binding on other courts at the same or a lower level in the hierarchy. The same decision must result from another situation in which the material or relevant facts are the same. The law evolves by means of opinion changing as to which facts are relevant, and by novel situations arising.

1.2.2 Civil law system

The civil law system is used by most of continental Europe and parts of Latin America. The law is all written down in statutes in a very logical and organized (codified) way across all subject areas. In such systems, precedent is not normally recognized as a source of law, although it can be used as a supplementary source. This results in a top-down system, a codified law book, which is based upon broad principles and then broken down into legal topics similar to those of the common-law countries.

In the civil law system, case law is illustrative, and the court relies more on commentaries from professors and judges published in books and journal articles. The civil law system – which is based on ancient Roman law – arose from many countries being given the Napoleonic Code when occupied during the Napoleonic era. Since then national laws have diverged, but remain basically similar.

1.3 Court system

England and Wales, Scotland, and Northern Ireland have their own hierarchy of courts, although they are all divided into two sections: criminal and civil.

1.3.1 England and Wales

The lowest criminal courts are the Magistrates Courts, which deal with minor offences. More serious cases are heard in the Crown Court in front of a judge and jury. The Crown Court also hears cases that are appealed from the Magistrates Courts on factual points. Cases can be appealed on points of law to the High Court (Queen's Bench Division). Appeals against conviction and sentence go to the Court of Appeal (Criminal Division).

Civil cases are heard in the County Courts at first instance for minor claims. More serious cases are dealt with by the High Court, which is divided into three divisions:

- The Queen's Bench Division hears civil claims involving tort, such as personal injury, other negligence actions and contract.
- The Chancery Division hears cases involving areas such as land, wills and trusts, as well as intellectual property, company and tax cases.
- The Family Division hears cases relating to family law such as divorce.

Cases may be appealed to the Court of Appeal (Civil Division), and in turn these may be appealed to the House of Lords. It should be noted, however, that appeals can only be brought with permission – either from the judge hearing the original case or from a Court of Appeal judge.

The House of Lords is currently the supreme court of appeal, although the government intends to replace the existing system of Law Lords operating as a committee of the House of Lords with a Supreme Court. The Constitutional Reform Act 2005 creates the Supreme Court of the United Kingdom. The Supreme Court will not start operating until a new building is fully functional, and the current preferred choice is Middlesex Hall, which is situated on Parliament Square, London. Following renovation of Middlesex Hall the first court sitting is not expected until 2008. Lord Falconer has said that moving the UK's top court from Parliament is an integral part of demonstrating the independence of the Law Lords from government.

The Queen's Bench Division also has a supervisory role: it is responsible for supervising subordinate bodies and tribunals in the exercise of their powers. This is achieved primarily by means of the procedure known as judicial review, in which the decisions of any inferior court, tribunal or other decision-making public body may be challenged or called into question on any one of three possible grounds:

- illegality – where the decision-maker acted beyond his/her powers
- unfairnesss – where there has been a procedural irregularity or breach of natural justice, such as not permitting applicants to put their case properly or bias

- irrationality – where the decision that has been reached is one that no properly informed decision-maker could rationally reach.

Procedure in the civil courts is now governed by the Civil Procedure Rules, which took effect in April 1999 after the Woolf Report *Access to Justice*, which instigated the most wide-ranging changes to civil litigation since the turn of the 20th century. These were developed from a number of overriding objectives: the Rules sought to change the adversarial nature of litigation and to introduce a fairer, faster and cheaper system of civil justice in which the courts exercised more control over the proceedings. Previous rules regarding civil litigation conduct (the Rules of the Supreme Court, known as 'The White Book' and the County Court Rules, known as the 'Green Book') were almost completely replaced by the Civil Procedure Rules, which comprised an entirely new regime for dealing with civil disputes.

1.3.2 Scotland

There are three levels of court procedure in criminal matters in Scotland.

The lowest criminal courts are the District Courts, which are presided over by justices of the peace and in some cases stipendiary magistrates. These courts deal with minor offences such as breach of the peace and shoplifting, and their powers to sentence are limited. Next are the Sheriff Courts, which deal with minor offences over which a sheriff presides alone, and more serious offences, except murder and rape, which are dealt with by a sheriff sitting with a jury. A sheriff sitting alone has limited sentencing powers in comparison to a sheriff sitting with a jury. The most serious offences in Scotland are heard by the High Court of Justiciary. This is also the final appeal court for all criminal matters in Scotland.

The principal forms of civil procedure in Scotland are small claims, summary cause and ordinary procedure in the Sheriff Court, and Court of Session procedure. Small claims are intended to be simple and cheap and designed for all claims under £750. Summary cause is for sums between £750 and £1,500. Ordinary cause procedure and Court of Session procedure are more formal with full written pleadings. The Outer House of the Court of Session can hear most types of civil case. The Inner House of the Court of Session is generally the court of appeal from the Outer House, sheriffs and certain tribunals. Thereafter appeals in civil cases can be made to the House of Lords which will be replaced by the new Supreme Court.

1.3.3   Northern Ireland

The highest court in Northern Ireland is the Supreme Court of Judicature, which consists of the Court of Appeal, the High Court and the Crown Court. There are then the lower courts: the County Courts with criminal and civil jurisdiction, and the Magistrates Courts. Cases which start in either the Crown Court or the High Court can be appealed to the Court of Appeal in Belfast, and, where leave is given, to the House of Lords. Cases which start in either the County Courts or the Magistrates Courts can only be appealed as far as the Court of Appeal in Belfast; and unlike the equivalent in England and Wales, this is not split into a Civil Division and a Criminal Division.

1.3.4   Tribunals

In addition to the courts there are also a number of specialized tribunals, which hear appeals on decisions made by various public bodies and government departments. Tribunals cover areas such as employment, immigration, social security, tax and land. Three tribunals relate to areas of law covered in this book.

1   The Information Tribunal considers appeals arising from decisions and notices issued by the Information Commissioner. It was previously called the Data Protection Tribunal, until its name changed as a result of the Freedom of Information Act 2000.
2   The Regulation of Investigatory Powers Act 2000 (RIPA) provides for an independent tribunal made up of senior members of the legal profession, appointed by the Queen. The role of the Investigatory Powers Tribunal is to consider all complaints against the intelligence services (Security Service, SIS and GCHQ), and those against law enforcement agencies and public authorities in respect of powers granted by RIPA, and to consider proceedings brought under Section 7 of the Human Rights Act 1998 against the intelligence services and law enforcement agencies in respect of these powers.
3   The other tribunal which is relevant to the topics covered in this book is the Copyright Tribunal (see 2.6).

In August 2001, Sir Andrew Leggatt's *Review of Tribunals: one service, one system*[2] was published. It gave a picture of an incoherent and inefficient set of institutions which, despite the best efforts of the thousands of people who work in them, provided a service to the public which was well short of what people are entitled to and what could be achieved.

On 11 March 2003 the government announced a major shake-up to create a unified tribunals service. It stated that it would publish a white paper outlining plans to:

- increase accessibility to tribunals
- raise customer service standards
- improve administration.

The White Paper was published in July 2004 and entitled *Transforming Public Services: complaints, redress and tribunals* (Cm 6243). It states that where a mistake occurs we are entitled to complain and to have the mistake put right with the minimum of difficulty. The process for putting things right or removing uncertainty must be proportionate – in other words, there should be no disproportionate barriers to users in terms of cost, speed or complexity, but misconceived or trivial complaints should be identified and rooted out quickly.

The July 2004 White Paper accepted Sir Andrew Leggatt's key recommendation that tribunals provided by central government should be brought together into a unified system within what is now the Department for Constitutional Affairs. It saw, however, the new body as much more than a federation of existing tribunals, but rather as a new type of organization with two central pillars: administrative justice appeals and employment cases. Its task, together with that of a transformed Council on Tribunals, will be not just to process cases according to law. Its mission will be to help to prevent and resolve disputes, using any appropriate method and working with its partners both in and out of government, and to help to improve administrative justice and justice in the workplace, so that the need for disputes is reduced.

The government has created in law the post of Senior President of Tribunals to oversee the system. It also plans to create an Administrative Justice Council, based on the Council of Tribunals, to supervise the work of tribunals in England, Scotland and Wales and to look at the whole system of redress.

The new Tribunals Service is being launched in April 2006, providing common administrative support for the main central government tribunals.[3]

1.4   Sources of law

The primary sources of law are legislation and case law, with textbooks, journal articles, encyclopaedias, indices and digests making up a body of secondary sources.

Legislation in the UK can apply to the country as a whole; or, bearing in mind the impact of devolved government, there can also be Scottish legislation, Welsh legislation and Northern Irish legislation.

United Kingdom primary legislation consists of public and general Acts, and local and personal Acts – such as ones which are of a specific and limited nature like the Land at Palace Avenue, Kensington (Acquisition of Freehold) Act 2002. Acts of Parliament typically have a section just before any schedules which is headed 'short title, commencement, extent' and which outlines the short title by which the Act is known; the arrangements for the coming into force of the Act; and whether the Act applies to particular countries. Either there will be an extent section at the end of the Act setting out the geographical extent of the Act, or it will be silent on the matter, in which case the Act applies to the whole of the UK.

When considering Acts of Parliament, one needs to ask whether an Act is yet in force – few Acts come into force immediately on being passed. The reader should look for a commencement section at the end of the Act (which would appear before any schedules). It will either give a specific day for commencement or else it will refer to 'a day to be appointed' which will then be prescribed in one or more commencement orders in the form of Statutory Instruments. If the Act doesn't contain a commencement section, this means that the Act came into force on the date it received Royal Assent. Where an Act has been brought into force, the question to ask is whether the Act is still – wholly or partly – in force. This isn't always easy to establish. For example, an Act could be repealed by another Act, but one would then need to check whether the repealing Act has yet come into force.

There are a number of commercially available annotated versions of statutes such as Halsbury's statutes, or the Blackstone's statutes series, or those available on the online service LexisNexis.[4]

1.4.1 Progress of UK government legislation

UK government Bills can start in either the House of Commons or the House of Lords, although Bills whose main purpose is taxation or expenditure start in the House of Commons. Some Bills may have been preceded by a consultation document (Green Paper) and/or by a statement of policy (White Paper), although this is optional.

Bills are drafted by lawyers in the Parliamentary Counsel Office, which is part of the Cabinet Office. The daily Order Paper contains a Notice of Presentation of the Bill and this is the first reading of the Bill. The minister or a government whip then names a day for the Bill's second reading. The Bill is then allocated a Bill number and is printed by the Stationery Office – for example, Legal Deposit Libraries Bill [HC] Bill 26 of Session 2002/03. The text of Bills can also be found on the internet.[5] Explanatory notes are published to accompany the Bill. These normally include a summary of the main purpose of the Bill and a commentary on individual clauses and schedules – for example, Legal Deposit Libraries Bill Explanatory Notes [HC] Bill 26-EN of Session 2002/03.

The second reading debate is announced by the Leader of the House in a Business Statement. The second reading is the time for the House to consider the principles of the Bill. The debate on second reading is printed in Hansard.[6] After the second reading, the Bill has its Committee stage. This would normally take place in a Standing Committee, but it may be taken in a Committee of the whole House or a Special Standing Committee depending on the nature of the Bill.

The next stage is the consideration or report stage. The House can make further amendments to the Bill at that stage, but does not consider the clauses and schedules to which no amendments have been tabled. The final Commons stage of the Bill is the third reading. This enables the House to take an overview of the Bill as amended in Committee. No amendments can be made at this stage. Once it has passed its third reading in the Commons, the Bill is then sent to the House of Lords.

The legislative process in the House of Lords is broadly similar to that in the House of Commons. However, there are a few important differences:

• After the second reading, Bills are usually submitted to a committee of the whole House.

- There is no guillotine, and debate on amendments is unrestricted.
- Amendments can be made at the third reading as well as at Committee and consideration stage.

The House of Lords and House of Commons must finally agree the text of each Bill. In practice, in order for this to happen a Bill can travel backwards and forwards between the two houses several times. If the Lords have not amended a Commons Bill, they must inform the Commons of that fact.

Once the text of a Bill has been approved by both houses, the Bill is then submitted for Royal Assent. The House of Commons *Weekly Information Bulletin*[7] can be used in order to monitor the progress of Bills through parliament.

Statutory Instruments are regulations, orders or rules made under the authority of an Act of Parliament. They often provide the detail required for the application of the Statute such as what forms to fill in, the level of fees to be paid or provisions for the commencement of an Act (i.e. when it comes into force). Statutory Instruments are 'revoked' rather than 'repealed'.

In addition to primary legislation in the form of Acts of Parliament and Statutory Instruments, there is also a body of what one might refer to as 'quasi-legislation' and other regulatory materials. This includes statutory codes of practice, departmental circulars and material emanating from governmental or non-governmental bodies which would have relevance in legal proceedings – particularly where questions of standards or reasonableness are at issue (see, for example, the codes of practice in Section 8.6).

1.4.2   Law reports

Cases in the courts are reported in numerous series of law reports. Until 1865 in England case reporting was undertaken by private court reporters, and the resultant publications are known as the nominate reports, because they are usually known by the name of the reporter. These have been gathered together in a collection called the English Reports. In 1865 the reporting of cases was systematized by the Incorporated Council of Law Reporting, which started publishing series of reports organized according to court, collectively known as the Law Reports. These are recognized as being the most authoritative in the hierarchy of reports.

The main series of law reports in England and Wales are:

- The Law Reports 1865 – , which is in four separate series: Chancery Division (Ch.), Appeal Cases (AC), Family Division (Fam.) and Queen's Bench (QB)
- Weekly Law Reports 1954–
- All England Law Reports 1936– .

In Scotland, the most authoritative reports are produced by a non-profit-making body, the Scottish Council of Law Reporting, but most reporting is undertaken by commercial publishing companies. The main reports are the Session Cases and these commenced in their present form in 1907. Previously, like the English Law Reports, the reports were known by the names of the editor and were collectively referred to as the nominate reports. The other common reports are:

- Scots Law Times
- Scottish Civil Law Reports 1987–
- Scottish Criminal Case Reports 1981–
- Greens Weekly Digest 1986– .

In Northern Ireland the official law reports are the Northern Ireland Law Reports. There are also the Northern Ireland Judgments Bulletin, the Irish Reports and the Irish Law Times Reports.

In addition, there are many specialized reports covering different areas of law. The most comprehensive list of citations in the UK is Donald Raistrick's *Index to Legal Citations and Abbreviations*.[8]

The starting point for research on English law is *Halsbury's Laws of England*, and in Scotland it is *Stair's Institutions of the Law of Scotland*. When using sources of legal information it is vital to make sure that the books, journal articles or web pages you use are up to date, or that at the very least you are aware of the changes that have taken place since they were written. Bear in mind that the law is changing rapidly in the areas covered by this book. The free web-based sources may not have been annotated or amended, so it is often necessary to use commercial subscription services in order to get the most up-to-date information.

Textbooks and other secondary sources aren't formal sources of law, but they do nevertheless have relevance in the courts. Writings by highly regarded authors are frequently cited in court as persuasive sources. There are a number of guides to law libraries and legal research. These include:

Clinch, P. (2000) *Legal Information: what it is and where to find it*, Europa Publications.
Clinch, P. (2001) *Using a Law Library: a student's guide to legal research skills*, 2nd edn, Blackstone Press.
Holborn, G. (2001) *Butterworths Legal Research Guide*, 2nd edn, Butterworths.
McKie, S. (1993) *Legal Research: how to find and understand the law*, Cavendish Publishing.
Pester, D. (2003) *Finding Legal Information: a guide to print and electronic resources*, Chandos Publishing.
Thomas, P. A. and Knowles, J. (2001) *Dane and Thomas: how to use a law library*, 4th edn, Sweet and Maxwell.

1.4.3   Public international law

The law governing the legal relations between states is known as 'public international law' and it is distinct from internal domestic law. Public international law covers topics such as the recognition of states, the law of war, treaty-making and diplomatic immunity. It can also apply to individuals where it operates at an international level but only through international courts and tribunals. This covers areas such as the law on asylum, human rights or war crimes. Sources of public international law include treaties and the case law of international courts and tribunals.

1.4.4   Websites

1.4.4.1 Parliamentary websites

United Kingdom Parliament www.parliament.uk
Northern Ireland Assembly www.niassembly.gov.uk
National Assembly for Wales www.wales.gov.uk/
Scottish Parliament www.scottish.parliament.uk
Tynwald (Parliament of the Isle of Man) www.tynwald.org.im

1.4.4.2 Government, legislation and law reports

Directgov www.direct.gov.uk is a portal to the websites of central government. *OPSI* www.opsi.gov.uk has the texts of statutes and statutory instruments.

TSO (The Stationery Office) www.tso.co.uk is an online index to TSO publications.

Government News Network www.gnn.gov.uk contains press releases of central government departments.

Parliament website for Bills www.parliament.uk/bills/bills.cfm.

POLIS (Parliamentary Online Indexing Service) www.polis.parliament.uk contains parliamentary debates.

BAILII (British and Irish Legal Information Institute) www.bailii.org provides access to British and Irish legal cases and legislation.

House of Lords Judicial Office www.parliament.the-stationery-office.co.uk/pa/ld/ldjudinf.htm.

Her Majesty's Courts Service www.hmcourts-service.gov.uk/.

Scottish Court Service www.scotcourts.gov.uk/.

Northern Ireland Court Service www.courtsni.gov.uk/.

1.4.4.3 Legal information portals

Legal Resources in the UK and Ireland (Delia Venables) www.venables.co.uk provides a set of links to useful legal resources designed to be of use to the legal community.

LawLinks (Sarah Carter) http://library.kent.ac.uk/library/lawlinks.

The Statutory Publications Office (SPO), an office within the Department for Constitutional Affairs, is producing a Statute Law Database of United Kingdom legislation. The database under development currently contains the text of all Acts that were in force on 1 February 1991, and all Acts and printed Statutory Instruments passed since then. It also contains local legislation, both primary and printed secondary. The main task of the SPO editorial team is to apply the effects of amending legislation to primary legislation. The key feature of the central database maintained by the SPO is that it will provide a historical view of primary legislation for any specific day from the base date of 1 February 1991, and any prospective legislation.

1.5   European Union

The European Union is said to comprise three 'pillars':

- The European Communities (EC – the European Community, and Euratom – the European Atomic Energy Community)
- common foreign and security policy
- justice and home affairs.

The law derives from the first pillar, and the roles of the Commission, the European Parliament and the ECJ relate almost exclusively to it.

The first source of EU law is the treaties establishing the Communities and the Union, the subsequent amending treaties, and the treaties of accession of additional member states. Under the normal principles of public international law, the treaties require incorporation into UK domestic law. However, the novel feature of the European Communities Act 1972 was that it gave effect to all future obligations under Community law without further enactment. The second source of EU law is the secondary legislation made in Brussels which forms part of UK law, as does the third source, the decisions of the ECJ at Luxembourg. The body of European Union law is known as the 'acquis communitaire'. European law consists of four main strands.

1.5.1   Primary legislation

1 Treaties are referred to as the 'primary' legislation of the Community as they form the constitution and give the structure of institutions and extent of powers. The principles of European law derive from the 1957 Treaty of Rome, but this has been amended by a number of other treaties such as the Maastricht Treaty and the Treaty of Amsterdam.

1.5.2   Secondary legislation

2 Regulations are binding in their entirety. They are directly applicable and do not need to be transposed into national law by the respective member states in order for them to take effect. An example of a regulation would be Regulation (EC) No 1049/2001 regarding public access to European Parliament, Council and Commission documents.

3 Directives are the main form of substantive law. They are formulated by the European Commission, where they are subject to extensive consultation, and are thereafter passed by a combination of the Parliament and the Council of Ministers. Directives only state the effects to be achieved and many directives leave the practical application to national discretion, so one needs to be aware of the non-harmonized details. Directives only take effect when enacted into national laws, which usually takes several years. The period of implementation is normally prescribed by each directive.

Taking the copyright directive 2001/29/EC as an example: the directive was published in the Official Journal on 22 June 2001 and Article 13 of the directive states that 'member states shall bring into force the laws, regulations and administrative provisions necessary to comply with this directive before 22 December 2002.' In fact, the European Commission was keen for the copyright directive to come into force at roughly the same time as the electronic commerce directive, and for that reason the time allowed for implementation was 18 months rather than the period of two years that had been expected.

With the copyright directive, Article 5 on exceptions and limitations is an example of harmonized and non-harmonized details within a directive. Article 5 has one compulsory exception, but then provides for a series of optional exceptions: member states can choose the ones that they wish to implement. Where there is a compulsory exception, the law is harmonized throughout the European Union; the remaining exceptions are optional and therefore the law is not harmonized because there is scope for each member state to select a different mix of exceptions to implement.

4 Decisions are from the Commission or the Council of Ministers, not from the European Court of Justice. These are generally of restricted application and importance. Normally these are addressed to member states.

1.6   Legal concepts/terminology
1.6.1   Criminal law

A crime is defined as an offence where the state acts against the individual to defend a collective interest. Criminal law is the branch of law which defines crimes and fixes punishments for them. The punishments are fines, probation, community service (which are seen as alternatives to custody) or a prison sentence. Also included in criminal law are rules and procedures for preventing and investigating crimes and prosecuting criminals, as well as the regulations governing the constitution of courts, the conduct of trials, the organization of police forces and the administration of penal institutions. In general, the criminal law of most modern societies classifies crimes as: offences against the safety of the society; offences against the administration of justice; offences against the public welfare; offences against property; and offences threatening the lives or safety of people.

1.6.2   Civil law

Civil law deals with disputes between individuals or organizations. The state's role is simply to provide the means by which they can be resolved. 'Civil law' in the context of distinguishing between civil law on the one hand and criminal law on the other has a different meaning to that of the legal system known as the 'civil law system' which is used in most of continental Europe (see 1.2.2). A civil claim results in a remedy, such as the payment of damages by way of compensation being granted to one party against the other, or restitution – injunction/interdict.

1.6.3   Tort (England, Wales, Northern Ireland)/delict (Scotland)

When a contract (see 1.6.4) cannot apply, third-party agreements called torts might apply. These encompass mainly obligations and duties of care. These duties of care are owed to those foreseeably affected by one's actions, balanced by a concern not to extend this to remote and generalized effects. A standard test of reasonableness has to be applied, whereby you must take reasonable care to avoid all acts and omissions which you can reasonably foresee would be likely to injure your neighbour.

Torts are essentially civil wrongs that provide individuals with a cause of action for damages in respect of breach of a legal duty. They include negligence, and as far as information professionals are concerned, professional negligence covers things like the accuracy of information; and they also include defamation. In deciding whether an information professional's actions were negligent, they would be judged against the actions of their fellow professionals. (Chapter 9 deals in more detail with professional negligence as it relates to information professionals.)

Basically, rights in tort are civil rights of action which are available for the recovery of unliquidated damages by persons who have sustained injury or loss from the acts, statements or omissions of others in breach of a duty or in contravention of a right imposed or conferred by law, rather than by contract. Damage includes economic as well as physical damage.

1.6.4   Contract law

A contract, in law, is an agreement that creates an obligation binding upon the parties involved. It is a promise or set of promises which the law will enforce. There must be two or more separate and definite parties to the contract for the contract to be valid. There must be an offer, acceptance, intention to create legal relations (and capacity to do so) and consideration supporting those promises (although consideration is not required in Scotland). There has to be a mutual exchange of promises for a contract to arise.

In general, contracts may be either oral or written. Certain classes of contract, however, in order to be enforceable, must be written and signed. These include contracts involving the sale and transfer of real estate, and contracts to guarantee or answer for the miscarriage, debt or default of another person.

In England, Wales and Northern Ireland, the Supply of Goods and Services Act 1982 implies terms into a contract, such as implying that the service must be carried out with reasonable care and skill. Customers in Scotland continue to rely on their common law rights. This Act is particularly relevant to information professionals. However, please note that the parties can agree that the implied rights should not apply to the provision of the service but any exclusion or restriction shall be subject to the terms of the Unfair Contract Terms Act 1977.

Under the Unfair Contract Terms Act 1977 a person cannot exclude or restrict his/her liability for death or personal injury resulting from negligence. Only if the exclusion clauses satisfy a test of reasonableness can someone exclude or restrict liability for other loss or damage resulting from negligence. It would be for the party seeking to impose a contract term to demonstrate to the court that it was reasonable, should they be challenged.

The Unfair Terms in Consumer Contracts Regulations 1999: SI 1999/2083 provide that a term which has not been individually negotiated in a consumer contract is unfair if, contrary to the requirement of good faith, it causes a significant imbalance in the rights and obligations of the parties to the detriment of the consumer.

Chapter 10 considers contracts and licensing in more detail, especially as they relate to the work of information professionals, such as in the case of contracts for searching online databases or having access to proprietary information.

1.7   Summary

In this chapter we have looked at the different types of legal system – the common law system (1.2.1) and the civil law system (1.2.2) – and also the court system (1.3). The chapter outlined primary and secondary sources of law (1.4), and the importance of ensuring that the information used is totally up to date.

As the United Kingdom is a member of the European Union, the chapter also looked at the role of EU law (1.5), and concluded with a brief outline of key legal concepts: criminal law (1.6.1), civil law (1.6.2), the law of tort/delict (1.6.3) and the law of contract (1.6.4).

It is important to recognize that where legal matters are concerned there are very few clearly right or wrong answers, hence many issues have to be resolved in court. Dealing with legal issues is often a matter of risk management. Bearing in mind that it isn't always clear whether something is considered to be legal, one has to consider how organizations and individuals can minimize the risk of legal action being taken against them.

Throughout the United Kingdom, the law is uniform in many respects. The laws of England and Wales and Northern Ireland are particularly close, while there are a number of differences with the law of Scotland. This book is based upon the laws of the United Kingdom, and while it will be of interest to information professionals working in other parts of the world, the reader should bear in mind that it is written from a UK perspective.

The next chapter deals with the topic of copyright law – an area that is extremely complex, and one with which information professionals have to grapple regularly.

Notes and references

1   Available at www.hri.org/docs/ECHR50.html.
2   Available at www.tribunals-review.org.uk/.
3   See www.dca.gov.uk/legalsys/tribunals.htm.
4   See www.lexisnexis.com/.
5   See www.parliament.the-stationery-office.co.uk/pa/pabills.htm.
6   See www.parliament.uk/hansard/hansard.cfm.
7   See www.publications.parliament.uk/pa/cm/cmwib.htm.
8   Raistrick, D. (1993) *Index to Legal Citations and Abbreviations*, 2nd edn, Bowker-Saur.

2 Copyright

2.1   Introduction

Information professionals have a duty to foster the fullest possible access to information for their users while respecting the intellectual property protections afforded to people for their creativity and innovation. This chapter outlines the general principles of copyright law (2.2), including the rights of authors as the first owners of copyright (2.3). It then considers the legal and regulatory environment within which we operate (2.4), which includes international treaties and conventions, European directives and UK statute law. These are supplemented by case law, which can help to clarify particular points of law. The exceptions or permitted acts are considered (2.5), in particular fair dealing and library privilege. It is necessary to consider licensing where people wish to copy beyond the extents and purposes that are set out in statute law, and the chapter looks at the licences available through the Copyright Licensing Agency, the Newspaper Licensing Agency, the Design Artists Copyright Society, Ordnance Survey and the Office for Public Sector Information (2.6). The application of copyright law in the electronic environment is considered (2.7), including how copyright applies to the internet, the question of deep linking and the licensing of electronic resources. The implications of database regulations are outlined (2.7.2), including how they impact upon not only electronic databases but also hard-copy ones such as reference directories. Finally, a number of ethical and professional issues are considered (2.8), including the conflict which stems from the desire to provide access to information while recognizing the need to protect copyright.

2.2   General principles

Copyright is the right to prevent the copying of work which has been created by intellectual effort. It protects information and ideas where these have been reduced into the form of a 'work'. Copyright is augmented by 'database right' – a *sui generis* ('of its own kind or type' constituting a class of its own) right to prevent extraction and re-utilization of all or a substantial part of a database.

Copyright subsists in:

- original literary, dramatic, musical or artistic works
- sound recordings, films or broadcasts
- the typographical arrangement of published editions.

It is said that copyright 'subsists' rather than 'exists' because copyright cannot exist by itself but only within the work which has been created (see also Figure 2.1).

Books
Articles
Photographs
Films and videos
Sound recordings
Artistic works
Musical works
Computer programs
Databases
Typographical arrangements

Figure 2.1   What is protected by copyright?

Article 27 of the Universal Declaration of Human Rights[1] (adopted by the United Nations General Assembly on 10 December 1948) says:

(1) Everyone has the right freely to participate in the cultural life of the community, to enjoy the arts and to share in scientific advancement and its benefits.
(2) Everyone has the right to the protection of the moral and material interests resulting from any scientific, literary or artistic production of which he is the author.

There are clearly tensions between the need to give authors protection for their work and the need to allow people access to material for the betterment of society, and to promote education, science and scholarship. That is why the monopoly rights that the law confers on the owners of copyright have a number of built-in safeguards. These include a number of permitted acts or copyright exceptions such as fair dealing (see 2.5.1). Another safeguard is the limit put on the period of copyright protection, after which works enter the public domain. (The public domain comprises the body of all creative works and other knowledge – writing, artwork, music, science, inventions and others – in which no person or organization has any proprietary interest.)

Copyright protection is automatic. It is not necessary to go through a registration process before copyright can be claimed. The corollary of this is that there isn't a comprehensive database of works protected by copyright with details of their rights owners – something which would make the process of obtaining copyright clearance much easier.

Legal deposit[2] is not a prerequisite for claiming copyright protection (for further information about the laws relating to legal deposit see Chapter 14). One myth is that if there is no copyright symbol on a work then it is not protected by copyright. Most countries (160 states as at January 2006) around the world are signatories to the Berne Copyright Convention, and this provides for the automatic protection of works without any formality. While it is true that the copyright symbol © is not necessary for a work to have copyright protection, it is, however, advisable to put a copyright notice on a work that you create as a reminder to those who make use of that work of your rights. You could use the copyright notice to tell potential users both the nature and the amount of copying that you are willing to permit. For example:

> You are allowed to redistribute this newsletter in its entirety, on a non-commercial basis. This includes making it available (in full and as published) on your corporate intranet. However, individual sections may not be copied and/or distributed without the prior written agreement of the publishers.

In general, the author of a work is the first owner of any copyright in it. However, where the work is made by an employee in the course of their employment, the employer is the first owner of any copyright in the work subject to any express written agreement to the contrary. This only applies to employees, not to contractors, so the mere fact that a work has been commissioned and paid for does not give ownership of the copyright to the commissioning party. It is important, therefore, to ensure that appropriate mechanisms are in place to deal with the ownership of the rights in content. For example, an organization may wish to publish information on a website. That information may come from a number of sources such as external developers, consultants and internal employees. The organization in question will therefore need to be sure that it secures assignment of rights from any third parties, and it should also be certain that any employees created the content during the course of their employment. It is all too often the case in practice that assignments are not obtained, which can cause problems if the organization wishes to sell, copy or license any of the copyright. It is therefore of the utmost importance that organizations regularly audit their rights to ascertain any ownership difficulties.

2.3   Economic and moral rights

Copyright owners have a number of exclusive rights to their work. Section 16(1) of the Copyright, Designs and Patents Act (CDPA) 1988 sets out the economic rights of a copyright owner. These are the rights to:

- copy the work (which includes storing the work electronically)
- issue copies of the work to the public
- rent or lend the work to the public
- perform, show or play the work in public
- communicate the work to the public
- make an adaptation or translation of the work.

If anyone other than the copyright owner undertakes any of these activities without permission or licence, unless it is under one of the statutory exceptions, that would be a primary infringement of the copyright.

There are also some actions which could be said to be secondary infringements (CDPA 1988 ss22–6):

- importing an infringing copy
- possessing or dealing with an infringing copy
- providing the means for making infringing copies
- permitting the use of premises for infringing performance
- providing apparatus for infringing performance.

There are also a number of moral rights (see sections 77–85 of the CDPA 1988):

- the right of paternity
- the right of integrity
- the right to object to false attribution
- the right of disclosure.

The right of paternity is the right of the author to be identified as such. This right of attribution or paternity is not infringed unless the author has asserted his/her right to be identified as the author of the work. That is why you will often find a statement at the beginning of a book along the lines of: 'Joe Bloggs asserts his right to be identified as the author of this work in accordance with the terms of the Copyright, Designs and Patents Act 1988 (CDPA).'

The right of integrity is the right of the author to prevent or object to derogatory treatment of their work.

The right to object to false attribution is the right of persons not to have literary, dramatic or musical works falsely attributed to them; and this right applies both to copyright owners and non-copyright owners alike.

The right of disclosure is the right to privacy of a person who commissions the taking of a photograph or the making of a film for private and domestic purposes.

A number of remedies are available for copyright infringement, both civil and criminal. The Copyright, etc. and Trade Marks (Offences and Enforcement) Act 2002 was passed in order to harmonize and rationalize enforcement provisions dealing with copyright and trade mark theft. The maximum penalties for wilful copyright infringement were brought into line with those already provided for wilful trade mark infringement. Consequently people could potentially face up to ten years in prison and/or an unlimited fine, where previously the maximum prison sentence was two years.

The range of available remedies for infringement is set out in Chapter VI of the CDPA 1988. These include damages, an injunction, delivery up of infringing copies, an account of profits or an undertaking to take out an appropriate licence. Many copyright cases are not settled in court, but are instead agreed informally as out-of-court settlements. In these instances, no legal precedent is set, and we are usually none the wiser as to the terms of the settlement.

Where copyright infringement occurs, people need to consider the risks involved. They should take into account not only the financial consequences of infringement, but also the potential risk of having a public relations disaster on their hands, and the damage that this could do to their organization's reputation.

2.4   Legislative framework

The legislative and regulatory framework for UK copyright consists of four key components. These are:

- international treaties and conventions to which the UK is a signatory
- European directives which the UK as a member state of the EU is obliged to implement
- UK legislation in the form of Acts of Parliament and Statutory Instruments
- case law which clarifies how the law applies in a particular set of circumstances.

2.4.1   Berne Copyright Convention

The main copyright convention is the Berne Copyright Convention for the protection of literary and artistic works, to which most countries are signed up (160 states as at January 2006). The original agreement was drawn up in 1886 and since then there have been a number of revisions, the most recent revision dating from 1979. Under the convention authors are entitled to some basic rights of protection for their intellectual output.

Berne also recognizes the need for people to have access to protected works, and so it allows exceptions and limitations to the exclusive rights (see Figure 2.2), although these must pass a three-step test (see Figure 2.3).

Translation	(article 8)
Reproduction	(article 9)
Public performance	(article 11)
Communication to the public	(article 11)
Recording of musical works	
Broadcasting	(article 11)
Cinematic adaptations	(article 14)
Adaptations, arrangements and other alterations	(article 12)
Moral rights	(article 6)

Figure 2.2 Exclusive rights set out in the Berne Convention
(as amended in Paris, 1971)

1	that the exception only applies in special (defined) cases
2	provided that such reproduction does not conflict with the normal exploitation of the work
3	and does not unreasonably prejudice the legitimate interests of the author

Figure 2.3 Berne three-step test

The Berne three-step test is significant, because a substantially similar form of words is used in Article 5(5) of Copyright Directive 2001/29/EC, which was implemented in the UK through the Copyright and Related Rights Regulations 2003 (SI 2003/2498). In short this means that any copyright exceptions or permitted acts are only allowed within UK copyright law if they meet this three-step test.

The Berne convention is based upon three principles:

- reciprocal protection – among Berne Union members, each state must protect the works of others to the same level as those from their own countries, provided the term accorded is not longer than that for its own works
- minimum standards for duration and scope of rights – author's life plus 50 years or, for anonymous works, 50 years after being made available to the public
- automatic protection, with no registration.

The UK is a signatory to the Berne Convention.

2.4.2 Universal Copyright Convention

The Universal Copyright Convention (UCC) was agreed at a 1952 UNESCO conference in Geneva. The main features of the convention are:

- works of a given country must carry a copyright notice to secure protection in other UCC countries – it was this convention that established the copyright symbol ©
- foreign works must be treated as though they are national works – the 'national treatment' principle
- a minimum term of protection of life plus 25 years
- the author's translation rights may be subjected to compulsory licensing.

The two conventions are not mutually exclusive, and the UK is also a member of the Universal Copyright Convention.

2.4.3   TRIPS

The World Trade Organization (WTO) signed an agreement in 1994 which had an annex known as TRIPS – Trade Related Aspects of Intellectual Property Rights.[3] This is designed to ensure that intellectual property rights do not themselves become barriers to legitimate trade.

The three main features of the agreement are:

- the minimum standards of protection to be provided by each member on:
  — the subject matter to be provided
  — the rights to be conferred
  — permissible exceptions to those rights
  — the minimum duration of protection
- general principles applicable to all intellectual property rights (IPR) enforcement procedures in order that rights holders can effectively enforce their rights
- the agreement that disputes between WTO members about TRIPS obligations will be subject to the WTO's dispute settlement procedures.

The TRIPS agreement is often described as one of the three 'pillars' of the WTO, the other two being trade in goods and trade in services.

There is a TRIPS council comprising all WTO members which is responsible for monitoring the operation of the agreement and how members comply with their obligations to it. The UK is a signatory of TRIPS.

2.4.4 WIPO Copyright Treaty

The World Intellectual Property Organization (WIPO) is a United Nations body which is responsible for administering many of the international conventions on intellectual property. In December 1996 around 100 countries adopted the WIPO Copyright Treaty and the WIPO Performances and Phonograms Treaty. The WIPO Copyright Treaty of 1996 introduced a new right of communication to the public, and it also gave legal protection and legal remedies against circumvention of technological measures, in order to prevent unauthorized access to works. The European directive on the harmonization of certain aspects of copyright and related rights [2001/29/EC] implemented the 1996 WIPO treaties in the European Union.

2.4.5 European directives on copyright matters

Changes to UK copyright law are often the result of developments at a European level. The aim of the European Commission is to harmonize copyright laws in EU member states in order to achieve a level playing field for copyright protection across national borders. This will allow the single market to become a reality for new products and services containing intellectual property. There have been a number of European directives on copyright over the past decade or so.

2.4.5.1 On the legal protection of computer programs [91/250/EEC]

Computer programs are protected as literary works, which gives them the full protection of the Berne Copyright Convention. The term 'computer programs' includes preparatory design work leading to the development of a computer program provided that the nature of the preparatory work is such that a computer program can result from it at a later stage.

2.4.5.2 On rental and lending rights [92/100/EEC]

Authors and performers have an exclusive right to authorize or prohibit rental and lending of their works. 'Rental' means making available for use for a limited period of time and for direct or indirect economic or commercial advantage. 'Lending' means making available for use for a limited period of time and not for direct or indirect economic or commercial advantage. Libraries are generally allowed to lend books (Section 40A of the CDPA states that copyright is not infringed by the lending of a book by a public library if the book is within the public lending right scheme).

2.4.5.3 Harmonizing the term of copyright protection [93/98/EEC]

This directive extended the term of protection for copyright literary, dramatic, musical and artistic works and films from 50 to 70 years after the year of the death of the author, and gave a new right – publication right – to works in which copyright had expired and which had not previously been published.

2.4.5.4 On the legal protection of databases [96/9/EEC]

This introduced the new form of *sui generis* property protection for databases to prevent unfair extraction and re-utilization of their contents (see Section 2.7.2).

2.4.5.5 On the harmonization of certain aspects of copyright and related rights [2001/29/EC]

This enabled the EU and its member states to ratify the provisions of the two 1996 WIPO treaties – the Copyright Treaty and the Performers and Producers of Phonograms Treaty – and updated the law to incorporate new technology, including internet practices.

2.4.5.6 On the resale right for the benefit of the author of an original work of art (droit de suite) [2001/84/EC]

This directive provides an artist with the right to receive a royalty based on the price obtained for any resale of an original work of art, subsequent to the first transfer by the artist. The right does not apply, however, to resales between individuals acting in their private capacity, without the participation of an art market professional, or to resales by persons acting in their private capacity to museums which are not for profit and are open to the public.

Resale of a work of art incurs a royalty of between 0.25% and 4% depending upon the sale price. However, the total amount of resale royalty payable on the sale must not in any event exceed 12,500 euros. The directive has been implemented in the UK through the Artists Resale Right Regulations 2006: SI 2006/346.

2.4.5.7 On the enforcement of intellectual property rights [2004/48/EC]

This requires all member states to apply effective, dissuasive and proportionate remedies and penalties against those engaged in counterfeiting and piracy and to create a level playing field for right holders in the EU. Implementation was required by 29 April 2006.

Having published a range of measures to tighten up copyright law over the past decade or so, it is clear that there is now a European Commission focus on enforcing intellectual property rights in order to ensure that those earlier measures have maximum impact. In addition to directive 2004/48/EC on the enforcement of intellectual property rights, in July 2005 the European Commission published COM(2005) 276 final on criminal measures aimed at ensuring the enforcement of intellectual property rights. [In order to monitor the progress of EU legislation, check the European Parliament legislative observatory.[4]]

   In view of the introduction of so many directives over a relatively short period of time, the Commission issued a staff working paper in July 2004 – SEC(2004) 995 [5] – containing a review of the EC legal framework in the field of copyright and related rights. It assesses whether there are any inconsistencies in the definitions or in the rules on exceptions and limitations between the different directives, and whether these hamper the operation of the *acquis* (that is to say the body of Community law) or whether they have a harmful impact on the fair balance of rights and other interests, including those of users and consumers.

2.4.6   UK legislation

The principal UK copyright legislation is the Copyright, Designs and Patents Act 1988, which came into force on 1 August 1989. The CDPA 1988 has been amended on a number of occasions – by the Broadcasting Acts of 1990 and 1996, the Copyright, etc. and Trade Marks (Offences and Enforcement) Act 2002, the Copyright (Visually Impaired Persons) Act 2002, the Legal Deposit Libraries Act 2003, and by secondary legislation (Statutory Instruments) which interpret and modify it including:

- SI 1992/3233 – the Copyright (Computer Programs) Regulations 1992
- SI 1995/3297 – the Duration of Copyright and Rights in Performances Regulations 1995

- SI 1996/2967 – the Copyright and Related Rights Regulations 1996
- SI 1997/3032 – the Copyright and Rights in Databases Regulations 1997
- SI 2003/2498 – the Copyright and Related Rights Regulations 2003.

All of these Statutory Instruments implement European Union directives. On 2 December 2005 the Chancellor of the Exchequer announced that he had asked Andrew Gowers to lead an independent review to examine the UK's intellectual property framework. The review will report in the Autumn of 2006.

The Patent Office is responsible for developing and carrying out UK policy on all aspects of intellectual property. It develops UK law on intellectual property, and promotes UK interests in international efforts to harmonize and simplify intellectual property law. The Intellectual Property and Innovation Directorate of the Patent Office deals with policy on copyright, rights in performances and design right.

2.4.7   Supplementary case law

No matter how well a piece of legislation is drafted, there will always be 'grey' areas of interpretation, or situations requiring further clarification about how the law applies to a particular set of circumstances, so the fourth component in the regulatory and legislative regime for copyright is that of case law. Under the English common law tradition, case law plays a key role.

If you want to find out more about case law relating to copyright, there isn't one single handy place where all such case law can be found. There are, however, a number of specialized series of law reports in the intellectual property field, such as the European Copyright and Design Reports (ECDR),[6] as well as W. R. Cornish's *Cases and Materials on Intellectual Property*.[7]

Matters relating to EU law are adjudicated by the European Court of Justice (ECJ) and the Court of First Instance, and these are published in the Common Market Law Reports (CMLR)[8] and the official Report of Cases brought before the ECJ, commonly known as European Court Reports (ECR). A number of the broadsheets publish law reports, such as *The Times*, *The Independent* and *The Daily Telegraph*.

Other useful sources of information on copyright case law include the journal *European Intellectual Property Review*,[9] the British and Irish Legal Information Institute (BAILII),[10] commercial online information systems such as Westlaw, Lexis and Lawtel[11] and the RSS feeds of relevant sites.[12]

2.5   Acts permitted in relation to copyright works

Chapter III of the CDPA covers acts permitted in relation to copyright works, otherwise known as exceptions. All of the UK's copyright exceptions have to conform to directive 2001/29/EC on the harmonization of certain aspects of copyright and related rights in the information society. Article 5(5) of the directive states that 'the exceptions and limitations . . . shall only be applied in certain special cases which do not conflict with a normal exploitation of the work or other subject matter and do not unreasonably prejudice the legitimate interests of the author.' This is based on the Berne three-step test (see Figure 2.3).

The Patent Office took the view that it would not introduce the test as such into UK law as a general constraint on exceptions, but that it would continue with the existing practice in the CDPA of using the test as a standard in framing exceptions to rights. In other words, all exceptions to copyright must first pass the Berne three-step test before they can be considered for possible inclusion in statute law, but there is no need for the wording of the three-step test to appear before each exception in the legislation.

The main copyright exceptions of interest to librarians have been fair dealing for research and private study and library privilege. Both of these have had their scope narrowed by SI 2003/2498. This Statutory Instrument implemented directive 2001/29/EC in UK law and it narrowed both the exception of fair dealing for the purposes of research or private study and library privilege, so that they both now relate only to copying undertaken for non-commercial purposes.

2.5.1   Fair dealing

Fair dealing is effectively a defence against accusations of infringement rather than a licence to copy (see Figure 2.4). Section 29(1) of the CDPA says

1	Fair dealing has not been defined by statute.
2	It must fit into one of the following three categories: • research for a non-commercial purpose or private study • criticism and review • reporting current events.
3	In the case of research for a non-commercial purpose or private study, multiple copying would not be fair dealing.
4	Courts are left to decide what constitutes 'fair dealing' on a case-by-case basis.
5	It relates to quality as well as quantity of what is being copied.

Figure 2.4 What is fair dealing?

that 'Fair dealing with a literary, dramatic, musical or artistic work for the purposes of *research for a non-commercial purpose* does not infringe any copyright in the work provided that it is accompanied by a sufficient acknowledgement', while section 29(1C) says that 'Fair dealing with a literary, dramatic, musical or artistic work for the purposes of *private study* does not infringe any copyright in the work.' Tucked away in a section of minor definitions (s178) there is a definition which makes it clear that private study is also non-commercial: ' "private study" does not include any study which is directly or indirectly for a commercial purpose.'

The problem is that the CDPA does not define what is meant by the phrase 'fair dealing'. It is therefore left to the courts to decide on a case-by-case basis whether or not a particular instance of copying was fair – a point made by Lord Denning in Hubbard v. Vosper [1972] 2 QB 84 CA, which pre-dates the CDPA.

The phrase 'fair dealing' is commonly thought to mean that the copying must not unfairly deprive the copyright owner of income for their intellectual property. Copyright owners earn income not just from sales of the original work, but also from photocopying undertaken under licensing schemes operated by collective licensing societies such as the Copyright Licensing Agency (CLA). This income is a just return for the creative work of the author and the financial investment made by the publisher.

If you rely on the fair dealing exceptions to justify copying activity, then you should minimize the risks of copyright infringement by considering the following points:

1 To be considered fair dealing, the copying must fit within one of the following three categories:

   - research for a non-commercial purpose or private study s29(1)
   - criticism and review s30(1)
   - reporting current events s30(2) (this does not cover photographs).

2 Multiple copying for the purpose of non-commercial research or private study would not normally be considered to be fair, nor would systematic single copying. Therefore the copying should normally be restricted to making a single copy.

3 Multiple copying for the purposes of criticism and review, or reporting current events, is permitted.

4 CILIP recommends that copying under the exception for fair dealing for the purposes of non-commercial research and private study shall be kept within the limits set out in the Library Regulations.[13] The CILIP copyright poster states that the agreed safe copying limit is one chapter or 5% of extracts from a published work, or one article from any one issue of a journal or periodical.

5 If the copying is likely to have a significant economic impact upon the copyright owner, then it would not be considered to be fair dealing.

6 Ask yourself whether you intend to copy a 'substantial' part. The legislation does not define what is meant by 'substantial', although it is clear from case law that 'substantial' relates not just to quantity but also to quality. For example, if you were to copy a two-page executive summary from a market research report, and that contained the most valuable findings from the report, the rights owner might argue that the copying was unfair. In a quick guide to copyright and moral rights, the Society of Authors[14] mentions one case where four lines from a 32-line poem were held to amount to a 'substantial part'.

7 What is the purpose of the copying? If the copying is undertaken to support research for a commercial purpose, then fair dealing for research cannot be used as a defence (see Figure 2.5).

1	Copying for a commercial purpose has not been defined by statute.
2	The European Court of Justice has the final say.
3	The test is whether the research is for a commercial purpose, not whether it is done by a commercial body.
4	When deciding whether or not research has a non-commercial purpose, businesses will only need to consider what is known at the time of copying.
5	Some research in a commercial environment could be classed as non-commercial, such as copying to support private study for law exams.

Figure 2.5 What constitutes copying for a commercial purpose?

There are no formal guidelines as to what would count as commercial copying, although there are a number of useful indicators: the British Library and the Copyright Licensing Agency have produced joint guidance on the changes to UK copyright law which came about through SI 2003/2498,[15] and Charles Oppenheim set out a number of examples of what he considers would be commercial and what would be non-commercial copying.[16]

The legislation does not provide us with a definition of what is meant by copying for a non-commercial purpose or copying for a commercial purpose. The Intellectual Property and Innovation Directorate at the Patent Office believes that to try and define it would result in less flexibility for librarians and researchers. In any case, it would ultimately be for the ECJ to decide precisely what research for a commercial purpose means. We do, however, have a number of helpful pointers to try and determine what would be copying for a commercial purpose. The test is whether the research is for a commercial purpose, not whether it is done by a commercial body. Research carried out may have no immediate commercial goal but may possibly have an unforeseen commercial application at a later date. The law cannot expect you to do more than decide what is the case on the day you ask for the copy. This could be relevant when the commercial purpose is as yet unknown or undefined. If there is no commercial purpose on the day the copy is requested, then it would seem reasonable to sign the copyright declaration form as non-commercial (see Figure 2.8), which is required for all copying under the library regulations (SI 1989/1212), but ultimately only the courts and the ECJ can decide. If it is known that research is directly funded by a commercial organization and is related to a product or service which will be going into the market, then it is likely to be for a commercial purpose.

Where the copying is undertaken within the scope of the fair dealing provisions, this would normally require acknowledgement. However, Section 30(3) of the CDPA 1988 does say that 'no acknowledgement is required in connection with the reporting of current events by means of a sound recording, film or broadcast where this would be impossible for reasons of practicality or otherwise.'

Copyright legislation does not set out percentages or numbers of words that can legitimately be copied under the exceptions. The recommended limits set out in Figure 2.6 should be given with a health warning to the effect that they are merely guidance, and a court would make a judgment about what was fair dealing based on the circumstances of an individual case. The guidance is based on the premise that fair-dealing copying for non-commercial research or private study purposes should observe the same limits that are set out in the Library Regulations (SI 1989/1212); the 5% limit for books is based on guidance in the CILIP copyright poster.[17]

> *Fair dealing for research for non-commercial purposes and private study only*
>
> Books   Up to a maximum of 5% of extracts or one complete chapter
> Journals   One article from a single issue of a journal

Figure 2.6 Guidance on what you are allowed to copy

2.5.2 The Library Provisions in the CDPA 1988

Sections 38–43 of the CDPA deal with copying by librarians and archivists, and they should be read in conjunction with SI 1989/1212 – the Copyright (Librarians and Archivists) (Copying of Copyright Material) Regulations 1989 as amended by SI 2003/2498 – the Copyright and Related Rights Regulations 2003.

Library privilege applies to staff who work in 'prescribed libraries' and who carry out photocopying on behalf of their users (see Figure 2.7). Schedule 1 of SI 1989/1212 sets out which libraries are 'prescribed'. These include:

- public libraries
- national libraries
- libraries in educational establishments
- parliamentary and government libraries
- local authority libraries
- libraries whose main purpose is to encourage the study of a wide range of subjects (including libraries outside the UK).

The regulations specifically exclude libraries that are conducted for profit.

1	Library privilege only applies to 'prescribed' (not-for-profit) libraries.
2	It provides an indemnity for librarians copying on behalf of their users as long as the conditions are met.
3	It only applies to copying for non-commercial purposes or private study.
4	Library users must sign a statutory declaration form.
5	It is important to retain the statutory declaration because it is the librarian's indemnity. The minimum period that these should be kept for is six years plus the current year, taking account of the Limitation Act 1980 [this act does not relate to Scotland, where the Prescription and Limitation (Scotland) Act 1973 applies].
6	Librarians should be cautious about giving out advice to their users on what constitutes copying for a commercial purpose. They must not knowingly be party to advising or telling people how to fill in the declaration or they could be liable for any infringement too.

Figure 2.7 Library privilege

Libraries have special privileges to copy:

- for their readers (ss38–9)
- for other libraries (s41):
  — any library in the UK can supply a copy of an item, but only 'prescribed libraries' can receive copies
- for preservation (s42) under the following conditions:
  — the work is in the permanent collection for reference or lending only to other libraries and archives
  — the copy made will only be used for these purposes
  — where it is not reasonably practicable to purchase a copy of the item
- for replacement (s42) of all or part of a work for a prescribed library provided that all of the following conditions as set out in the Library Regulations (SI 1989/1212) are met:
  — the copy is required to replace an item which has been lost, damaged or destroyed
  — the work being replaced was in the permanent collection for reference or lending only to other libraries
  — the copy made will only be used for these same purposes
  — a copy cannot reasonably be purchased
  — the requesting library provides a declaration saying it is a prescribed library and giving the purposes for which it requires the copy (i.e. if the item has been lost, destroyed or damaged)
  — the requesting library pays a sum equivalent to but not exceeding the cost (including a contribution to the general expenses of the library or archive) attributable to its production.

Libraries can also copy certain unpublished works (s43):

- if the document was deposited before it was published
- if the copyright owner has not prohibited copying
- if the reader pays a sum equivalent to but not exceeding the cost (including a contribution to the general expenses of the library or archive) attributable to its production
- if a statutory declaration is signed, which must state that:
  — the work was not published before it was deposited

— the copy is for research for a non-commercial purpose or private study and will not be further copied
— a copy has not previously been supplied.

Library privilege covers copying undertaken by library staff on behalf of library users, whether they be local users or interlibrary users. It cannot be claimed by the individual users themselves. Library privilege covers literary, dramatic or musical works, including typographical arrangements and illustrations, but it does not cover artistic works.

Under library privilege, library staff can make one copy of an article from an issue of a periodical, or copy a reasonable proportion of a non-periodical work, provided that a number of conditions are met:

• the user signs the necessary statutory declaration form
• the user pays an appropriate sum so that the library is able to recover the costs of production of the photocopy
• no more than one article from a periodical issue or a reasonable proportion of a non-periodical work is copied
• the librarian is satisfied that the criteria set out in the legislation are met.

The statutory declaration form (see the sample copyright declaration form in Figure 2.8) which library users are required to sign must state:

• that a copy has not previously been supplied (by any librarian)
• that the copies are for research for a non-commercial purpose or private study and will not be further copied
• that they are not aware that anyone with whom they work or study has made, or intends to make, at or about the same time as this request, a request for substantially the same material for substantially the same purpose.

The Library Regulations (SI 1989/1212) do not require the declaration form to be precisely the same as the one which appears in Schedule 2 to the SI, but that it is 'substantially in accordance' with that form (see Figure 2.8). If the declaration is false the copy is an infringing copy and the reader is responsible.

While it is certainly the case that librarians have previously relied upon the

DECLARATION: COPY OF ARTICLE OR PART OF PUBLISHED WORK

To:
        The Librarian of..Library
        [Address of Library]

Please supply me with a copy of:
        * the article in the periodical, the particulars of which are
        [ ]

        * the part of the published work, the particulars of which are
        [ ]

required by me for the purposes of research for a non-commercial purpose or private study

2. I declare that –
(a) I have not previously been supplied with a copy of the same material by you or any other librarian;
(b) I will not use the copy except for research for a non-commercial purpose or private study and will not supply a copy of it to any other person; and
(c) to the best of my knowledge no other person with whom I work or study has made or intends to make, at or about the same time as this request, a request for substantially the same material for substantially the same purpose.

3. I understand that if the declaration is false in a material particular the copy supplied to me by you will be an infringing copy and that I shall be liable for infringement of copyright as if I had made the copy myself.

                                † Signature ....
                                Date ....

Name ....
Address ....
              ....
              ....

* Delete whichever is inappropriate.
† This must be the personal signature of the person making the request. A stamped or typewritten signature, or the signature of an agent, is *not* acceptable.

Figure 2.8 Copyright declaration form

fair dealing and library privilege exceptions as their main justification for the copying of copyright works, the CDPA does contain a number of other exceptions. For example, there are exceptions relating to public administration which permit copying for parliamentary and judicial proceedings (s45), Royal Commissions and statutory enquiries (s46), material open to public inspection or on official register (s47), material communicated to the Crown in the course of public business (s48), public records (s49) and acts done under statutory authority (s50). The Copyright (Visually Impaired Persons) Act 2002 was implemented in October 2003 and it introduced two new copyright exceptions. These are outlined in the chapter on disability discrimination (see 12.3).

More often than not the business community will experience difficulty trying to fit copying into any of the copyright exceptions or permitted acts, and they are advised to look to the copyright licences offered by the collective licensing societies as a possible solution.

2.6   Licensing

What copyright law does not allow can often be done with the copyright owner's consent through an appropriate licence – usually in exchange for payment (Chapter 10 deals with contracts and licensing agreements). The CDPA allows for the setting up of collective licensing bodies such as the Copyright Licensing Agency (CLA) or the Newspaper Licensing Agency (NLA). Where there is a dispute between a collecting society and users or groups representing users, these can be referred to the Copyright Tribunal, which is administered by a Secretary who is a civil servant working in the Patent Office.[18] The Copyright Tribunal is not a cheap and quick source of resolution because its decisions are legally binding and so parties are likely to make similar provisions to those that they would make for a court case. The decisions of the Copyright Tribunal are appealable to the High Court (or in Scotland to the Court of Session) only on a point of law.

2.6.1   Copyright Licensing Agency

The Copyright Licensing Agency (CLA) is one of the UK's largest reproduction rights organizations. It is a not-for-profit company which was established in 1982 by the Publishers Licensing Society (PLS) and the Authors Licensing and Collecting Society (ALCS); it also now works closely with the Design Artists Copyright Society (DACS). The CLA licenses photocopying from magazines, books and journals, and takes action against infringers.

The CLA offers a range of licences, according to the type of organization applying.[19] There are licences for business, law firms, pharmaceutical companies, public administration, higher education and schools. There is also a licence available for press cuttings agencies. As required by s136 of the CDPA,[20] licence holders are given an indemnity against liability for infringement provided that the licence terms are complied with.

The CLA regularly publishes a 'list of excluded categories and excluded works',[21] which lists the publishers and/or the individual titles that cannot be copied under the terms of the licence agreement. It also lists a number of countries whose works are covered by the licence. There are a number of 'excluded categories' such as printed music, workbooks, work cards or assignment sheets, tests or public examination papers, industrial house journals, photographs and all UK newspapers.

Key features of the standard business licence are:

- scanned copies can be distributed by e-mail
- there is no limit to the number of photocopies or scanned copies of licensed material which may be made or distributed
- photocopying and scanning of artistic works such as photographs, diagrams and illustrations are included in the licence
- copies can be made and distributed from copies received from licensed press cuttings agencies and copyright-fee-paid copies from document delivery services.

While copies can be scanned and distributed by e-mail, the standard business licence does not permit these electronic copies to be stored in a central repository available to others in the organization, such as a company intranet, a networked computer drive or a shared system such as Lotus Notes.[22] The CLA has been discussing with rights-owners the possibility of offering an enhanced business licence which would cater for those requirements, but it remains to be seen whether this will get sufficient rights-holder support. Under the standard business licence electronic copies can, however, be retained permanently as long as they are housed on a standalone PC or on a non-networked drive.

One geographic limitation to bear in mind regarding the CLA's scanning licences is that they don't cover the scanning of content from other countries, only UK content.

The licence fee is usually based on a rate per professional employee, and the interpretation of what is meant by a professional employee will differ from sector to sector. There is one licence available from the CLA which is not based upon a rate per professional employee, and that is the small business licence which is available for businesses employing up to 50 employees. Businesses are charged a flat fee which is based upon the total number of staff. There are two bands – one for businesses employing up to 10 people, and the other for those employing between 11 and 50 employees. The small business licence incorporates the same terms as the business licence.

The CLA exists in order to collect licence fees from organizations wishing to make copies of items and then passes those fees on to authors, publishers and visual artists. In order for the fee distributions to be fair to authors and publishers, it is necessary to gather information on what material is being copied. It is for this reason that licence holders are required to complete an information audit in which they tell the CLA what journals they subscribe to and what books they have purchased. Surveys are also undertaken to record what is being copied. The fees are then distributed to authors, publishers, and visual creators and artists, through the ALCS, the PLS and the DACS respectively.

2.6.2 Newspaper Licensing Agency

Set up in January 1996, the NLA operates a licensing scheme to collect royalties on behalf of newspaper publishers. The NLA licence covers UK national and regional papers, and a number of foreign titles. There are a number of different types of licence available, such as licences for professional practices, schools, public relations agencies and trade or professional associations.

The NLA licence covers the photocopying on paper of newspaper articles, either on an ad-hoc basis or as part of a press cuttings service. The standard licence permits the copying of a maximum of 250 copies of any one article. It covers paper-to-paper copying only unless you opt to pay for an electronic extension. It is not possible to have an electronic licence in its own right, but only as an extension to the main licence. This permits in-house electronic scanning of cuttings taken from newspapers covered by the NLA for circulation by e-mail or by electronic means such as an intranet. However, the licence only allows these to be retained electronically for up to seven days.

The NLA licence does not cover the copying of photographs, illustrations or advertisements. The copying that is permitted is intended for management information purposes only, and thus it specifically excludes: copying for distribution internally to a sales force for use as a sales aid; inclusion in an in-house publication; inclusion in the company's annual report and accounts; or copying for marketing or promotional purposes. Such copying would require the user to obtain permission directly from the newspaper publishers.

In the summer of 2005, the NLA launched eClips, a centralized digital database of newspaper articles, giving press clippings agencies and their customers a system for delivering a wider range of better quality news clippings. It includes content from News International, and this is the first time that News International content has been included in an NLA digital licence. According to the NLA press release about eClips, 'end users will continue to pay the same fee for their NLA licences. Press clipping agencies are being charged an additional cost, which they are expected to recoup due to the operational savings that the database will provide. PCAs have no obligation to use the service.'[23]

2.6.3   Design Artists Copyright Society

Formed in 1983, DACS represents visual creators, artists and photographers. It licenses the use of artistic works such as photographs, sculptures, charts, maps, cartoons and diagrams. DACS also pursues cases of copyright infringement on behalf of its members.

Many artists create their works as a result of a commission, and they might directly administer and control their primary rights, but they may not be able to control their secondary rights. DACS manages this for them through their 'Payback' campaign. Some of the rights that are often collectively licensed and administered include off-air recording right, reprographic right, cable retransmission right, and terrestrial and satellite broadcast rights.

DACS lobbied on behalf of its members for the introduction of Artists Resale Right (*droit de suite*) under which an artist gets a percentage each time a work is sold after the first sale. The Artists Resale Right was the subject of a 2001 directive,[24] and the right came into force for living artists on 14 February 2006. The royalty payment is payable where the resale involves art dealers or other art market professionals as sellers, buyers or intermediaries. This royalty is not payable where the resale takes place directly between private individuals or where the resale price is below a certain limit (see also Section 2.4.5.6).

2.6.4 Ordnance Survey[25]

The Ordnance Survey provides a licensing system to enable people to make use of mapping products such as maps and aerial photographs. There are licences available for education, local authorities, commercial and business, legal procedures and planning permissions. These licences are used by customers ranging from solicitors, shopkeepers and estate agents through to engineers. Under these licences, users pay an annual fee in order to be able to make unlimited copies of paper maps for internal business use or to publish Ordnance Survey mapping externally for display and promotion purposes, as long as this does not result in any direct financial gain from the use of the mapping.

Ordnance Survey Northern Ireland v. Automobile Association (2001)
Ordnance Survey (OS) launched a High Court action against the Automobile Association in 1996 after the AA was caught copying dozens of OS maps. Cartographers at OS trapped the copiers by putting faults, such as tiny kinks in rivers, in dozens of maps. These helped to prove that maps in 26 million published guides, which the AA claimed as its own work, were straightforward copies.

In 2000 the AA had already admitted breaching crown copyright of 64 maps and agreed to pay £875,000 compensation. In this separate case more than 500 publications were involved with more than 300 million copies printed.

Outcome: The Automobile Association agreed to pay £20m in compensation. The money was paid over a period of two years and covered back-dated royalties, interest, legal costs and an advance on the AA's coming royalties for the next year.

2.6.5 The Office for Public Sector Information

OPSI – the Office for Public Sector Information – is a division of the Cabinet Office. It incorporates Her Majesty's Stationery Office and is at the heart of information policy, setting standards, delivering access and encouraging re-use of public sector information (see Chapter 6). The department provides online access to UK legislation, licenses the re-use of Crown copyright material, manages the Information Fair Trader Scheme (see Section 6.2.3), maintains the Government's Information Asset Register (see Section 6.2.2) and provides advice and guidance on official publishing and Crown copyright.

In March 1999 the White Paper *The Future Management of Crown Copyright*[26] announced that unrestricted copying and reproduction of certain categories of Crown copyright material would be permitted. As a result, copyright is waived for material such as court forms, legislation and government press notices in order to encourage its widespread use for reference and onward dissemination to all with interests in these areas. The word 'waiver' can be a bit misleading, because crown copyright is still asserted in order to protect the material against use in a misleading or derogatory manner. But the OPSI waiver means that the Crown does not seek to exercise its legal right to license formally, restrict usage or charge for the reproduction of the content.

The waiver does stipulate a set of terms which must be complied with in order for the copying to be permitted. These terms include:

- all reproduction of the material should be made from an official version
- the material should be reproduced accurately
- care should be taken that the material reproduced is from the current or up-to-date version
- the material should not be used in a derogatory or misleading manner
- the material should not be used to advertise or promote a particular product or service
- the material is properly acknowledged.

OPSI issues guidance to government departments, agencies and all users of Crown-copyright-protected material in the form of a series of guidance notes, which are available on the OPSI website.[27] Each guidance note covers a category of material and sets out what copying is permitted and under what conditions.

In addition to the Crown copyright material for which a waiver applies as set out in the OPSI guidance notes, more material can be copied under a 'click-use' licence (see Section 6.2.1) from OPSI.[28] The main purpose of the click-use licence is to provide users with a fast system which lets them re-use a wide range of core government information that is central to the process of government and is subject to Crown copyright protection. The click-use licence does not cover computer programs, software, personal identity documents, or value added products or services that have been developed by government; there are also many departments with government trading fund status whose material is outside the remit of the click-use licence.

2.6.5.1 Reproducing short extracts

OPSI's policy on the re-use of crown copyright extracts[29] allows extracts of up to 250 words to be re-used without the need to apply for a licence, in order to simplify the process and reduce unnecessary administration and delay for re-users of Crown copyright material.

This covers both core and value added text. It does not, however, cover:

- text that appears in tables, diagrams and forms
- cases where a department states that the material may not be re-used
- the re-use of official imprints and departmental logos unless you have the permission of the department concerned.

People wishing to reproduce short extracts of crown copyright material should also bear in mind the terms of the copyright waivers as set out above.

2.6.5.2 Advisory Panel on Public Sector Information

The Advisory Panel on Public Sector Information (APPSI) is chaired by Professor Richard Susskind. It was formed in April 2003 and was initially known as the Advisory Panel on Crown Copyright. The panel has three key roles:

- to advise Ministers on how to encourage and create opportunities in the information industry for greater re-use of government information
- to advise the Controller of HMSO about changes and opportunities in the information industry, so that the licensing of Crown copyright information is aligned with current and emerging developments
- to advise on the impact of the complaints procedures under the Information Fair Trader Scheme.

The Panel is charged with advising ministers strategically on how to open up opportunities for greater re-use of government information by the private and voluntary sectors of the economy, and advising the Controller of HMSO about changes and opportunities in the information industry.

2.6.5.3 Parliamentary copyright

In addition to Crown copyright material, OPSI manages parliamentary copyright on behalf of the parliamentary authorities. It provides guidance on the levels of copying of parliamentary material that are permitted through the 'Dear Librarian' letter (see Figure 2.9). This states that people are entitled to make one photocopy of a document in its entirety so long as no more than one copy is made for any one individual and that the copies are not distributed to other individuals or organizations; they can also make multiple copies of extracts of up to 30% of a work or one complete chapter, whichever is the greater (see also Chapter 6 on the re-use of public sector information.)

The 'Dear Librarian' letter permits users to copy the text from any single title or document in its entirety provided that:

- no more than one photocopy is made for any one individual
- copies are not distributed to other individuals or organizations.

There is an exception for schools and places of higher education, which are allowed to provide a single copy to each student.

The guidelines also permit unlimited photocopies of extracts from any title or document provided that the extracts from any single work do not exceed 30% or one complete chapter or equivalent, whichever is the greater.

The categories of parliamentary material covered by these guidelines include:

- Lords and Commons Official Reports (Hansard)
- House Business Papers, including Journals of both Houses, Lords Minutes, the Vote Bundle, Commons Order Books
- Commons Public Bill Lists
- Statutory Instruments Lists
- Weekly Information Bulletin
- Sessional Information Digest.

Figure 2.9   Parliamentary material that can be copied under the 'Dear Librarian' letter[30]

2.7   Electronic copyright

Works which are 'published' in electronic form, such as electronic journals, PDF documents on the internet, CD-ROM or online databases, are protected by copyright law.

2.7.1   Internet

Content on websites and in e-mail messages is protected by copyright law.

In a single web page there can be many different copyrights. For example, the textual articles are literary works; the graphics are artistic works; sound files are sound recordings containing musical works; and the HTML coding and metadata are literary works. People wishing to undertake copying of material on the internet which falls outside any of the permitted acts should check to see if there is a copyright notice on the web page. If the copying they wish to undertake is not covered in the copyright notice, or if there is no copyright notice on the website, then you should ask for permission by contacting the webmaster. It is safest to work on the basis that there is no implied licence to copy material which is available on the internet.

Librarians not only need to consider copyright when copying material from the internet, they also need to bear in mind that, under the Copyright Rights in Databases Regulations 1997,[31] many websites will fall under the definition of a database and will have the protection of database right (see section 2.7.2). An important legal case which dealt with database right was that of the British Horseracing Board (BHB) v. William Hill EUECJ C-203/02 (9 November 2004).[32] The ECJ judgement shows that in order for database right to apply there must have been a substantial investment in the obtaining, verification and presentation of the contents of the database, and that this must be distinct from any investment involved in the creation of the contents of the database.

Copying in relation to any description of work includes the making of copies which are transient or are incidental to some other use of the work – CDPA s17(6). When you look at a web page, for example, you will have automatically made more than one copy simply by virtue of the way in which the technology works – the copy that you see on the screen as well as the copy that is automatically saved to your web browser's cache. It is for this reason that directive 2001/29/EC has one mandatory exception. Article 5.1 requires member states to provide an exception to the reproduction right for certain temporary acts which are transient or incidental, and so SI 2003/2498 inserts s28A into the CDPA:

> Copyright in a literary work, other than a computer program or a database, or in a dramatic, musical or artistic work, the typographical arrangement of a published edition, a sound recording or a film, is not infringed by the making of a temporary copy which is transient or incidental, which is an

integral and essential part of a technological process and the sole purpose of which is to enable —

(a) a transmission of the work in a network between third parties by an intermediary; or
(b) a lawful use of the work;

and which has no independent economic significance.

2.7.1.1 Right of communication to the public

The copyright owner has the right to prevent anyone else from communicating the work to the public by electronic transmission. This includes broadcasting the work and also making the work available by electronic transmission so that members of the public may access it from a place and at a time individually chosen by them. If you want to include another person's content on your website it is essential that you obtain their permission.

Remedies available to a copyright owner who finds that someone has made use of his or her content without permission include damages and an injunction to stop the inclusion of the material on the website.

2.7.1.2 Hyperlinking and deep linking

Hyperlinking is an integral part of the way in which the web works, allowing people either to jump from one website to another or to navigate from one page within a site to another page on the same site. There have been quite a number of legal cases which have considered the use of hyperlinks, and in particular deep links, and whether or not these are legitimate, although the vast majority of these cases have been heard in non-UK jurisdictions.

In June 2005 the Department of Trade and Industry published a *Consultation Document on the Electronic Commerce Directive: the liability of hyperlinkers, location tool services and content aggregators*. This set out three types of hyperlink:

1 Linking takes you to a home page of a particular website: this is also known as 'shallow linking'.
2 Deep linking occurs when a link takes you directly to a specific page (or part of a page) of a website.

3 Framing occurs when a webpage is linked to another site which appears in a 'frame' of the original website visited, and the uniform resource locator (URL) remains that of the original website.

The use of deep links can be problematic for a number of reasons:

1 If the website that you are linking to has banner advertisements on its home page, for which the site owner gets an income based upon the number of 'click throughs', then you should avoid linking to a page further down within the site because it could be argued that, by deep linking within the site, you are depriving the site owner of income.
2 By deep linking to a page within a site, you might be said to be encouraging people to go directly to a page when the site owner might want you to see a set of terms and conditions before viewing any pages on their site. Indeed, by getting people to circumvent the page containing terms and conditions of use, you might actually be stopping people from seeing that the site owner has clearly stated in those terms and conditions of use that deep linking is not permitted.
3 Linking may be judged to be an infringement of database right. In Stepstone v. OFiR [2000 EBLR 87] a German court took the view that Stepstone's website, which provided a database of job vacancies, was protected by the database right, and that OFiR's activities amounted to the repeated and systematic extraction of insubstantial parts of Stepstone's database, which prejudiced Stepstone's legitimate interests.
4 The use of frames technology can also be problematic. With frames it is possible to link from one website to another without users realizing that they have linked through to an external site. This could suggest a false association with the other site.

Looking at some of the legal cases that have addressed the question of deep linking, one is led to the conclusion that the law is still uncertain in this particular area. In the author's opinion, however, to respond to this by avoiding the use of links altogether is an overreaction to the perceived risks. I would advise anyone wishing to make use of hyperlinking and deep linking to bear in mind the points outlined in Figure 2.10.

1	Make it clear what is being done and who you are linking to.
2	Avoid using frames technology which could result in your appearing to pass off someone's content as your own.
3	Ideally, the hyperlink should open in a new page.
4	Use a disclaimer about the content of external sites.
5	Check the terms and conditions on sites that you wish to link to.
6	Do not circumvent anti-linking measures.
7	Link to the home page if that will do.
8	Avoid deep linking that is commercially unfair (i.e. which will lead you to benefit commercially at the expense of the owner of the site you are linking to).
9	Inform the content owners that you wish to link to their site. This is a matter of good netiquette and may lead them to create a reciprocal link from their website.

Figure 2.10 Points to consider when deep linking

2.7.2   Database regulations

The Copyright and Rights in Databases Regulations (SI 1997/3032) came into force on 1 January 1998. They implement council directive 96/9/EC on the legal protection of databases. The regulations introduce a new right – database right – which subsists if there has been a substantial investment in obtaining, verifying and presenting the contents of the database. In order for a database to qualify additionally for full copyright protection, it must be the author's own intellectual creation by virtue of the selection and arrangement of the contents. Some databases might qualify for both copyright and database right. The regulations do not consider a database to be limited to electronic information, but rather as any collection of independent works, data or other materials which are arranged in a systematic or methodical way and are individually accessible by electronic or other means. Collections of data such as directories, encyclopaedias, statistical databases, online collections of journals, multimedia collections and many websites would fit this definition of a database.

As with copyright, there are a number of exceptions to database right. However, the number of exceptions is far fewer than is the case for copyright. Fair dealing with a database is permitted so long as the person extracting the material is a lawful user of the database, and as such that person must show that their purpose is illustration for teaching, research or private study and not for any commercial purpose, and that the source is indicated. The regulations state that 'the doing of anything in relation to a database for the purposes of research for a commercial purpose is not fair dealing with the database.' They distinguish clearly between research or private study and research for commercial purposes. This was the first time that such a distinction was made in UK copyright law, and this principle was extended in SI 2003/2498 to cover all copyright-protected material.

Schedule 1 of the Regulations sets out a number of exceptions to database right for public administration and these relate to:

- parliamentary and judicial proceedings
- Royal Commissions and statutory inquiries
- material open to public inspection or on an official register
- public records
- actions taken under statutory authority.

In the case of copyright the period of protection for a database is normally 70 years from the end of the year of death of the author if there is one, or the end of the year of first publication if there isn't a personal author. In the case of database right, the period of protection is for 15 years from its creation or from its being made available to the public if this occurs during the 15-year period. Importantly, any substantial new investment would qualify the database for a new 15-year term of protection. Many databases are maintained continually and this can involve a significant investment. As such, they can potentially end up being protected for an indefinite period.

British Horseracing Board v. William Hill was a key case exploring the meaning and significance of database right (for further information see Section 2.7.1).

2.7.3 Licensing of electronic resources

One of the problems with electronic information is that its use is normally governed by a licence or contract rather than by copyright law, and these licences often differ on key points from one supplier to another. It is for this reason that a number of initiatives [33] have been undertaken to try and come up with a standard licence for electronic resources (see also Section 10.4 – Consortia and standard licences).

With electronic information, as with hard-copy information, it is important to make a distinction between single copying and multiple copying. If, for example, you send an e-mail to several people which contains a scanned item in which you do not own the rights, you will have undertaken multiple copying. In those circumstances it cannot be said to be covered by the provisions for fair dealing for non-commercial purposes or private study.

2.7.3.1 JISC/PA Guidelines on Fair Dealing in an Electronic Environment

In 1998, JISC (Joint Information Systems Committee) and the Publishers Association (PA) published *Guidelines for Fair Dealing in an Electronic Environment*.[34] These guidelines were intended specifically for the higher education sector. The main aim of the JISC/PA working party was to identify any possible areas of agreement between representatives of JISC and the PA on a practical definition of fair dealing of materials in electronic form, and, if possible, the necessary mechanisms that might be used to provide a workable monitoring system (see Table 2.1). The agreement contains the following definitions:

- electronic publication: publication created in electronic format or originally in paper form and converted under copyright law
- part: one article from a journal issue, one chapter from a book, or 10% of other works
- issue: collection of articles issued at the same time under same issue number.

Table 2.1   JISC/PA guidelines on fair dealing in an electronic environment

Acceptable	Not acceptable
Viewing on screen	
Printing to paper – one copy of a part	
Copying to disk – part	Copying to disk – all
Transmission to enable printing – part	Transmission to enable printing – all
Transmission for permanent storage – part	Transmission for permanent storage – all
	Posting on a network or website open to the public
	Copying and transmitting an image, or a set of images, with little or no text associated with them is probably not fair dealing

2.7.4 Electronic copyright management systems

Electronic copyright management systems (ECMS) can provide a techno-logical solution for rights-owners wishing to ensure that their intellectual property is not copied or redisseminated in an unauthorized manner. They can provide robust and reliable tamper-proof mechanisms for controlling the usage of copyright material. An ECMS has two key roles. One relates to track-ing and monitoring usage, and therefore deals with the area of security and authentication, and the other concerns payment issues through the licens-ing of material and charging of royalties.

In principle, the copyright exceptions or permitted acts apply to digital infor-mation. However, if the rights-owners have made use of technical measures to prevent access to their work(s), the copyright exceptions are rendered worthless, because it would be illegal to try and break any copy protection that is in place. SI 2003/2498 implements the provisions of directive 2001/29/EC into UK law, and this makes it an offence to break through a tech-nical protection measure or to remove or alter information from an ECMS.

CDPA 1988 s296ZE sets out the remedy available where effective tech-nological measures prevent a person from carrying out a permitted act. Basically the person affected can issue a notice of complaint to the Secretary of State for Trade and Industry. A class action is also possible where a repre-sentative of a group of affected people submits a complaint to the Secretary of State. The Secretary of State can then give directions to the publisher to rectify the situation.

2.7.5 Electronic signatures and copyright declaration forms

Section 7 of the Electronic Communications Act 2000 implemented the pro-visions of directive 1999/93/EC[35] relating to the admissibility of electronic signatures as evidence in legal proceedings, while the Electronic Signatures Regulations 2002 (SI 2002/318) implemented the provisions relating to the supervision of a certification-service provider,[36] its liability in certain cir-cumstances and relevant data protection requirements. These regulations define electronic signatures as 'data in electronic form which are attached to or logically associated with other electronic data and which serve as a method of authentication'.

The Library Regulations (SI 1989/1212) require the requester to sign the statu-tory declaration form. It is not acceptable for a librarian to sign the declaration form on behalf of the user. Schedule 2 to these Regulations says that 'this must be the personal signature of the person making the request. A stamped or typewritten signature, or the signature of an agent, is NOT acceptable.' What would be the status of an electronic signature? The Patent Office understands that the Library Regulations already cover e-signatures.[37] The Regulations require that the signature must be in writing, and writing is defined in the CDPA s178 as including any form of notation or code, whether by hand or otherwise.

Librarians can receive copyright declaration forms which have been signed electronically. The problem is that they must fulfil the requirements for a personal signature. The signature has to have a unique link to the requester which cannot easily be used by others. In short, this means that the signature must be linked to an authentication system. At the time of writing the British Library is in the process of launching a service as part of BL Direct which will enable users of the service to sign copyright declaration forms using digital signatures, in a way which satisfies the legal requirements.

2.8   Ethical and professional issues and conflicts

Library and information service professionals find themselves in a difficult situation, playing the role of 'piggy in the middle' – acting as guardians of intellectual property while at the same time being committed to supporting their users' needs to gain access to copyright works and the ideas that they contain.

CILIP's Ethical Principles and Code of Professional Practice for Library and Information Professionals[38] states that information professionals should strive to achieve an appropriate balance, within the law, between demands from information users, the need to respect confidentiality, the terms of their employment, the public good and the responsibilities outlined in the Code. It also says that information professionals should defend the legitimate needs and interests of information users, while upholding the moral and legal rights of the creators and distributors of intellectual property. The key point here is that commitment to providing users with information has to be tempered by the need to do so within the limits of the law, which includes respecting copyright law.

Similarly, the EIRENE code of practice for information brokers[39] also deals with a number of copyright-related issues, stating that 'a broker shall abide by copyright law' (A.3) and that he/she should 'clarify their copyright position vis-à-vis the information suppliers and inform the client of their copyright obligations as regards the information provided' (B.1).

The CLA has a whistleblower's line. There was an instance when a disaffected librarian, after leaving their job, rang the whistleblower's line to inform the CLA of the systematic copyright infringement of their former employer which had been undertaken over a long period of time. This led to the company paying out £50,000 in damages and costs, and also taking out a CLA licence.[40]

It is not the role of the librarian or information professional to police the copying undertaken by their users on behalf of rights-owners. For example, the CLA makes clear in its guidance about the sticker scheme for walk-in users of public libraries that librarians are not required to monitor private copying or police the use of the sticker scheme. It is for each patron at a self-service copier to decide whether or not their copying is for commercial purposes and, if so, whether to ask for a sticker.

However, librarians should do everything they can to ensure copyright compliance within their organizations. This could, for example, include:

- putting up the CILIP posters next to photocopying machines or publicly accessible computers
- including guidance about copyright on intranets
- developing a set of frequently asked questions about copyright which covers the activities that users are most likely to wish to undertake
- making the users of electronic products aware of the key points of the terms and conditions of the relevant licence agreement(s).

Figure 2.11 (on next page) shows some helpful sites that offer advice on copyright.

2.9   Summary

In this chapter we have covered the general principles of copyright law (2.2); the legal and regulatory environment which governs the use of copyright material (2.4); the exceptions or permitted acts such as fair dealing and library privilege (2.5); licensing issues (2.6); the application of copyright law in the electronic environment (2.7); and a number of ethical and professional issues (2.8).

CILIP's information and advisory service (for CILIP members only)	info@cilip.org.uk
Libraries and Archives Copyright Alliance (LACA lobbies the government and the EU on all aspects of copyright on behalf of UK libraries, archives and information services and their users.	www.cilip.org.uk/laca
IPR helpdesk	www.ipr-helpdesk.org
Intellectual Property (UK government-backed website)	www.intellectual-property.gov.uk
JISC Legal Information Service (for the FE and HE sectors)	www.jisc.ac.uk/legal

Figure 2.11 Where to go to seek copyright advice

In the next chapter we will look at the general principles of data protection; the eight principles of good information handling; the rights of individuals; and the responsibilities of those who process personal data.

2.10   Further information
British Library
Website copyright pages: www.bl.uk/copyright

CILIP
7 Ridgmount Street, London WC1E 7AE
Tel: 020 7255 0620 (CILIP Information Services)
E-mail: info@cilip.org.uk (members only)
Website: www.cilip.org.uk

Copyright Licensing Agency
Saffron House, 6–10 Kirby Street, London EC1N 8TS
Tel: 020 7400 3100; Fax: 020 7400 3101
E-mail: cla@cla.og.uk
Website: www.cla.org.uk

Design Artists Copyright Society
33 Great Sutton Street, London EC1V 0DX
Tel: 020 7336 8811; Fax: 020 7336 8822
Website: www.dacs.org.uk

European Commission – Copyright and Neighbouring Rights
http://europa.eu.int/comm/internal_market/copyright/index_en.htm

IPR helpdesk (a project of the European Commission DG Enterprise)
www.ipr-helpdesk.org

Newspaper Licensing Agency
7–9 Church Road, Wellington Gate, Tunbridge Wells TN1 1NL
Tel: 01892 525273; Fax: 01892 525274
E-mail: copy@nla.co.uk
Website: www.nla.co.uk

Office for Public Sector Information
Enquiry Officer, Office for Public Sector Information, The Licensing
Division, St Clements House, 2–16 Colegate, Norwich NR3 1BQ
Tel: 01603 621000; Fax: 01603 723000
Contact page on website: www.opsi.gov.uk/about/contact-us/index.htm
Website: www.opsi.gov.uk

Ordnance Survey
Customer Service Centre (Copyright), Romsey Road, Southampton
SO16 4GU
Tel: 023 8030 5030
E-mail: customerservice@ordnancesurvey.co.uk
Website: www.ordnancesurvey.co.uk

Patent Office
Enquiry Unit: 0845 9500505
E-mail: enquiries@patent.gov.uk
Website: www.patent.gov.uk

World Intellectual Property Organization

Copyright and Related Rights Sector, 34 chemin des Colombettes, CH-1211 Geneva 20, Switzerland
Tel: 0041 22 338 9111; Fax: 0041 22 733 5428
E-mail: copyright.mail@wipo.int
Website: www.wipo.int

Notes and references

1   See www.unorg/Overview/rights.html.
2   Publishers and distributors in the United Kingdom and the Republic of Ireland have a legal obligation to send one copy of each of their publications to the Legal Deposit Office of the British Library within one month of publication. The other five legal deposit libraries (the National Library of Scotland, Edinburgh; Bodleian Library, Oxford; University Library, Cambridge; Trinity College, Dublin; and the National Library of Wales, Aberystwyth) are entitled to claim free of charge a copy of everything published in the United Kingdom, providing they make a claim in writing within a year of the date of publication.
3   See www.wto.org/english/tratop_e/trips_e/t_agm0_e.htm.
4   See www.europark.eu.int/oeil/index.jsp?language=en.
5   See http://europa.eu.int/comm/internal_market/copyright/docs/review/sec-2004-995_en.pdf.
6   European Copyright and Design Reports, Sweet and Maxwell.
7   Cornish, W. R. (2003) *Cases and Materials on Intellectual Property*, 4th edn, Sweet and Maxwell.
8   Published by Sweet and Maxwell.
9   Published by Sweet and Maxwell.
10   See www.bailii.org.
11   See www.westlaw.co.uk, www.lexisnexis.com and www.lawtel.co.uk.
12   One way of keeping up to date with case law on copyright is to subscribe to the RSS feeds of relevant sites such as Out-law.com, IPKat (ipkitten.blogspot.com), Mondaq.com and the IPR newsfeed (www.ipr-helpdesk.com) using an RSS newsreader such as Bloglines (www.bloglines.com).
13   SI 1989/1212 – the Copyright (Librarians and Archivists) (Copying of Copyright Material) Regulations 1989 as amended by SI 2003/2498 (commonly known as the Library Regulations).
14   The Society of Authors (2002) *Copyright and Moral Rights: quick guide 1*.
15   See www.bl.uk/services/information/copyrightfaq.html.

16 Oppenheim, C. (2002) Directive on copyright, *Library and Information Update*, **1** (5), 26–7.

17 See www.cilip.org.uk/professionalguidance/copyright/formsandposters/posters.htm.

18 Details of Copyright Tribunal cases can be found on the Patent Office website at www.patent.gov.uk/copy/tribunal/index.htm.

19 To see details of the full range of licences available from the CLA (which includes licences for schools, further education, higher education, business, government and public bodies), see www.cla.co.uk/licensing/index.php.

20 CDPA s136 – implied indemnity in schemes or licences for reprographic copying.

21 See www.cla.co.uk/support/excluded.html.

22 In the case of the pharmaceutical licence, electronic copies can be systematically stored on a shared network, server or intranet.

23 New digital database from the Newspaper Licensing Agency, 21 June 2005 (see press releases section of www.nla.co.uk).

24 Directive 2001/84/EC of the European Parliament and of the Council, 27 September 2001, on the Resale Right for the Benefit of the Author of an Original Work of Art, *Official Journal* L 272 (13 October 2001), 0032–6.

25 The Ordnance Survey website (www.ordnancesurvey.co.uk) has a number of useful publications on copyright such as *Copyright 4: copying our paper maps for business use* (www.ordnancesurvey.co.uk/oswebsite/business/copyright/copyright4/), as well as a set of FAQs.

26 See www.opsi.gov.uk/advice/crown-copyright/future-management-of-crown-copyright-guidance/.

27 See www.opsi.gov.uk/advice/crown-copyright/copyright-guidance/.

28 See www.opsi.gov.uk/click-use/index.htm.

29 See www.opsi.gov.uk/advice/crown-copyright/copyright-guidance/re-use-of-crown-copyright-extracts.htm.

30 For full details see www.opsi.gov.uk/advice/crown-copyright/copyright-guidance/guidance-for-librarians.doc.

31 The Copyright and Rights in Databases Regulations 1997: SI 1997/3032.

32 See the text of the judgment at www. curia.eu.int.

33 These include John Cox Associates (www.licensingmodels.com), ECUP (European Copyright Users Platform, www.eblida.org/ecup/licensing), ICOLC (International Coalition of Library Consortia, www.library.yale.edu/consortia/statement.html) and the NESLi2 licence for journals (www.nesli2.ac.uk/model.htm).

34   See www.ukoln.ac.uk/services/elib/papers/pa.

35   Directive 1999/93/EC of the European Parliament and of the Council of 13 December 1999 on a Community Framework for Electronic Signatures L13/12, published 19 January 2000.

36   A person who issues certificates or provides other services related to electronic signatures.

37   Statement by the Libraries and Archives Copyright Alliance (LACA) concerning electronic signatures on copyright declaration forms, June 2002, available at www.cilip.org.uk/professionalguidance/copyright/advice/e-signatures.htm.

38   See www.cilip.org.uk/professionalguidance/professionalethics/code.

39   EUSIDIC (European Association of Information Services), EIIA (European Information Industry Association) and EIRENE (European Information Researchers Network) (1993) *Code of Practice for Information Brokers*.

40   CLA (1996, 2 December) *Whistle Blower Leads to £50,000 Court Settlement for the Copyright Licensing Agency*, press release.

3 Data protection

3.1 Introduction

Information professionals process personal data as part of their daily work. Examples include the maintenance of user registration records, circulation records and management statistics on usage of the information service. They might be responsible for a contact database, or maintain an intranet or a website through which they collect and process personal data. In addition to the need to comply with the Data Protection Act 1998, CILIP members also need to abide by CILIP's Ethical Principles and Code of Professional Practice for Library and Information Professionals.[1] The Code states that information professionals should 'protect the confidentiality of all matters relating to information users, including their enquiries, any services to be provided, and any aspects of the users' personal circumstances or business'.

This chapter outlines the general principles of data protection (3.2), including the eight principles of good information handling (3.3). There is a section covering the processing of personal data (3.4), and the need to take additional care when processing sensitive personal data. The chapter then looks at notification (3.5) and the need for data processors to register with the Office of the Information Commissioner. Information professionals need to demonstrate good practice when processing personal data, but they are, of course, data subjects in their own right, who want to be able to protect their own information (3.6), and who should be aware of the rights that they themselves have as data subjects (3.8). The impact of data protection on employment is explored (3.9), including the contentious question of whether it is permissible to monitor an employee's internet, telephone or e-mail usage. Data protection compliance audits (3.11) can help to ensure that the data protection system in place is effective and that it works smoothly; the very fact that an audit is undertaken can help to raise awareness of data protection issues and the need for compliance. The chapter then deals with issues relating to websites and intranets (3.12), such as the use of cookies[2] and other invisible tracking devices, and the problem of spam or unsolicited commercial e-mail (3.12.2). Privacy or data protection statements are also considered. These are key documents and it is well worth spending time on drafting them, because they will govern what an organization can do with personal data. The chapter concludes by considering the implications of data protection for librarians (3.13), including the question of how public librarians handle requests for access to electoral roll data (3.14).

3.2   General principles

The Data Protection Act 1998 (DPA) came into force on 1 March 2000. It sets out how personal data should be handled. As far as the DPA is concerned, personal data means data which relate to an identified or identifiable living individual (see Figure 3.1, which sets out what constitutes personal data). The data could be about anyone in the world because the DPA applies either if control of the data is UK-based or if the data itself is held in the UK.

The DPA sets out the rules for the processing of personal information and it applies to personal data held on computer and in some paper records where these form part of a 'relevant filing system'.[3] In essence, for manual records to be covered by the DPA, they need to fulfil three criteria:

- they are not automatically processed
- they are structured by reference to individuals or criteria relating to individuals
- they contain specific information about individuals that is readily accessible.

Some manual records are covered by the DPA regardless of whether they are part of a relevant filing system. They include records relating to health matters, educational matters, housing matters and social security matters. The DPA also covers other media such as tape recordings and CCTV footage.

In Durant v. Financial Services Authority [2003] EWCA Civ 1746, the judge considered what is meant by a 'relevant filing system'. The Court of Appeal took the view that the Act intended to cover manual files 'only if they are of sufficient sophistication to provide the same or similar ready accessibility as a computerized filing system'.

The DPA defines personal data in section 1(1) as:

data which relate to a living individual who can be identified –

(a)   from those data, or

(b)   from those data and other information which is in the possession of, or is likely to come into the possession of, the data controller,

and includes any expression of opinion about the individual and any indication of the intentions of the data controller or any other person in respect of the individual.

The Court of Appeal judgment in Durant v. FSA [2003] EWCA Civ 1746 provides further guidance on what constitutes personal data (for further information about the Durant case see Section 3.2). The CA concluded that data will relate to an individual if it 'is information that affects [a person's] privacy, whether in his personal or family life, business or professional capacity'.

If in doubt as to whether information relates to an individual, ask yourself whether the information in question is capable of having an adverse impact upon the individual. The Court identified two notions which will assist those who need to determine whether the information relates to an individual:

1   Is the information biographical in a significant sense?
2   The information should have the individual as its focus.

Mere mention of an individual's name does not constitute personal data, unless its inclusion affects that individual's privacy. So the mere reference to an individual's name where that name is not associated with any other personal information, or the incidental mention in the minutes of a meeting of an individual's attendance at that meeting, would not normally be personal data.

In cases where the information in question can be linked to an identifiable individual, the following are examples of personal data:

* information about the medical history of an individual
* an individual's salary details
* information concerning an individual's tax liabilities
* information comprising an individual's bank statements; and
* information about individuals' spending preferences.

Figure 3.1   What constitutes personal data?

Any manual filing system 'which, for example, requires the searcher to leaf through files to see what and whether information qualifying as personal data of the person who has made the request [for access to his personal data] is to be found there, would bear no resemblance to a computerised search.' It would not, therefore, qualify as a relevant filing system.

The judgment concluded that:

a 'relevant filing system' for the purposes of the Act, is limited to a system:

1) in which the files forming part of it are structured or referenced in such a way as to clearly indicate at the outset of the search whether specific information capable of amounting to personal data of an individual requesting it under section 7 is held within the system and, if so, in which file or files it is held; and

2) which has, as part of its own structure or referencing mechanism, a sufficiently sophisticated and detailed means of readily indicating whether and where in an individual file or files specific criteria or information about the applicant can be readily located.

Where manual files fall within the definition of a relevant filing system, the content will either be so sub-divided as to allow the searcher to go straight to the correct category and retrieve the information requested without a manual search, or will be so indexed as to allow a searcher to go directly to the relevant page/s.

Following the Durant judgment, it is likely that very few manual files are covered by the provisions of the DPA. However, it should be borne in mind that section 69 of the Freedom of Information Act 2000 amends the Data Protection Act 1998 to insert a right of access to unstructured personal data held by public authorities.

On 29 November 2005 the House of Lords rejected a petition by Michael Durant to hear an appeal against the Court of Appeal's ruling in the case which he brought against the Financial Services Authority. This is, however, unlikely to be the end of the story for a number of reasons. Mr Durant is reported to be bringing proceedings before the European Court of Human Rights for breaches of the ECHR under Article 6 (on the right to a fair trial) and under Article 8 (on the rights concerning private and family life). The European Commission could also take formal action against the United Kingdom for incorrectly implementing data protection directive 95/46/EC.

While the Data Protection Act 1984 wasn't prompted by legislation at an EU level, the DPA 1998 was introduced in order to ensure that UK law complied with the EU data protection directive.[4] Article 1 of the directive aims to protect the individual's rights to privacy. This principle is enshrined in

Article 8 of the European Convention on Human Rights:[5] 'Everyone has the right to respect for his private and family life, his home and his correspondence.' It is important to recognize that the UK's data protection legislation is based on these human rights foundations (see Figure 3.2).

1980: OECD guidelines (*Recommendation of the Council Concerning Guidelines Governing the Protection of Privacy and Transborder flows of Personal Data*) adopted by the Council 23 September 1980)

1981: Council of Europe convention (108/81) for the protection of individuals with regard to automatic processing of personal data

1984: First UK Data Protection Act (now repealed)

1990: United Nations guidelines concerning computerized personal data files adopted by the general assembly on 14 December 1990

1995: EU directive (95/46/EC) on the protection of individuals with regard to the processing of personal data and on the free movement of such data

1997: EU Telecommunications Data Protection Directive (97/66/EC), now repealed and replaced by 2002/58/EC

1998: Data Protection Act

1998: Human Rights Act

2000: Data Protection Act came into force

2000: Human Rights Act came into force

2000: Freedom of Information Act

2000: Regulation of Investigatory Powers Act

2002: EU directive (2002/58/EC) on privacy and electronic communications

2003: The Privacy and Electronic Communications (EC Directive) Regulations 2003 (SI 2003/2426)

2004: The Privacy and Electronic Communications (EC Directive) (Amendment) Regulations 2004 (SI 2004/1039)

2005: Freedom of Information Act came into force

Figure 3.2   Legislative history of data protection laws

3.3   The eight data protection principles

The DPA says that those who record and use personal information must be open about how the information is used and must follow the eight principles of 'good information handling' (see Figure 3.3). These eight principles are set out in Schedule 1 to the Act. Since the eight principles are enshrined in law, data controllers are required to ensure that their handling of personal data is in line with these principles.

Data must be:

- fairly and lawfully processed
- processed for limited purposes (notified to the Commissioner and to the data subject)
- adequate, relevant and not excessive
- accurate
- not kept for longer than is necessary
- processed in line with the data subject's rights
- kept secure
- not transferred to countries without adequate protection.

Figure 3.3   The eight principles of good information handling

3.3.1   First principle

The first data protection principle says that personal data should be processed fairly and lawfully. The information must be processed in a way which complies with the general law and in a manner which is fair to individuals. The whole ethos of the legislation is that for processing to be fair there should be transparency. So the data subject needs to be told the identity of the data controller, the purpose for which the information is going to be processed, and any other information necessary to ensure that the processing is fair.

3.3.2   Second principle

The second data protection principle says that data must only be obtained for a specified purpose. You need to let individuals know the reason(s) why you are collecting the data. If you subsequently decide that data collected for one purpose would be useful for another purpose, you should first let the data subjects know what you are intending to do and give them an opportunity to opt out.

3.3.3   Third principle

The third data protection principle says that personal data shall be adequate, relevant and not excessive in relation to the purpose for which it is processed. So you should only collect the minimum data necessary to fulfil the purpose for which you are processing it. This principle should be borne in mind when designing forms, and in the case of online forms you might want to make some of the fields optional.

3.3.4 Fourth principle

The fourth data protection principle says that personal data shall be accurate and where necessary kept up to date. This requires data controllers to take reasonable steps to ensure the accuracy of the data. Upon a data subject's request you should correct, change or delete inaccurate details.

3.3.5 Fifth principle

The fifth principle requires that personal data should not be kept for longer than is necessary. Data controllers should have a clear policy on how long they keep data, and at the end of that period the data should be reviewed or destroyed as appropriate. But there are circumstances in which the destruction of personal data can be construed as unfair or damaging. Experian's guide to the DPA[6] uses an example to illustrate this: 'If sales records needed for the calculation of agreed retrospective discounts are destroyed, the customer can claim that their destruction is detrimental to his business.'

In a university library, for example, there could be a policy along the lines of 'Data will be held for up to twelve months after you leave the university, unless there are any outstanding payments or other breaches of the university library regulations, in which case we may retain the data for six years after you leave the university'.

3.3.6 Sixth principle

The sixth data protection principle states that personal data shall be processed in accordance with the rights of data subjects under the DPA. In other words, you are obliged to comply if a data subject wishes to assert his or her rights, and should do nothing to undermine those rights.

3.3.7 Seventh principle

Appropriate technical and organizational measures should be used to protect against unauthorized or unlawful processing of personal data and against accidental loss or destruction of, or damage to, personal data. There has been a steady stream of stories in the press about companies that have failed to keep personal data secure, and where customer information, including credit card details, has been accidentally made available to anyone through their website. It should be pointed out that the seventh principle covers not just technical measures, but also organizational measures. For example, library staff need to be careful about the positioning of VDUs at enquiry desks, ensuring that third parties cannot see screen contents. They also need to be wary of speaking on the telephone about a person's record within earshot of third parties.

The interpretation of this principle in Schedule 1 of the DPA says that 'the data controller must take reasonable steps to ensure the reliability of any employees of his who have access to the personal data.' Therefore it is necessary to consider, for example, whether you should ask temporary staff who are given access to personal data to sign a confidentiality agreement, or how you might ensure that visitors to your organization are not inadvertently given access to personal data.

The Privacy and Electronic Communications (EC Directive) Regulations 2003: SI 2003/2426 take the seventh data protection principle a stage further with regard to the security of public electronic communications services. Where there is a significant risk to security, service providers are required to inform subscribers of the nature of that risk – see Figure 3.4.

Regulation 5 of the Privacy and Electronic Communications (EC Directive) Regulations SI 2003/2426 says:

5. – (1) Subject to paragraph (2), a provider of a public electronic communications service ('the service provider') shall take appropriate technical and organisational measures to safeguard the security of that service.
(2) If necessary, the measures required by paragraph (1) may be taken by the service provider in conjunction with the provider of the electronic communications network by means of which the service is provided, and that network provider shall comply with any reasonable requests made by the service provider for these purposes.
(3) Where, notwithstanding the taking of measures as required by paragraph (1), there remains a significant risk to the security of the public electronic communications service, the service provider shall inform the subscribers concerned of –

(a)   the nature of that risk;
(b)   any appropriate measures that the subscriber may take to safeguard against that risk; and
(c)   the likely costs to the subscriber involved in the taking of such measures.

(4) For the purposes of paragraph (1), a measure shall only be taken to be appropriate if, having regard to –

(a)   the state of technological developments, and
(b)   the cost of implementing it, it is proportionate to the risks against which it would safeguard.

(5) Information provided for the purposes of paragraph (3) shall be provided to the subscriber free of any charge other than the cost to the subscriber of receiving or collecting the information.

Figure 3.4   Security of public electronic communications services

3.3.8   Eighth principle

The eighth data protection principle requires that personal data shall not be transferred to a country or territory outside the European Economic Area (EEA) unless that country or territory ensures an adequate level of protection for the rights and freedoms of data subjects in relation to the processing of personal data.

The EEA consists of the 25 member states of the European Union plus Norway, Iceland and Liechtenstein. No distinction is made between transfer to others within an organization or transfer to third parties.

The eighth data protection principle causes practical difficulties for companies wishing to do business across national borders. There are, however, a number of initiatives to minimize those difficulties:

1 The US Department of Commerce developed a 'safe harbor' agreement, which was approved by the European Union in July 2000,[7] but this only covers US companies who have agreed to abide by the 'safe harbor' principles.

2 The European Union has recognized the adequacy of the protection of personal data [8] for the following countries:

   - Switzerland
   - Argentina
   - Guernsey
   - Isle of Man
   - USA (companies signed up to the safe harbor agreement)
   - USA (transfer of air passenger name record to the United States Bureau of Customs and Border Protection)
   - Canada.

3 The European Commission has adopted [9] a decision setting out standard contractual clauses ensuring adequate safeguards for personal data transferred from the EU to countries outside the Union. The decision obliges member states to recognize that companies or organizations using such standard clauses in contracts concerning personal data transfers to countries outside the EU are offering 'adequate protection' to the data.

In a number of instances, transfer of personal data to non-EEA countries is acceptable, and these are outlined in Schedule 4 of the DPA. They include the following:

1 Individuals have given their consent.
2 It is necessary for the performance of a contract.
3 It is necessary for reasons of substantial public interest.
4 It is necessary for legal reasons (in connection with legal proceedings, obtaining legal advice, etc.).
5 The data subject has requested it.
6 It is necessary to protect the vital interests of the data subject.
7 The transfer is part of the personal data on a public register.

3.4   Processing of personal data

The DPA regulates the processing of information about individuals, and it defines processing widely to cover everything that can be done with personal information such as the obtaining, recording, holding, disclosing, blocking, erasure or destruction of personal data.

The DPA requires that personal data be processed fairly and lawfully. Personal data will not be considered to be processed fairly unless certain conditions are met. These conditions are set out in Schedule 2 of the Act. Processing may only be carried out where one of the following conditions has been met:

1 Individuals have given their consent to the processing.
2 The processing is necessary for the performance of a contract with the individual.
3 The processing is required under a legal obligation.
4 The processing is necessary to protect the vital interests of the individual.
5 The processing is necessary to carry out public functions.
6 The processing is necessary in order to pursue the legitimate interests of the data controller or third parties (unless it could prejudice the interests of the individual).

The Act treats sensitive personal data differently, giving it added protections. Figure 3.5 outlines what is meant by 'sensitive personal data'. The added

This refers to personal data about an individual's

- racial or ethnic origin
- religious or political beliefs
- trade union membership
- physical or mental health
- sex life
- criminal record.

Figure 3.5   Sensitive personal data

protections state that it is necessary not only to comply with the fair processing conditions, but also to comply with further conditions which are set out in Schedule 3 of the Act. One of the conditions in Schedule 2 must apply plus one of the following conditions from Schedule 3:

1 Data subjects have given their explicit consent.
2 They are required by law to process the data for employment purposes.
3 It is necessary to protect the vital interests of the data subject or another person.
4 Processing is carried out in the course of its legitimate activities by any body which exists for political, philosophical, religious or trade union purposes, and which is not established or conducted for profit.
5 The information has been made public by the data subject.
6 It is necessary for the administration of justice or legal proceedings.
7 It is necessary for defending legal rights.
8 The processing is necessary for medical purposes and is undertaken by a health professional or someone with an equivalent duty of confidentiality.
9 It is necessary for equal-opportunities monitoring.

3.5   Notification

The DPA says that those who record and use personal information must notify the Office of the Information Commissioner that they process personal data. Entries in the register[10] of data controllers consist of:

- the data controller's name and address
- a description of the personal data being processed

- the categories of data subject to which they relate
- data classes such as employment details
- a description of the purpose(s) for which data is or may be processed
- a description of recipient(s) to whom the data will be disclosed
- the names of countries or territories outside the EEA to which the data is or might be transferred either directly or indirectly by the data controller.

Those who process personal data must provide access to the data that they hold on a person in order for the data subject to be able to check and correct their records and prevent certain types of processing.

A data controller may only have one register entry. Therefore, even in the case of large organizations, there should only be a single entry on the register. Data controllers register for one year at a time at a notification fee of £35 for the year. They must ensure that the register entry for their organization is up to date and any changes must be notified [11] to the Office of the Information Commissioner within 28 days. Changes to the register entry can be made at any time free of charge.

It should be noted that there are a number of people posing as data protection 'agencies' who offer to register your company on your behalf. They send out notices on headed notepaper requesting sums of £95 and upwards. Indeed, some people are even posing as collectors of data protection and are attending business premises requesting payment for data protection registration. These 'collectors' produce identification cards and receipt books. They have no connection with the Office of the Information Commissioner, and anyone approached in this way is advised not to make any payment and to notify the local police. In fact, notification is relatively simple and the cost is only £35, and it can be done by companies themselves following the guidelines that are available on the website of the Office of the Information Commissioner. [12]

If you process personal data, then you need to ensure that you are registered with the Office of the Information Commissioner and that your register entry adequately covers the scope of your operations. It is important that it is clear who within the organization has ultimate responsibility for data protection matters; you also need to be clear about who would handle access requests, who would handle contractual or data transfer issues, and who would deal with complaints by customers about issues relating to their personal data.

3.6   How to protect your information

Personal information is a valuable commodity. Think before you supply anyone with your personal data, and always ask yourself why an organization is asking for information about you. Does it need all of the information or is it asking for more information than is necessary? You may not have to provide it. It may, for example, be asking about your income, hobbies, interests or family life for possible future marketing campaigns. If someone wants to use your information for a purpose other than the reason for which the data is being collected, you should be told about it and given a choice. Of course, there will be times when you will need to give your personal information for legal reasons. If this is the case, it should be clearly explained. It is important to read the data protection clauses at the end of documents very carefully and to ensure that you make full use of the 'opt-out' or 'opt-in' choices. Sometimes an organization will put several tick boxes at the end of a document and they may use a mixture of opt-ins and opt-outs. It is well worth taking the time to read through the wording of such documents to ensure that you have made the choices you intended. Figure 3.6 outlines the steps you should take to protect your privacy online.

1	Limit the disclosure of your personal information.
2	Set up a separate e-mail account for e-commerce activities.
3	Reject cookies planted in your computer by intrusive businesses.
4	Use tools to protect privacy and enable you to surf anonymously. Tools available are listed at www.epic.org/privacy/tools.html.
5	Learn about your legal rights and be prepared to use them.

Figure 3.6   Five steps to protecting your privacy online [13]

A number of different 'preference services' are available if, for example, you want to stop unwanted marketing material being sent to you, or if you want to stop receiving uninvited telesales calls or telemarketing faxes (see Figure 3.7).

Mailing Preference Service (MPS), Freepost 22, London W1E 7EZ	020 7766 4410
Telephone Preference Service	0845 070 0707
Fax Preference Service	0845 070 0702
E-mail Preference Service	www.e-mps.org/en

Figure 3.7   Preference services

The Privacy and Electronic Communications (EC Directive) (Amendment) Regulations 2004: SI 2004/1039 enable corporate subscribers to register their telephone numbers with the Telephone Preference Service. Since 25 June 2004, anyone making promotional and/or fundraising calls to any business has been required to ensure that they are not calling a business number which is registered on the TPS. If a business wants to register its number(s) on the TPS list, it must do so in writing. Registration is renewable annually.

Meanwhile, British Telecom have introduced 'BT Privacy at Home'. One of the key features of this free service enables users to see who's calling before answering the phone with a free caller display.[14]

3.7   Identity theft

Identity theft is said to be Britain's fastest growing fraud. If a thief steals your identity, he/she might then use it in order to open a bank account or set up a number of credit cards in your name. As the saying goes, 'Prevention is better than cure.' The victims of identity theft have to spend a considerable amount of time contacting each of the separate companies against which there are bad debts. It is not simply a case of calling up the credit reference company and asking for the bad debts to be removed from your credit record on the grounds that they were undertaken without your knowledge. If you become a victim of identity theft, you could find yourself being refused a credit card or mortgage, or being prevented from setting up a bank account. Indeed, it may only be when you apply for a credit card, bank account or mortgage that you realize that someone has stolen your identity.

In order to avoid becoming a victim of identity theft, the best advice is to look after your personal information very carefully (see Figure 3.8). In order to do this, you need to be extremely cautious about giving out information such as your mother's maiden name or your date of birth. If you undertake electronic commerce transactions – such as buying books, music or DVDs online, or booking rail tickets, a flight or a holiday on the web – the companies may ask you first to register your details. If the registration process requires you to divulge your mother's maiden name or your date of birth, think very carefully before giving out the correct information. Do you have confidence that the information is secure?

One of the most effective ways of looking after your personal information is to invest in a shredder. It is becoming more and more common for thieves to steal people's rubbish with the aim of gathering useful snippets of information which can then be used to steal a person's identity. To minimize the risks involved, it is advisable to shred documents such as bank statements or council tax bills, as well as marketing literature from financial institutions trying to sell you a particular product – your own details may be printed on the application form.

- Think before giving out key information such as your mother's maiden name or your date of birth.
- Password-protect access to your computer.
- Use passwords to protect documents.
- Invest in a shredder.
- Check your credit record – if your identity has been stolen, the record may show details of bad debts that you have no knowledge of.
- Don't put anything in your dustbin that could be of use to identity thieves.
- Use a screensaver with a password which activates after a period of inactivity.
- Encrypt sensitive data.

Figure 3.8   Tips for avoiding identity theft

3.8   Rights of the data subject

The DPA gives certain rights to individuals. They are allowed to find out what information is held about them on computer and in some paper records. This is known as the 'right of subject access'. To assert this right, you need to write to the data controller at the organization which you believe holds the information. You should ask for a copy of all the information held about you to which the DPA applies (see Figure 3.9). If you are not sure who to write to within an organization, it is best to address your letter to the Company Secretary, Chief Executive or the contact name given on the register of data controllers kept by the Office of the Information Commissioner.[15]

Some decisions are made via an automatic process. If you wish to be informed of the logic involved in certain types of automated decisions which the controller may take (for example, your performance at work or creditworthiness), after 'Section 7(1)' in the letter, you should add 'including information under Section 7(1)(d)'.

In response, you should receive a copy of the information held about you. The DPA (s8) says that the information should be in permanent form,

> Your address
> The date
>
> Dear Sir or Madam
>
> Please send me the information which I am entitled to under section 7(1) of the Data Protection Act 1998.
>   If you need further information from me, or a fee, please let me know as soon as possible.
>   If you do not normally handle these requests for your organization, please pass this letter to your Data Protection Officer or another appropriate official.
>
> Yours faithfully

Figure 3.9   Sample letter requesting a copy of the information held about you

unless the supply of such a copy is not possible or would involve disproportionate effort, or the data subject agrees otherwise. This means that the
information will usually be provided on paper and may therefore be sent as
a computer printout, in a letter or on a form. You should also receive a
description of why your information is processed, anyone it may be passed
to or seen by, and the logic involved in any automated decisions. The DPA
requires that the information should be in an intelligible or understandable
form, and so any codes should be explained.

Data controllers are obliged to reply. If you do not receive a reply to your
request within 40 calendar days, you should send the organization a reminder
by recorded delivery. If you still don't receive a reply fairly quickly, or if the
information you receive is wrong or incomplete, you should contact the Office
of the Information Commissioner. The Commissioner can help you to get
a reply and, if one of the principles has been broken, enforcement action can
be taken against the data controller.

It is best for you to send your request by recorded delivery in the first
instance, and it is important to keep a copy of the letter and any further correspondence. In many cases you will be asked to provide more details in order
to confirm your identity. It will obviously help if you provide the data controller with these details as quickly as possible. You are generally entitled to
receive a reply within 40 calendar days of providing these details, as long as

you have paid the fee if required. There are different periods for copies of credit files (seven working days) and for school pupil records (15 school days). Many organizations choose not to charge a fee at all, but where a fee for access to information held about a data subject is levied, this cannot normally be more than £10. However, in the case of certain medical or educational records the amount can be up to £50; in the case of credit records the fee is normally £2.

Usually you can see all the personal data held about you. However, there are some exceptions (see Figure 3.10) – for example, if providing you with the information would be likely to affect the way crime is detected or prevented, the catching or prosecuting of offenders, or the assessing or collecting of taxes or duty. It should also be noted that material which infringes the privacy of third parties might be withheld. In some cases your right to see certain health and social work details may also be limited. If you think that information is being unreasonably held back from you, you should contact the Office of the Information Commissioner.

The rights that a data subject has are:

Personal data collected for:

- national security
- crime and taxation
- health, school education and social work
- certain types of regulatory activity
- journalism, literature and art
- research, history and statistics
- legal proceedings
- domestic purposes.

Figure 3.10 Exemptions

1 Right of access to personal data – individuals have a right to know the identity of the data controller, the purposes for which their data will be used, where the data has come from and where it has gone to. They also have a right to be given any other information that is necessary to make the processing fair, such as details of likely disclosures (i.e. who is likely to have seen the data) or transfers.

2 Right to prevent processing that is causing, or likely to cause, unwarranted and substantial damage or distress to the individual, or to anyone else – according to Experian,[16] examples of causing substantial damage or distress

include sending letters to dead people or to their family relating to the deceased, or revealing payment details to a third party without consent.

3 Right to prevent processing for the purposes of direct marketing.

4 Right to be given an explanation about how any automated decisions taken about you have been made.

5 Right to claim compensation – data subjects are entitled to claim compensation through the courts if damage has been caused as a result of a data controller not meeting any requirements of the DPA, and in particular if they have broken any of the data protection principles. If damage is proved, the court may also order compensation for any associated distress. Data subjects can claim compensation for distress alone in very limited circumstances (e.g. because of intrusion by the media).

6 Right to correction, blocking, erasure or destruction of inaccurate data.

7 Right to request an assessment by the Information Commissioner of the legality of the processing that is occurring. However, the Information Commissioner is not obliged to respond to such a request.

3.8.1 Credit reference agencies

Credit reference agencies hold information to enable credit grantors to exchange information with each other about their customers. They also have access to the electoral roll and to publicly available financial information which will have a bearing on an individual's credit worthiness, including County Court judgments and Scottish decrees. If you want to see the information that the credit reference agencies hold about your financial standing – your 'credit file' – the main credit reference agencies are:

- Equifax plc, Credit File Advice Service, PO Box 1140, Bradford BD1 5US
- Experian Ltd, Consumer Help Service, PO Box 8000, Nottingham NG80 7WF
- Callcredit plc, Customer Services Team, PO Box 491, Leeds LS3 1WZ.

You should send a fee of £2 and provide your full name and address (including postcode), any other addresses you have lived at during the last six years, and details of any other names you have used or been known by in that time. Unless the agencies require any further information to locate the file, they have seven working days from the receipt of the letter in which to supply you with a copy of your file.

The credit reference agency will only send you information about your financial situation, unless you have specifically requested other information, such as that outlined in Figure 3.9.

3.9   Data protection and employment

The Office of the Information Commissioner has published a four-part *Employment Practices Data Protection Code*:

- Part 1 – recruitment and selection
- Part 2 – records management
- Part 3 – monitoring at work
- Part 4 – medical information.

The aim of the Employment Code is to strike a balance between a worker's legitimate right to respect for his or her private life and an employer's legitimate need to run its business. Compliance with the code will: increase trust in the workplace; protect organizations from legal action; encourage workers to respect personal data; aid organizations in meeting other legal requirements such as the Human Rights Act 1998 and the Regulation of Investigatory Powers Act 2000; assist global business in complying with similar legislation in other countries; and help to prevent illegal use of information by workers. By contrast, a failure to comply with the code can lead to prosecution of both the company and/or the individual. Many companies would regard a serious breach of data protection rules as being a disciplinary offence.

As mentioned earlier (see Section 3.2), data protection covers personal data held on computer and in some paper records where these form part of a relevant filing system. In respect of the Employment Code, this includes information such as salary details, e-mails, notebooks and application forms of applicants, former applicants, employees, agency workers, casual workers, contract workers, volunteers and work experience placement workers.

Before an employer can store and process sensitive personal data (see Figure 3.5) at least one of the conditions set out in Schedule 3 must be met (see Section 3.4). For example:

- it is necessary for the purposes of exercising any right or obligation – for

example, to ensure health and safety, to avoid discrimination or to check immigration status
- the data subject has freely given explicit consent to the processing.

Employees are entitled to see their data. Requests must be made in writing and the company must respond within 40 calendar days and can charge up to £10. There are exemptions from disclosure in areas such as criminal investigations or management planning (promotions, transfers or redundancies).

3.9.1   Recruitment and selection
The section of the Employment Code relating to recruitment and selection covers any data on applicants, employees, agency workers and casual workers (current and former) which are stored on a computer or on paper in a relevant filing system. It relates to the processing of data – that is, obtaining, keeping, using, accessing, disclosing or destroying it. This also applies to sensitive personal data, which includes information about racial or ethnic origin, political opinions, religious beliefs, physical or mental health or sex life. Figure 3.11 gives a checklist for employers to follow in order to make sure that they are in compliance with the Employment Code.

3.9.2   Employment records and references
Part 2 of the Employment Code covers records management issues relating to personal data stored on computer or on paper in a relevant filing system. It relates to the processing of data – that is, obtaining, keeping, using, accessing, disclosing and destroying it. This also applies to sensitive personal data (see Figure 3.5), which includes information about racial or ethnic origin, political opinions, religious beliefs, physical or mental health and sex life.

References are subject to the DPA. The writer of a confidential reference is not obliged to provide the data subject with access to its contents, but the recipient of a reference is obliged to show the data subject the references if a subject access request is received. The employee is therefore able to obtain a copy of the reference from their new employer or would-be employer. It makes no difference whether the reference is marked 'confidential' or not. If the reference was fraudulent or negligent, the writer of the reference could be sued for compensation.

Recruitment and selection

1 If possible, use the company name in recruitment advertisements.
2 Only ask for information that is relevant to the selection process.
3 When short-listing, use objective methods such as selection matrices and interview guides in order to avoid subjective decisions.
4 Check that your selection criteria do not discriminate in terms of race, age, gender, etc.
5 Keep CVs locked away. Only give access to those involved in the recruitment process.
6 Explain what information will be checked if applicable, and how (e.g. reference and qualification checks). Ask permission from the applicant if taking up references that they did not provide. If these checks suggest discrepancies, allow the applicant the opportunity to explain the inconsistencies.
7 Take interview notes. Store them securely. Ensure the notes are relevant and justifiable for the process (e.g. make no assumptions based on age, appearance, etc.). Candidates have the right to see these notes.
8 Advise unsuccessful applicants if you intend to keep their details on file for future vacancies. Give them the opportunity to ask to have their details removed.
9 Only transfer information from recruitment records to employment files where this information is relevant to ongoing employment.
10 Remember that workers have the right to see their personal details.
11 Keep personal data on staff secure.
12 Include a privacy statement when seeking to capture personal data.

Employment records

1 Ensure that new employees are aware of any information kept about them, how it will be used and who it will be disclosed to.
2 Only collect necessary information and destroy it when no longer required.
3 Ask the individual to check the accuracy of information.
4 Put systems in place to avoid accidental loss or unauthorized access.
5 Place confidentiality clauses in contracts.
6 For discrimination reasons, keep sickness and accident records separate from absence records. Only disclose information for legal reasons or if the individual has given their consent.
7 Make sure the information is secure when being sent. Use passwords where possible.
8 Anonymize any information where practical (e.g. the author of an employment reference).
9 Establish the identity of the person making the request for information. Only disclose information if you think it reasonable and appropriate.

Figure 3.11 Employment compliance checklist

According to the Institute of Management, an employer does not have the right to demand an employee's home telephone number, unless it is specified in the contract that the employee has a duty to be available outside normal working hours. Telephone calls made by a manager to an employee at home could be held to be an invasion of privacy under the Human Rights Act 1998. Even when an employee has indicated a willingness to be called at home, managers should respect privacy and not make unnecessary or inappropriate calls.[17]

3.9.3   Employee monitoring

One of the most controversial parts of the Employment Code relates to monitoring at work of such things as e-mail, internet usage, telephone calls or CCTV footage. The DPA does not prevent monitoring. However, employers should ensure that the introduction of monitoring is a proportionate response to the problem that it seeks to address. Staff should also be made aware that such monitoring might occur. In making that decision, employers should be absolutely clear about the benefits that monitoring will bring, whether there will be an adverse impact upon workers, whether comparable benefits can be obtained with a lesser impact, and the techniques available for carrying out monitoring.

The monitoring of employees' electronic communications such as telephone calls, fax messages, e-mails and internet access is governed by the Regulation of Investigatory Powers Act 2000 (RIPA), the Human Rights Act 1998 (HRA) and the Telecommunications (Lawful Business Practice) (Interception of Communications) Regulations 2000: SI 2000/2699.

While RIPA covers the content of communications, Part 11 of the Anti-Terrorism, Crime and Security Act 2001 covers access to communications data, which includes:

- traffic data – information such as a telephone number you call, when you made the call, where you were when you made the call and the location of the person you call
- service data – information about what telecommunications services you use, and when
- subscriber data – information about you that is held by your service provider, such as your name and address.

In March 2003 the Home Office issued two consultation papers on communications data.[18] The following statutory instruments are also relevant:

- the Regulation of Investigatory Powers (Communications Data) Order 2003: SI 2003 3172
- the Retention of Communications Data (Code of Practice) Order 2003: SI 2003 3175.

SI 2003/3172 specifies additional public authorities for the purposes of Section 25(1) of the Regulation of Investigatory Powers Act 2000. Public authorities specified for the purposes of Section 25 are entitled to acquire communications data under the provisions in Chapter II of Part I of the 2000 Act. The Order specifies which individuals within those public authorities, and the public authorities already listed in the 2000 Act, are entitled to acquire communications data. SI 2003/3172 also:

- places restrictions on the grounds on which they may acquire communications data and the types of communications data they may acquire
- lists the individuals holding an office, rank or position within each public authority who may acquire communications data
- sets out the rank or position of individuals who can acquire communications data and the particular grounds for acquiring it.

In December 2005 the European Union passed a directive on data retention. All 25 member states will have to impose data retention obligations on the telecommunications service and network providers operating within their jurisdiction. This will mean that all telephone and internet traffic data is to be retained by ISPs, telecommunications companies and mobile operators for use by police authorities. The purpose of the measure is the prevention, investigation and prosecution of criminal and terrorist activity.

The simple listening-in, in real time, to telephone calls without recording them does not involve the processing of personal data and therefore falls outside the scope of the DPA. However, if an employer carries out monitoring involving an interception which results in the recording of personal data, then it will need to ensure compliance with the DPA, and that it has also taken account of other relevant statute law such as the RIPA and the HRA.

Monitoring of employees should only be undertaken if there are specific business benefits, and when an impact assessment has concluded that the impact of monitoring on workers is justified by the likely benefits. In making that assessment employers should consult trade unions or other workers' representatives. Where employers undertake monitoring in order to ensure compliance with regulatory requirements or to ensure that the company's policies are not breached, it is important to make sure that the rules and standards are clearly set out and that workers are fully aware of them. Workers should be told what monitoring is taking place and the reasons for it, and they should be periodically reminded that monitoring is undertaken unless covert monitoring can be justified. There should be proper safeguards in place to ensure that information obtained through monitoring is kept securely. One aspect of this would be to limit strictly those who have access to the information, and to include in their contracts a confidentiality clause. Another point would be to take care if sensitive personal data (see Section 3.4) are collected, so that the requirements of Schedule 3 are complied with. It may be that where an organization undertakes monitoring, it gleans information which might be interesting but which is not strictly relevant to the purpose for which the monitoring was originally put in place. If this happens the employer must avoid using that information unless it is quite clearly in the employee's interest to do so or it reveals activity which no reasonable employer could be expected to ignore. Figure 3.12 contains guidance for employers on monitoring at work, taken from the Employment Practices Data Protection Code.

While employees of a company might know that monitoring of phone conversations is routinely undertaken, that will not automatically be true of those making calls to or receiving calls from employees of the company. They should therefore be made aware that the telephone call may be monitored. E-mail is subject to the DPA. The ability for employees to send messages around the world at the touch of a button has its own problems, such as attracting negative publicity – as was demonstrated by the case of Claire Swire,[19] who became a household name after an e-mail reached thousands of people around the world in a matter of minutes. Another potential problem is that e-mail might increase an employer's liability to actions for defamation, racial or sexual harassment; it can also increase the chance of employees unintentionally creating contractual commitments for which their employers may be responsible. The CIPD (Chartered Institute of Personnel and Development) publishes a booklet on data protection aimed at HR practitioners.[20] Figure 3.13 provides a checklist about the monitoring of electronic communications, while Figure 3.14 offers the employer an e-mail and internet access monitoring checklist.

1	Covert monitoring should not normally be considered. It will be rare for covert monitoring of workers to be justified. It should therefore only be used in exceptional circumstances.
2	Deploy covert monitoring only as part of a specific investigation and cease once the investigation has been completed.
3	If embarking on covert monitoring with audio or video equipment, ensure that this is not used in places such as toilets or private offices.
4	There may be exceptions to this in cases of suspicion of serious crime but there should be an intention to involve the police.
5	Check any arrangements for employing private investigators to ensure your contracts with them impose requirements on the investigator to collect and use information on workers in accordance with your instructions and to keep the information secure.
6	In a covert monitoring exercise, limit the number of people involved in the investigation.
7	Prior to the investigation, set up clear rules limiting the disclosure and access to information obtained.
8	If information is revealed in the course of covert monitoring that is tangential to the original investigation, delete it from the records unless it concerns other criminal activity or equivalent malpractice.
9	Where private use of a vehicle is allowed, monitoring its movements when used privately, without the freely given consent of the user, will rarely be justified.
10	If the vehicle is for both private and business use, it ought to be possible to provide a 'privacy button' or similar arrangement to enable the monitoring to be disabled.
11	Where an employer is under a legal obligation to monitor the use of vehicles, even if used privately, for example by fitting a tachograph to a lorry, then the legal obligation will take precedence.
12	Make sure, either in the policy or separately, that details of the nature and extent of monitoring are set out.
13	Check that workers using vehicles are aware of the policy.
14	[Where there is any doubt seek legal advice.]

Figure 3.12   Guidance on covert monitoring[21]

3.10   The business case

Ensuring that your organization processes data in accordance with policies

1   If your organization does not have a policy on the use of electronic communications, decide whether you should establish one.

2   Review any existing policy to ensure that it reflects data protection principles.

3   Review any existing policies and actual practices to ensure that they are not out of line, e.g. whether private calls are banned in the policy but generally accepted in practice.

4   Check that workers are aware of the policy and if not bring it to their attention.

5   Interception occurs when, in the course of its transmission, the contents of a communication are made available to someone other than the sender or intended recipient. It does not include access to stored e-mails that have been opened.

6   The intended recipient may be the business, but it could be a specified individual.

7   Check whether any interception is allowed under the Lawful Business Practice Regulations (SI 2000/2699).

8   Take any necessary action to bring such monitoring in line with RIPA and these Regulations.

9   Automated systems can be used to provide protection from intrusion, protection against malicious code such as viruses and trojans, and to prevent password misuse. Such systems may be less intrusive than monitoring of communications to or from workers.

10 If telephone calls or voice-mails are monitored, or will be monitored in the future, consider carrying out an impact assessment.

11 If voice-mails need to be checked for business calls when workers are away, make sure they know this may happen and that it may be unavoidable that some personal messages are heard.

12 In other cases, assess whether it is essential to monitor the content of calls and consider the use of itemized call records instead.

13 Ensure that workers are aware of the nature and extent of telephone monitoring.

14 Remember that expectations of privacy are likely to be significantly greater at home than in the workplace.

15 If any workers using mobiles or home telephone lines, for which you pay, are currently subjected to monitoring ensure that they are aware of the nature and the reasons for monitoring.

16 If e-mails and/or internet access are presently monitored, or will be monitored in the future, consider carrying out an impact assessment.

17 Check that workers are aware of the nature and extent of e-mail and internet access monitoring.

18 Ensure that e-mail monitoring is confined to address/heading unless it is essential for a valid and defined reason to examine content.

19 Encourage workers to mark any personal e-mails as such and encourage them to tell those who write to them to do the same.

20 If workers are allowed to access personal e-mail accounts from the workplace, such e-mails should only be monitored in exceptional circumstances.

21 It may be practicable – for example when soliciting e-mail job applications – to provide information about the nature and extent of monitoring.

22 In some cases, those sending e-mails to a workplace address will be aware that monitoring takes place without the need for specific information.

Continued on next page

Figure 3.13   Monitoring electronic communications – checklist [22]

23	If e-mail accounts need to be checked in the absence of workers, make sure they know this will happen.
24	Encourage the use of a marking system to help protect private or personal communications.
25	Avoid, where possible, opening e-mails that clearly show they are private or personal communications.
26	Check whether workers are currently aware of the retention period of e-mail and internet usage.
27	If it is not already in place, set up a system (e.g. displaying information online or in a communication pack) that informs workers of retention periods.

Figure 3.13 *Continued*

1	Use simple, clear disclaimers on e-mails and web pages where necessary.
2	The policies on authorized access and acceptable use should be available at the login screen.
3	Inform workers of the extent to which information about their internet access and e-mails is retained in the system and for what length of time.
4	Do not retain data for any longer than you need to.
5	Make sure that sensitive data is adequately secured.
6	Take into account the possibility of unintentional access of websites by workers when you are reviewing the results of any monitoring.
7	Train staff to exercise caution when using e-mail, just as much as with other written documents.
8	Handle complaints in a fair, consistent, and common-sense manner as they arise.
9	Ensure that any precautions taken are proportionate to the level of risk.
10	Where there is any doubt seek legal advice.

Figure 3.14 E-mail and internet access monitoring checklist

and procedures that meet the requirements of the DPA makes sound business sense. It is important that, in their dealings with users of their information services, information professionals build up a relationship of trust with them. Having a well-thought-out data protection policy and a privacy statement will go a long way towards inspiring confidence in users.

Privacy is a strategic business issue that needs to be applied enterprise-wide. Many organizations recognize that they need to take privacy and data protection issues seriously, and that a failure to do so ultimately has the potential to harm their relationships with customers, business partners or employees. The consequences of not keeping data secure can manifest themselves in a number of different ways such as security breaches, hacking, credit card details getting into the wrong hands, or computer viruses causing disruption. Where companies fail to protect the personal data of customers, clients, employees or partners, the consequence might be that a fine is imposed. But once news of an incident of poor management of personal data gets out, it can have a dramatic impact upon the organization's reputation, and it might even have a negative impact on the company's share price and result in a loss of clients.

In cases where the Information Commissioner's Office issues an enforcement notice and this is then breached, a company risks potential criminal prosecution.

A couple of examples of where things went wrong include: a large US bank[23] that paid millions to settle a complaint that it sold customer data, including account numbers and balances, social security numbers and home phone numbers, to telemarketers; and an online ad agency which was hit with charges that it would violate consumer privacy if it merged anonymous user names with data from a company it acquired. After the Federal Trade Commission launched a probe, the agency's share price fell by over 20% in a week.[24]

3.11   Data protection compliance audits

A data protection compliance audit is a systematic and independent examination to determine whether activities involving the processing of personal data are carried out in accordance with an organization's data protection policies and procedures, and whether this processing meets the requirements of the DPA.

The key factors involved in data protection audits are that they should involve a systematic approach; that they should, where possible, be carried out by independent auditors; that they should be conducted in accordance with a documented audit procedure; and that their outcome should be a documented audit report.

There are a number of reasons why data protection audits should be carried out:

- to assess the level of compliance with the DPA
- to assess the level of compliance with the organization's own data protection system
- to identify potential gaps and weaknesses in the data protection system
- to provide information for a data protection system review.

The audit is a mechanism for ensuring that personal data is obtained and processed fairly, lawfully and on a proper basis. When carrying out a data protection audit in any area of an organization there are three clear objectives:

- to verify that there is a formal documented and up-to-date data protection system in place in the area
- to verify that all the staff in the area involved in data protection are aware of the existence of the data protection system, and that they understand and use that system
- to verify that the data protection system in the area actually works and is effective.

Undertaking a data protection audit facilitates compliance with the DPA. The very fact that an audit is taking place serves to raise awareness of data protection issues among both management and staff, and can act as a training tool. Additionally, where weaknesses are identified and then addressed, this can lead to improved customer satisfaction because it pro-actively tackles areas that might otherwise have led to complaints.

The auditor needs to check that the data protection procedures in place comply with the data protection legislation in the context of other pieces of legislation such as the Human Rights Act; that they comply with data subjects' rights; that there are clear policies, codes of practice, guidelines and procedures in place; that where personal data is processed there are proper quality assurance safeguards to ensure that the information is accurate, complete, up to date, adequate, relevant and not excessive; and that there are formal retention policies in place to ensure that appropriate weeding and deletion of information occurs automatically.

The Information Commissioner's Office has produced a useful guide to data protection compliance auditing.[25] It contains a step-by-step guide to data protection auditing with a series of forms, checklists and basic auditing guidance to help ensure that even small organizations with limited auditing experience are able to undertake compliance audits.

3.12   Issues concerning websites and intranets

Anyone who hosts a website which processes personal data needs to ensure that users of that site are aware of:

- the identity of the person or organization responsible for operating the website
- the purposes for which the data collected is processed
- any other information that is needed in order to ensure the fairness of the processing of the data, such as whether the site uses cookies.

This requirement to process data fairly and lawfully can be addressed by developing a privacy policy statement (see Figure 3.15) which covers information about the data that you collect, the reasons for collecting it, and details of who it is passed on to. It is important that the statement provides users with information which enables them to ensure that the processing of the data is fair. If, for example, your site uses invisible tracking devices such as cookies or web bugs, this could hardly be said to be fair unless you have made that clear to potential users of your site.

The following should be included:

- your company's name and address, so that customers can contact you if they need to
- the information that is gathered about a customer
- what you will do with this information
- if cookies are used to track a customer's movements, then this must be specifically drawn to their attention
- details of how the customer will be contacted
- if your company is planning on sharing or disclosing personal information to any of its group companies or third parties, the customer must be informed of this
- the customer must have the opportunity to object to being marketed to
- details of the rights of customers to access their personal data and rectify any inaccuracies
- how long you intend to hold the data on your system
- the choices available to customers about the processing of their personal information
- how data security is managed.

You must give the notice to your customers before they are asked to complete their details online.

Figure 3.15   What should be in a data protection/privacy statement

It is well worth investing time in developing a privacy statement, because it will govern what you are able to do with the data that you collect. Consumers are likely to have real concerns about giving out personal data through a website. They may be reluctant to engage in electronic transactions unless they can be reassured about the privacy of their personal data. Privacy policies are therefore a vital step towards encouraging openness and trust in electronic commerce among visitors to websites. An individual who looks at a website's data protection or privacy statement is able to make an informed choice about whether or not to entrust their personal data to that organization, and whether or not they are willing to do business with that company. To assist in the process of putting together a data protection statement the OECD has developed a privacy statement generator.[26]

The data protection statement should be placed in a prominent position on the organization's website. Recognizing that people can get to pages within a website by a number of different routes, you should ensure that wherever personal data is being collected the data subject always has the option to click on a link to see the privacy statement or at least an outline of the basic messages and choices. A data protection statement could also be placed onto the intranet or the library catalogue, depending on whether or not these are used to collect, process or hold personal data.

Websites and intranets might be used to collect or process personal data in a number of ways. For example, they might include a directory of employees, clients or business partners, or they might have a series of biographical information pages about members of staff, including photographs. Websites or intranets can also be used to collect data by means of online registration forms, requests for information or online research surveys. They might make use of invisible tracking devices such as cookies or web bugs. A key question that needs to be considered is whether or not any of the categories of data being collected fall within the definition of sensitive personal data (see Section 3.4), in which case there are stricter safeguards to be considered.

3.12.1 Privacy and Electronic Communications (EC Directive) Regulations

Directive 2002/58/EC[27] on the processing of personal data and the protection of privacy in the electronic communications sector was implemented in the UK by the Privacy and Electronic Communications (EC Directive) Regulations: SI 2003/2426. These were subsequently amended by the Privacy and Electronic Communications (EC Directive) (Amendment) Regulations 2004: SI 2004/1039. See Figure 3.16.

The Directive replaced the Telecoms Directive[28] and it set an important precedent by adopting a harmonized opt-in approach to unsolicited commercial e-mail across the European Union.

1	Citizens have the right to determine whether their phone numbers for mobile or fixed lines, their e-mail addresses and physical addresses figure in public directories.
2	The use of privacy-sensitive location data indicating the exact whereabouts of mobile users is subject to explicit consent by the user. Moreover, users should have the option to block temporarily the processing of these location data such as 'cell of origin' data at any time.
3	Invisible tracking devices, such as cookies, that may collect information on users of the internet may only be employed if the user is provided with adequate information about the purposes of such devices and has the option to reject these tracking devices.
4	Unsolicited commercial e-mail is regulated, as are SMS messages and other electronic messages received on any mobile or fixed terminal.
5	The Regulations introduce protection for subscribers to electronic communications services.

Figure 3.16 Key features of the Privacy and Electronic Communications (EC Directive) Regulations

3.12.2 Spam

Spamming is the practice of bulk-sending unsolicited commercial e-mails in order to market and promote products and services. The e-commerce directive,[29] which was implemented in the UK in August 2002,[30] requires unsolicited commercial e-mail to be clearly identified as such in the title. This makes it easier for addressees to delete or filter out messages that they do not want to read. The Privacy and Electronic Communications (EC Directive) Regulations 2003 brought in further rules on the sending of spam, which require the prior consent of an individual before unsolicited commercial e-mail is sent unless there is an existing customer relationship.[31] It also makes it unlawful to send junk mail anonymously or using a false identity. In the UK this only applies to individual subscribers – that is, a residential subscriber, a sole trader or an unincorporated parternship in England, Wales and Northern Ireland.

In 2003 the All Party Internet Group (APIG)[32] held a public inquiry into stemming the flow of bulk unsolicited e-mail to UK internet users. The inquiry focused upon the following:

- the developing legislative situation (UK, EU, US and elsewhere)
- technical methods that may prevent spam reaching users
- social methods that may prevent problems with spam
- future trends in spam
- spam's effect on other platforms (e.g. mobile phones and other devices).

The European Union undertook a study which found that 'junk' e-mail costs internet users €10 billion a year worldwide.[33] This study identified a number of steps that can be taken to minimize junk mail:

1 Use the e-mail filters employed by your internet service provider (for example, it is possible within Hotmail to say that you only wish to receive e-mails from a list of people that you specify).
2 Contact one of the associations devoted to preventing junk e-mail such as CAUCE or EuroCAUCE.[34]
3 Use e-mail checking software such as Mailwasher.[35]

If you have a problem with spam, it is good advice not to reply or request to unsubscribe unless you recognize the sender. Doing so only confirms that you are a real recipient. If you receive unsolicited e-mail and you can tell from the subject or sender that it is spam, you should delete it without opening it. In many cases, the senders track the opening of e-mails and use this to confirm that the recipient is real. They then send more.

The Privacy and Electronic Communications (EC Directive) Regulations 2003 require the prior, positive consent (i.e. opt-in) for direct marketing via e-mail, SMS messaging and other electronic messaging services on any mobile or fixed terminal for new customers. In the case of existing customers[36] a modified opt-out system applies in relation to direct marketing by e-mail, mobile telephone or mobile text messaging.

Information about a user's movements within a site obtained by means of a cookie becomes personal data when it is combined with personal details submitted in a form. The cookie contains a unique identifier generated by the site, which is typically a series of numbers and letters intelligible only to the site, but it may also contain the user's account name and password or internet address. Cookies can be used to enable the website to 'recognize' a repeat visitor; the cookie links to information the website has collected about the user's previous visits. This can be helpful to the user as it means not having to enter a username and password on every visit. It can also help to develop the level of personalization of a website by storing user preference details. The directive permits cookies on an opt-out basis provided that: recipients of the cookie are aware that a cookie will be deposited on their machine; the purposes are clear for which the information collected via the cookie will be processed; and users are given an opportunity to opt out of receiving cookies.

Websites using cookies must ensure that their privacy policy or terms and conditions contain sufficient information to comply with the new requirements. They therefore need to provide users with information about data which is collected through the site, by whom, what will be done with the data, how long it will be kept, how it will be processed and how the user can disable cookies if they so wish.

The security provisions of the Privacy and Electronic Communications (EC Directive) Regulations 2003 include a new obligation on providers of publicly available electronic communications services. This is to inform users if there is a security risk to the network, where that security risk lies outside the scope of the provider's security measures. Service providers must also inform users of possible remedies, including an indication of any likely costs. This information should appear in the general terms and conditions of use for services such as e-mail accounts or real-time chat-room facilities.

Further information sources are given at the end of this chapter.[37]

3.13   The implications for librarians

Library and information services are likely to process personal data as part of their day-to-day operations. Examples might include:

- user registration records containing user names and addresses
- circulation records
- contact databases containing names, job titles, e-mail addresses and direct phone numbers
- staff records
- payroll and pension records
- management statistics on usage of the information service.

CILIP's Ethical Principles and Code of Professional Practice for Library and Information Professionals in no way affects legal obligations under the Act, but it does supplement them with professional principles which apply to user information. The CILIP guidelines state that information professionals are required to 'protect the confidentiality of all matters relating to information users, including their enquiries, any services to be provided, and any aspects of the users' personal circumstances or business'; and it also says that the conduct of members should be characterized by 'respect for confidentiality and privacy in dealing with information users'. In 2005 CILIP sought legal advice on the extent of police powers regarding the activities of library users (see Figure 3.17).

In 2005 CILIP obtained legal advice on rights of access to confidential information on library users following a number of instances where police had sought information from CILIP members on library users' activities.

The advice, which was provided by public law and human rights specialist James Eadie of Blackstone Chambers, on instructions from Bates Wells Solicitors, confirms that:

- all library sectors can be investigated
- police and security services investigating serious crime or terrorism in England and Wales have the right to seek information on books borrowed or internet sites accessed by certain library users
- they can also mount surveillance operations in libraries if they believe that national security is at risk, to prevent or detect crime, or in the interests of public safety.

Although the position is not clearcut, the powers are probably broad enough to permit the agencies concerned to insist on the installation of spyware in an appropriate case, the advice says.

According to the advice the police could apply for an order authorizing access to library records under the Police and Criminal Evidence Act 1984 where a serious arrestable offence had been committed, or under the Terrorism Act 2000 where they believed that the material was likely to be of substantial value to a terrorist investigation. Surveillance operations in libraries are also possible, under the Regulation of Investigatory Powers Act 2000. This could include monitoring a person's activities or communications, recording anything monitored with a surveillance device and engaging in covert surveillance to obtain private information about a person. Finally, under the Intelligence Services Act 1994, the Secretary of State can issue a warrant authorizing the security services to take action to protect national security against threats such as terrorism or to support the police.

The CILIP Ethical Principles make clear that librarians and information professionals have a duty of client confidentiality, so they cannot collude with fishing expeditions by the authorities. Nevertheless, they obviously have to respect the law of the land.

Figure 3.17   Police and security services have power to scrutinize
library records[38]

CILIP has also produced Top Tips on Data Protection,[39] covering topics such as: a parent requesting to have access to their child's library record; the use of CCTV cameras in libraries; and the collection of library statistics.

3.14 Electoral roll information in libraries

The Representation of the People Act 2000 along with the Representation of the People (England and Wales) (Amendment) Regulations 2002: SI 2002/1871 has established a framework whereby there are two versions of the electoral register. The full register, containing everyone's details, is available only for electoral and a limited range of other purposes. The edited register, which continues to be available for sale for any purpose, does not include the details of those who have chosen to 'opt out'.

Before the Representation of the People Act 2000 came into force, an elector brought a case to court against his local electoral registration officer (ERO) in Wakefield.[40] Mr Robertson was concerned that if he registered to vote he would have no right to object to the sale of his details for marketing purposes. In finding in Mr Robertson's favour the court ruled that the use of the electoral register for commercial purposes without an individual right of objection was in breach of the DPA.

Following the Robertson case, public librarians wanted clarification about how this would affect the making available of the registers in public libraries for inspection and consultation. The judge did say that EROs must consider and anticipate the purposes for which personal data are intended to be processed. If commercial data collection companies are allowed to access and copy the data in public libraries for free, then EROs are likely to be forced to clamp down on this as well. Staffordshire Libraries and Information Services have produced a poster entitled *Electoral Registers Clarification*, which can be accessed via the LACA website.[41]

At the end of August 2005 the Department for Constitutional Affairs published a consultation paper entitled *Electoral Registers: proposed changes to the Representation of the People Regulations*.

The consultation paper proposes the following:

1 The National Library of Wales should be supplied with a printed copy of the full electoral register, in the same way as the British Library and National Library of Scotland are so entitled.
2 Public libraries and local authority archives services should be included among the organizations able to request that a full electoral register be supplied to them free of charge by EROs, and to be able to make the register available for inspection.

3 The same restrictions on copying and the requirement of supervision would apply as already apply to the copies of the register made available for inspection by the ERO him/herself.

4 Public libraries may request the registers for the whole of their areas.

5 Information gained from an inspection of electoral registers should not be used for direct marketing purposes, and this restriction should also cover the copies that are made available by the British Library, the National Library of Wales, the National Library of Scotland and the Office for National Statistics, and the copies made available for inspection by the ERO.

6 The older registers should be available for historical and research purposes through public libraries and local authority archives services, but this should be done in a way which is consistent with data protection and human rights principles.

7 Where they are more than 10 years old the restrictions on public registers held by public libraries and local authority archives services should be relaxed so that researchers can make use of the registers as a historical source.

8 The relaxation of the restrictions for registers that are more than 10 years old should only apply where they are used for research purposes as set out in Section 33 of the DPA 1998, subject also to compliance with the 'relevant conditions' referred to in that section.

9 All full versions of the registers which are produced under the principal regulations from 2002 should only be viewed under supervision and information from them may only be recorded by way of handwritten notes.

The Information Commissioner has also expressed concerns[42] over other public registers such as the Register of Members ('Shareholders Register'), the Register of Directors and Secretaries, the Register of County Court Judgments and the Register of Medical Practitioners. Those who own shares, take on company directorships, get into debt or practise certain professions similarly have no choice but to have their details made available for marketing and other commercial purposes. Another potential danger is that the registers can also provide the basis for those wishing to establish false identities.

Having directors' home addresses on the public record at Companies House is a key part of making sure business activity remains transparent and accountable. But when threats were made against the directors of the

Cambridgeshire-based Huntingdon Life Sciences biotechnology firm by animal rights protesters, who had tracked down the directors using the information lodged at Companies House, the government decided that action needed to be taken to prevent such cases of intimidation. Legislation was introduced to bring those changes into effect. Section 45 of the Criminal Justice and Police Act 2001 inserted Sections 723B to 723F into the Companies Act 1985. Those sections provide for a system for granting confidentiality orders to directors and secretaries of companies formed under the 1985 Act and to directors, secretaries and permanent representatives of overseas companies with a place of business or a branch in Great Britain within the meaning of the 1985 Act. This was then followed up by the Companies (Particulars of Usual Residential Address) (Confidentiality Orders) Regulations 2002: SI 2002/912, which enable the Secretary of State to issue confidentiality orders to individuals if satisfied that the availability for inspection of the usual residential address of that individual in the records of the Registrar of Companies creates, or is likely to create, a serious risk that the individual, or a person who lives with them, will be subjected to violence or intimidation. The effect of an order is that all notifications to the Registrar of Companies subsequent to the granting of the order in respect of the usual residential address of the beneficiary of the order are kept as confidential records by the registrar which do not form part of the records available for public inspection.

Figure 3.18 lists some useful sources of help and advice on data protection.

Office of the Information Commissioner	www.ico.gov.uk
JISC Legal Information Service	www.jisclegal.ac.uk
Department for Constitutional Affairs	www.dca.gov.uk/foi/datprot.htm

Figure 3.18 Where to go to seek data protection advice

3.15   Radio frequency identification

RFID or radio frequency identification refers to tiny devices that can be fitted to any goods. They comprise a microchip and an antenna which are capable of transmitting messages to 'readers'. The readers use the message in accordance with their programmers' instructions. Generally, readers are situated a couple of metres or so away from the tags, although some experts believe that more powerful versions which are capable of reading information at greater distances can be built.

Libraries use RFID for a number of reasons:

- annual stock taking
- rapid checking that books are shelved in the correct area
- searching for specific items using a scanner
- self check-out of items
- self-return of items
- security
- library membership cards.

RFID can be employed as an electronic article surveillance system. A tag is applied to the items that are being monitored, and a detection corridor is set up at the exit to the library. If someone attempts to remove an item from the library illicitly, an alarm is triggered and a member of the library staff can check out why the alarm went off. With RFID technology in place, it is also possible to undertake a stock check extremely quickly.

However, the use of RFID tags in libraries and elsewhere has raised fears over civil liberties. The main concern is that if an item can be monitored then so can the movements of the person carrying the item, as well as their reading habits. Privacy campaigners are concerned that tags could be used for more sinister purposes, such as monitoring the whereabouts of customers and building profiles of customers' shopping preferences (or indeed their reading tastes) – without their knowledge.

Taking into account the requirements of the UK's data protection laws, RFID technology should not be misused in order to collect information on library users' reading habits and other activities without their consent or knowledge. Libraries should take a number of points into account when implementing RFID:

- tags should not be used to record personal information
- adequate and proper security measures should be in place in order to avoid the information being read by an unauthorized third party

- compliance with both data protection law and industry best practice should be ensured.

The main body advising EU governments on data protection (the Article 29 Working Party[43]) has warned that RFID tags could 'violate human dignity'. The committee says that RFID systems are 'very susceptible to attacks', and that it would be possible for people owning a radar to detect passports, banknotes, books, medicines or personal belongings of people in a crowd should those objects have microchips. Under most scenarios, the committee says that consent from individuals will be the only legal ground available to data controllers justifying the use of RFID technology.

BIC (Book Industry Communications)/CILIP RFID in Libraries Group	www.bic.org.uk, www.cilip.org.uk
RFID Implementation in Libraries: some recommendations for best practices	www.privacyrights.org/ar
RFID in Libraries: technological applications and privacy implications of Radio Frequency Indentification Tags in libraries [blog]	www.libraryrfid.net/wordpress/

Figure 3.19 Sources of further information on RFID

3.16 Summary

In this chapter we have considered the general principles of data protection (3.2), including the eight data-protection principles (3.3). The chapter also dealt with the legal requirements to be borne in mind before personal data can be processed (3.4), including the requirement for data controllers to notify the Office of the Information Commissioner that they process personal data (3.5). Recognizing that library and information professionals are data subjects in their own right, the chapter acknowledged that personal data is a valuable commodity which should be protected (3.6), and that data subjects have a number of rights under the DPA (3.8). Issues relating to employment matters were considered (3.9), including recruitment and selection, employment records and the controversial issue of whether it is permissible to monitor an employee's internet, telephone or e-mail usage. The chapter then discussed the role of data protection compliance audits (3.11) in ensuring that legislative requirements are met, and how the mere fact that an audit is undertaken can help to raise awareness of data protection issues within an organization. The chapter discussed issues relating to websites and intranets such as the use of cookies, the problem of unsolicited commercial e-mail, and the implications of the Privacy and Electronic Communications (EC Directive) Regulations (3.12.1). This section also looked at the role of the data protection or privacy statement in informing users of a service about how their data will be handled, and how it could – if well drafted – reassure users about doing business with that organization. The chapter then considered the implications of data protection for librarians (3.13), including the question of how public librarians should handle requests for access to electoral roll data (3.14), now that there are two versions of the electoral roll. Finally, the data protection implications of using RFID technologies in libraries were considered (3.15).

The next chapter considers freedom of information and includes an overview of the general principles of freedom of information; the use of publication schemes by public authorities as a means of outlining what they routinely publish or intend to publish; the rights of individuals to request information; and the rights of redress where people feel that the provisions of the Freedom of Information Act or the Freedom of Information (Scotland) Act have not been followed.

3.17   Further information

British Standards Institution

389 Chiswick High Road, London W4 4AL
Tel: 020 8996 9000
Website: www.bsi-global.com
(BSI publishes a data protection update service)

Department for Constitutional Affairs

Information Rights Division, 6th floor, 54 Victoria Street, London SW1P 6QW
Tel: 020 7210 8986
Website: www.dca.gov.uk/

Europa – Justice and Home Affairs – Data Protection
Website: http://europa.eu.int/comm/justice_home/fsj/privacy

JISC Legal Information Service
The JISC Legal Information Service, Learning Services, University of Strathclyde, Alexander Turnbull Building, 155 George Street, Glasgow G1 1RD
Tel: 0141 548 4939; Fax: 0141 548 4216
E-mail: info@jisclegal.ac.uk
Website: www.jisclegal.ac.uk/

OECD privacy statement generator
Website: www.oecd.org/sti/privacygenerator

Office of the Information Commissioner
Wycliffe House, Water Lane, Wilmslow, Cheshire SK9 5AF
Tel: 01625 545 745; Fax: 01625 524 510
E-mail: mail@ico.gsi.gov.uk

Registration/notification hotline:
Tel: 01625 545 740
E-mail: notification@ico.gsi.gov.uk
Website: www.informationcommissioner.gov.uk

Notes and references

1   See www.cilip.org.uk/professionalguidance/professionalethics/code.
2   A cookie is a small file that is placed on a user's hard drive by a website.
3   DPA 1998 s1.
4   Directive 95/46/EC on the protection of individuals with regard to the processing of personal data and on the free movement of such data.
5   Convention for the Protection of Human Rights and Fundamental Freedoms – see the Council of Europe conventions website at http://conventions.coe.int.
6   Experian (no date), *Data Protection Act 1998: a simplified guide to assist businesses holding personal information on customers, suppliers, directors, shareholders and others*, page 5.
7   See www.export.gov/safeharbor.
8   For up-to-date information on European Commission decisions on the adequacy

of the protection of personal data in third countries, see http://europa.eu.int/comm/justice_home/fsj/privacy/thridcountries/index_en.htm.

9   Commission decision of 27 December 2004 Amending Decision 2001/497/EC as Regards the Introduction of an Alternative Set of Standard Contractual Clauses for the Transfer of Personal Data to Third Countries (notified under Document Number C(2004) 5271), in *Official Journal* 385/74, 29 December 2004. See http://europa.eu.int/comm/justice_home/fsj/privacy/modelcontracts/index_en.htm. See also MEMO/05/3 for frequently asked questions on the standard contractual clauses and IP/05/12, 7 January 2005, *Data Protection: Commission approves new standard clauses for data transfers to non-EU countries* (both available via Europa Press Room).

10 See www.ico.gov.uk.

11 There is a notification helpline (01625 545740) and an e-mail address (notification@ico.gsi.gov.uk) for any questions about the notification process.

12 See www.ico.gov.uk.

13 Source: Consumers International (2001) *Privacy@net: an international comparative study of electronic commerce and data protection* (pamphlet).

14 See www.bt.com/btprivacy.

15 See www.ico.gov.uk.

16 Experian (no date), *Data Protection Act 1998: a simplified guide to assist businesses holding personal information on customers, suppliers, directors, shareholders and others.*

17 For further information see Institute of Management (2001), *Guidelines for Managers on the Human Rights Act 1998.*

18 Home Office (2003, March), *Access to Communications Data: respecting privacy and protecting the public from crime* and *Consultation paper on a Code of Practice for Voluntary Retention of Communications Data.*

19 See, for example, Email Woman in Hiding, BBC News Online, (16 December 2000), http://news.bbc.co.uk/1/hi/uk/1072391.stm.

20 CIPD (no date), *Data Protection*, Legal Essentials Series.

21 Source: Office of the Commissioner (2005) Chapter 3 of *The Employment Practices Code.*

22 Ibid.

23 Implementing Privacy Protection Should be Seen as an Asset, Not a Cost, *The Business Journal* (20 September 2002).

24 Privacy Risks Threaten Bottom Lines: why CFOs should worry about their companies' internet privacy policies, *CFO.com* (22 February 2001).

25 See www.informationcommissioner.gov.uk/cms/documentuploads/the_complete_audit_guide.pdf.

26 See www.oecd.org/sti/privacygenerator.

27 Directive 2002/58/EC of the European Parliament and of the Council of 12 July 2002 concerning the processing of personal data and the protection of privacy in the electronic communications sector (directive on privacy and electronic communications), 31 July 2002 L201/37, was adopted by the European Council on 25 June 2002 and came into force on being published in the *Official Journal of the European Communities* on 31 July 2002. Member states were required to implement its provisions into their national laws by 31 October 2003.

28 Directive concerning the processing of personal data and the protection of privacy in the telecommunications sector – 97/66/EC.

29 Directive 2000/31/EC of the European Parliament and of the Council of 8 June 2000 on Certain Legal Aspects of Information Society Services, in Particular Electronic Commerce, in the Internal Market, *Official Journal*, L178 (17 July 2000).

30 The Electronic Commerce (EC Directive) Regulations 2002: SI 2002/2013. See www.opsi.gov.uk/si/si2002/20022013.htm.

31 The Privacy and Electronic Communications (EC Directive) Regulations 2003 defined an existing customer relationship as a residential subscriber, a sole trader or an unincorporated partnership in England, Wales and Northern Ireland.

32 See www.apig.org.uk. For further details of the inquiry see www.apig.org.uk/archive/activities_2003.html.

33 See http://europa.eu.int/comm/justice_home/fsj/privacy/studies/spam_en.htm. See also Commission of the European Communities (2001), *Unsolicited Commercial Communications and Data Protections*, (January).

34 See www.cauce.org and www.euro.cauce.org/en.

35 See www.mailwasher.net.

36 The Privacy and Electronic Communications (EC Directive) Regulations 2003 defined an existing customer relationship as a residential subscriber, a sole trader or an unincorporated partnership in England, Wales and Northern Ireland.

37 The *IPR Helpdesk* has information about the regulation of unsolicited commercial communications (i.e. spam): see www.ipr-helpdesk.org (section on documents/intellectual property/information society). See also Fallows, D. (2003), *Spam: how it is hurting email and degrading life on the internet*, Pew Internet and American Life Project, www.pewinternet.org/PPF/r/102/report_display.asp.

38 A summary of the legal opinion is available on the CILIP website at www.cilip.org.uk/professionalguidance/rightsofaccess/default.htm. Personal

members of CILIP can access the full text in the members-only area of CILIP's website at www.cilip.org.uk/professionalguidance/rightsofaccess/legalopinion.htm.

39 See www.cilip.org.uk/professionalguidance/needadvice/toptips/ttdataprotection. htm (this page is on the members' only area of the CILIP website).

40 R. v. City of Wakefield Metropolitan Council & another ex parte Robertson (16 November 2001), [2002] 2 WLR 889.

41 See www.cilip.org.uk/professionalguidance/copyright/advice/er1.html.

42 In the Information Commissioner's Annual Report 2002, 22, www.ico.gov.uk/ documentUploads/annrep2002.pdf.

43 See http://europa.eu.int/comm/justice_home/fsj/privacy/workinggroup/ index_en.htm and http://europa.eu.int/comm/justice_home/fsj/privacy/ workinggroup/wpdocs/2005_en.htm.

4 Freedom of information

4.1 Introduction

Library and information professionals are uniquely placed and skilled to defend and deliver freedom of information. This chapter sets out the general principles of freedom of information (4.2). It considers the Freedom of Information Act 2000 (FOIA) (4.3) and then looks at how publication schemes are used as guides to what a public authority routinely publishes or intends to publish (4.4). The chapter outlines the copyright implications of complying with the FOIA (4.5). The impact of FOI on information professionals is considered, as is the role that they can play in facilitating access to information (4.6). The rights of an individual to make a request for information from a public authority are outlined, and also the process involved (4.7). The chapter looks at the exemptions in the Act, and how – while most of these require public authorities to consider a test of prejudice and a public interest test – there are some absolute exemptions. The chapter examines the appeals process (4.8) – where individuals consider that the FOIA has not been followed, they can apply to the Information Commissioner for a decision on whether or not the legislation has been adhered to (4.9). The chapter looks at the Environmental Information Regulations (4.10), as well as the separate freedom of information regime in Scotland (4.11). It then highlights the discrepancies which exist between the freedom of information and data protection legislation (4.12). A list of sources of further information and useful resources for keeping up to date is also provided (4.15).

4.2 General principles of freedom of information

Openness and transparency are now considered to be an essential part of any modern government, and about 60 countries around the world have adopted comprehensive access to information laws. An open government backed by a properly implemented and working freedom of information regime provides many benefits both to government bodies as well as to citizens.

The legal right to information is not limited to access to information laws, because each country has its own mix of legislation covering areas such as public records/archives, environmental protection, data protection and privacy, state secrets and media.

General Assembly Resolution 59(i), which was passed at its first session on 14 December 1946, states: 'Freedom of information is a fundamental human right and is the touchstone of all the freedoms to which the United Nations is consecrated.'

Freedom of information regimes exist in order to promote transparency and accountability. The public sector, by definition, is funded from the public purse, and as such has a responsibility to demonstrate that it is held to account for that expenditure. Key benefits of a fully-fledged freedom of information system are:

- participation in public debate
- improved administration and decision-making
- accountability in the spending of public money
- allowing the public to understand decisions made about them
- promoting public health and safety.

The Freedom of Information Act 2000 and the Freedom of Information (Scotland) Act 2002 give citizens a wide-ranging right to see all kinds of information held by the government and public authorities. They can use this legislation to find out about a problem affecting their community and to check whether an authority is doing enough to deal with it, to see how effective a policy has been, to find out about the authority's spending, to check whether an authority is doing what it says it is and to learn more about the real reasons for decisions. Public authorities can only withhold information if an exemption in the Act allows them to. Even exempt information may have to be disclosed in the public interest. If a member of the public thinks that information has been improperly withheld they can complain to the independent Information Commissioner (or the Scottish Information Commissioner), who can order disclosure.

4.3   The Freedom of Information Act 2000

The purpose of the FOIA[1] is to promote greater openness by public authorities (see Figure 4.1 for the types of public authorities covered by the Act).
The FOIA gives a general right of access to all types of 'recorded'[2] information held by public authorities; it sets out a number of exemptions from that
right and it also places a number of obligations on public authorities.

- central government
- local government
- non-departmental public bodies
- NHS bodies
- schools
- colleges
- universities
- the police
- House of Commons
- House of Lords
- Northern Ireland Assembly
- National Assembly of Wales

Figure 4.1   Public authorities covered by the Act

Around 100,000 public bodies are covered by the FOIA.[3] The list is set out
in Schedule 1 of the Act, and it has been amended by a number of statutory
instruments.

The FOIA does not apply to information held by the Security Service, the
Secret Intelligence Service, the Government Communications Headquar-
ters (GCHQ), the Special Forces or any unit or part-unit assisting GCHQ.

As far as libraries are concerned, relevant organizations covered by the Act
include:

- Advisory Council on Libraries
- British Library
- National Library of Wales
- Museums Libraries and Archives Council
- Staff Commission for Education and Library Boards (Northern Ireland).

The FOIA is enforced by the Information Commissioner whose role is to promote good practice, to approve and advise on the preparation of publication

schemes, to provide information as to the public's rights under the FOIA and to enforce compliance with the FOIA. He is also required to report annually to Parliament (Chapter 5 gives a more comprehensive overview of the role of the Information Commissioner). There is a separate FOI(S)A which was passed by the Scottish Executive on 28 May 2002[4] and is overseen by a Scottish Information Commissioner (see 4.11).

Responsibility for freedom of information and data protection comes within the remit of the Department for Constitutional Affairs.

There are three codes of practice issued under the FOIA and the Environmental Information Regulations which provide guidance to public authorities:

1 About responding to requests for information and associated matters.[5] This code provides guidance on:

- the provision of advice by public authorities to those making requests for information
- the transfer of requests from one public authority to another
- consultation with third parties to whom the information requested relates or who may be affected by its disclosure
- the inclusion in contracts entered into by public authorities of terms relating to the disclosure of information
- the development of procedures for handling complaints from applicants.

2 On the management of records.[6] This code aims to give advice to public authorities subject to the Public Records Act 1958 and the Public Records (Northern Ireland) Act 1923 as to desirable practice in record keeping, and also advises on the practices to be followed when transferring records to the National Archives (formerly known as the Public Records Office and the Historic Manuscripts Commission) or the Public Records Office of Northern Ireland in the context of the FOIA. The DPA, the Public Records Act 1958 and the Public Records (Northern Ireland) Act 1923 are amended. One of the most significant amendments to the DPA[7] is that the definition of 'data' has been extended, as far as public authorities are concerned, to cover all personal information held. This includes both 'structured' and 'unstructured' manual records, as noted in Chapter 3.2.

3 Code of practice on the discharge of the obligations of public authorities under the Environmental Information Regulations 2004.[8] This code covers:

- training
- proactive dissemination of information
- the provision of advice and assistance to persons making requests for information
- timeliness in dealing with requests for information
- charges
- transferring requests for information
- consultation with third parties
- Environmental Information Regulations and public sector contracts
- accepting information in confidence from third parties
- consultation with devolved administrations
- refusal of request
- review and complaints procedures.

Public authorities have two main obligations under the Act (as shown in Figure 4.2):

1	They have to produce a 'publication scheme' as a guide to the information that they hold which is publicly available.
2	They also have a duty to deal with individual requests for information.

Figure 4.2   Obligations of public authorities under the Freedom of Information Act 2000

4.4   Publication schemes

The FOIA places a duty on public authorities to adopt and maintain publication schemes, which must be approved by the Information Commissioner. A publication scheme is essentially a guide to information that a public authority routinely publishes or intends to publish; the word 'publication' should be defined widely to cover not just items to be found in bound or printed form, but also computer printouts, information downloaded from a website, etc. The emphasis is on information rather than documents. Such schemes must set out the types of information the authority publishes, and the format and details of any charges.

The FOIA has provided a tremendous opportunity for information professionals to play a key part in the development of publication schemes. They have considerable information management expertise that can be utilized in carrying out information audits so that public authorities can produce a detailed inventory of what they produce. The FOIA has also increased pressure on public authorities to have effective records management systems in place. Only by managing their records in a professional manner can public authorities be confident that they have a comprehensive overview of the information that they hold; that knowledge can then assist those authorities to respond to requests effectively and to speedily identify cases where an exemption might be relied upon. Public authorities need to have formal records management procedures in place, including proper retention, destruction and archiving policies. Sound principles of information handling and retrieval are the foundation of freedom of information.

The code of practice on records management recognizes that any freedom of information legislation is only as good as the quality of the records to which it provides access. The National Archives also point out that records management can exist without freedom of information but freedom of information cannot exist without records management.[9] Some civil servants appear more concerned about being able to fulfil the requirement to confirm or deny whether or not an item exists, based on the way in which records are managed, than they are with disclosure of the item.

Section 19(1)(c) of the FOIA requires public bodies to keep their publication schemes under review. They can submit a revised publication scheme for approval at any time after first approval. They are not permitted to remove a class of information from the scheme without first obtaining the approval of the Information Commissioner, and, following a modification to the guidance from the Commissioner,[10] 'where a public authority chooses to add new classes to those which are included in their approved publication scheme they will be required to inform the Commissioner.' It is important to ensure that, once the scheme has been approved and is active, the process is not seen as being complete. Publication schemes are time-limited, and although a public body may not be required to re-submit the scheme for as much as four years, the scheme itself should not be seen as in any way static.

Public authorities should be monitoring the access requests that they receive in order to determine whether information that is regularly being requested should be made available routinely, and the publication scheme amended accordingly. Indeed, it is good practice for authorities to keep a log of requests made for information which is not already included in their publication schemes, and to consider adding the class of information into which it falls as a new class to be covered by the scheme. The log itself could fall into a class for publication under the scheme.[11] It is advantageous for public authorities to add new classes of material into their publication schemes in response to requests that they had not anticipated initially, since the authority could then refer enquirers to their publication scheme for those items. Expanding the range of material covered by the publication scheme would therefore be likely to lead to a reduction in the number of individual freedom of information requests for specific pieces of information.

The Information Commissioner can approve model publication schemes for groups of similar bodies. There are model publication schemes available for a wide range of public bodies. These include:

- parish and town and community councils
- parish meetings
- fire authorities
- internal drainage boards
- district drainage commissioners
- information for health sector bodies
- passenger transport authorities
- port health authorities
- strategic health authorities
- primary care trusts
- opticians and optometrists
- mental health trusts
- general practitioners
- dentists
- community pharmacists
- ambulance trusts
- acute trusts
- universities.

It is left to the public authority to decide how to publish its scheme. The Information Commissioner's guidance[12] makes clear, though, that making the publication scheme available on the web is not sufficiently universal to render it the sole means by which a scheme is delivered. Public authorities must cater for the needs of those who do not have web access; they must also pay due attention to the needs of people with disabilities. They need to take account of their obligations under the Disability Discrimination Act (DDA) 1995. The scheme should be available to all who request it and, in normal circumstances, public authorities should not charge users for copies of it.

A publication scheme specifies classes of information which the public authority publishes or intends to publish. These classes might be described as groupings of information having one or more common characteristic. Including a class of information within a scheme commits the public authority to publishing the information that falls within it. It is therefore important that a public authority and its staff understand what material is covered, and that the coverage is clear to the user. Where it is intended that certain information is not included, this must also be clear to users.

If, for example, a public authority chose a heading such as 'recruitment', then it would be required to make available all information connected with the recruitment process. This is unlikely to be appropriate. It could, however, break this down further into headings for 'vacancies', 'induction' and 'job descriptions'. The lower-level headings then become the classes of information, rather than the broader heading of 'recruitment' – see Figure 4.3.

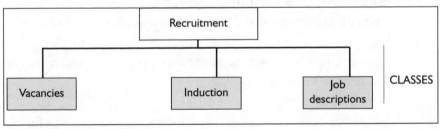

Figure 4.3 Classes of information

4.5 Copyright implications of the Freedom of Information Act 2000

Most documents disclosed under freedom of information, whether they are covered by a publication scheme or sent to an individual in response to a freedom of information request, will be subject to copyright protection.

Section 50 of the Copyright Designs and Patents Act 1988 (CDPA) states:

Acts done under statutory authority

50.-(1) Where the doing of a particular act is specifically authorized by an Act of Parliament, whenever passed, then, unless the Act provides otherwise, the doing of that act does not infringe copyright.

(2) Subsection (1) applies in relation to an enactment contained in Northern Ireland legislation as it applies in relation to an Act of Parliament.

(3) Nothing in this section shall be construed as excluding any defence of statutory authority otherwise available under or by virtue of any enactment.

The Freedom of Information Act does not, however, explicitly authorize the copying of material which is used in order to respond to an FOI request. What the Act authorizes is the public authority providing access to the material, and this need not necessarily be done by copying the information. The requirement set out in the FOIA could, for example, be achieved by the public authority making the item available for the requester to inspect at their premises, or providing a summary.

The Code of Practice under s45 of the FOIA says:

In some cases, it may . . . be appropriate to consult . . . third parties about such matters as whether any further explanatory material or advice should be given to the applicant together with the information in question. Such advice may, for example, refer to any restrictions (including copyright restrictions) which may exist as to the subsequent use which may be made of such information.[13]

What is clear is that the recipient of that information is not free to further reproduce the material in ways that would breach a third party's copyright. Under copyright law, the enquirer cannot make further copies of the documents without obtaining the permission of the copyright owner.

The Office for Public Sector Information (OPSI) has issued guidance on Freedom of Information publication schemes in relation to Crown Copyright.[14] This guidance draws a distinction between the supply of information held by public authorities under freedom of information legislation and the re-use of that information, and explains those circumstances where formal licensing is required. The guidance includes a sample form of words which can be used in order to explain who owns copyright in the information and contact details for obtaining a copyright licence.

Chapter 8 of the procedural guidance on the Freedom of Information Act 2000 produced by the Department for Constitutional Affairs sets out the interface between freedom of information and copyright:

Use of Crown Copyright

Public authorities should be aware that information which is disclosed under the Act may be subject to copyright protection. If an applicant wishes to use any information in a way that would infringe copyright, for example by making multiple copies, or issuing copies to the public, he or she would require a licence from the copyright holder . . .

Third Party Copyright

Public authorities complying with their statutory duty under sections 1 and 11 of the Freedom of Information Act to release information to an applicant are not breaching the Copyright, Designs and Patents Act 1988. The FOIA specifically authorises release of the information to an applicant, even if it is in such a form as would otherwise breach the copyright interests of a third party. However, the Copyright Designs and Patents Act 1988 will continue to protect the rights of the copyright holder once the information is received by the applicant.[15]

Section 50 of the Copyright Designs and Patents Act 1988 and Schedule 1 of the Database Regulations (SI 1997/3032) Reg. 20(2)(6) allows the supply of documents under the exceptions of 'Acts done under statutory authority'.

It is also worth mentioning that in the Environmental Information Regulations 2004 a public authority is entitled to refuse to disclose information to the extent that its disclosure would adversely affect intellectual property rights – Regulation 12(5)(c). Any intellectual property rights, including copyright protected material, a patented design, the constituents of a chemical which has yet to be marketed or other trade secret, may be protected by this exception where a potentially adverse effect can be reasonably anticipated and where the public interest in disclosure does not outweigh the adverse effects.

In the case of Scotland, the question of how copyright affects FOI is covered by Article 3 of the Freedom of Information (Scotland) Act 2002 (Consequential Modifications) Order 2004 SI 2004/3089.[16] The Regulations insert the following as Subsection (3) to Section 80 of the CDPA 1988:

> Section 50 of the Copyright, Designs and Patents Act 1988[8] and paragraph 6 of Schedule 1 to the Copyright and Rights in Databases Regulations 1997[9] apply in relation to the Freedom of Information (Scotland) Act 2002 as they apply in relation to this Act.

4.6 Freedom of information and library and information professionals

Representing its membership of around 23,000 information staff, the Chartered Institute of Library and Information Professionals (CILIP) attaches a high value to freedom of information, which is considered to be a core responsibility of its members.

CILIP's position statement on information access states that:

> CILIP is committed to promoting a society where intellectual activity and creativity, freedom of expression and debate, and access to information are encouraged and nurtured as vital elements underpinning individual and community fulfilment in all aspects of human life. It is the role of a library and information service that is funded from the public purse to provide, as far as resources allow, access to all publicly available information, whether factual or fiction and regardless of media or format, in which its users claim legitimate interest. [In some cases this will be limited to those areas reflecting the primary purpose of a parent institution; in others it will be generalist in nature].
>
> Access should not be restricted on any grounds except that of the law. If publicly available material has not incurred legal penalties then it should not be excluded on moral, political, religious, racial or gender grounds, to satisfy the demands of sectional interest. The legal basis of any restriction on access should always be stated.[17]

CILIP's Ethical Principles and Code of Professional Practice for Library and Information Professionals binds its members to uphold its policy on access to information:

> The conduct of information professionals should be characterized by commitment to the defence, and the advancement of, access to information, ideas and works of the imagination.[18]

Information professionals have a key role to play in facilitating freedom of access to information. Libraries, and information and advice centres of public authorities, can provide citizens with details of what freedom of information means to them. They can guide enquirers towards the information which their authority makes routinely available through the publication schemes, and they can also alert people to their rights of access to information not covered by the publication schemes.

Back in 1998, CILIP unsuccessfully argued the case for the FOIA to include a statutory right for public libraries to claim a deposit copy, without charge, of any publication produced by public authorities in their geographic area. They said that public libraries are, and will remain, the most widely used, accessible and popular point of access for most people to official information. This proposal was not adopted by the government.

In July 2005, the Governing Council of CILIP approved a position statement *Intellectual Freedom, Access to Information and Censorship*[19] which affirms the role of librarians as guardians of the unfettered right to information as CILIP policy. The Council's decision establishes the principle that access to information should not be restricted on any grounds except that of the law. If publicly available material has not incurred legal penalties then it should not be excluded on moral, political, religious, racial or gender grounds, to satisfy the demands of sectional interest.

It determined that the same holds true for the emerging networked society, where the opportunities provided by information and communications technologies have revolutionized the way information is made available, but the fundamental principle remains constant. Building on this approach, the *Council of Europe Guidelines on Public Access to and Freedom of Expression in Networked Information* also received endorsement by CILIP Council.[20]

The Council of Europe Guidelines detail a seven-point approach to the practical issues of enabling and managing access to information in the era of the internet and e-mail. In addition to emphasizing the right to unfettered access, they also stress the obligation to support information users in making their choices of information sources and services freely and confidently.

Employers of library and information staff are urged to embed these guidelines into their practice and to support the principle of uninhibited access to information, recognizing the discretion that library and information staff will need to exercise in meeting the legitimate interests of their users.

CILIP Scotland has set out in a very clear way the impact of freedom of information on library and information professionals (Figure 4.4).

The role of the information professional is to:

- help those who wish to get information from public sector bodies by suggesting how best to frame enquiries
- inform people about their right to appeal if information is withheld
- provide information on who deals with what (i.e. where to go for a particular topic)
- signpost websites and helplines with further information.

For those in the public sector additional roles will be important:

- helping to answer enquiries from external audiences
- providing a physical location for enquirers to consult material held by their organization
- creation of guides and indexes to publications and other material that is released by the organization
- facilitating links via websites and other means with material issued by related bodies in terms of function or subject coverage
- active involvement in ongoing development of publication schemes, encouraging growth to match interests of external audiences and lobbying for more proactive publishing
- taking an active part in organizing information more effectively through improved information architecture and collection procedures.

Figure 4.4   Freedom of information and the role of the information professional[21]

The Scottish Information Commissioner's website also has guidance in the form of a set of frequently asked questions (FAQs) on the relationship between libraries, archives and access to information through the Freedom of Information (Scotland) Act.[22]

It is also worth mentioning the work of the CILIP Freedom of Information Panel.[23] The role and activities of the Panel include:

- taking the recommendations of the National Information Policy[24]
- considering the international perspective, notably the work of FAIFE (IFLA Committee on Free Access to Information and Freedom of Expression) and the UK UNESCO Communications Committee
- preparing and updating a briefing/statement scoping the interests of CILIP in the legal and regulatory framework relating to access to information
- advising on the objectives of CILIP policy in this regard
- identifying the alliances and partnerships required to forward CILIP interests
- recommending a programme of activities necessary to achieve the objectives of CILIP in this regard.

4.7   Freedom of information rights and request procedures

The individual's right of access to information means that anyone, anywhere, can make a request for information from a public authority provided that the request satisfies all the relevant conditions (for procedure see Figure 4.5). The request must include sufficient information to enable the authority to identify the information requested. You do not have to live in the United Kingdom in order to ask for information, you do not have to be a British citizen and you do not have to say why you want the information. There are no limits on the kinds of information you can ask for, although there are limits on the information that the authority has to provide. Applicants have the right to be told what information is held by the public authority and they also have the right to receive the information (unless one of the exemptions disapplies or qualifies

---

When making a request, you must:
- ask for the information in writing, which includes fax and e-mail
- give your name and address
- describe the information you want.

When responding to requests, public authorities:
- must must respond to requests promptly, and in any event within 20 working days
- may charge a fee, which has to be calculated according to the Fees Regulations
- may extend the 20 working days by up to three months until the fee is paid (if required)
- must tell the requester whether they hold the information that is being requested
- must give reasons for any decision not to release the information requested and must tell the applicant of their right to complain.

Figure 4.5 Freedom of information requests procedure

that right). The right of access is fully retrospective. It covers information recorded both before and after the FOIA was passed. Applicants do not have to mention the FOIA or the DPA when requesting information.

When making a request under the FOIA, you can specify how you want the information to be given to you, and the public authority should give you the information in the form you prefer, if it is reasonably practicable to do this. The FOIA lists three ways in which you might ask for the information to be provided:

- as a copy, in permanent form or some other form acceptable to you
- by an opportunity to inspect the information
- as a summary or digest.

The authority can consider the cost when deciding how practical your preference is.

Public authorities have 20 working days within which to respond to requests, and in certain circumstances they can charge a fee, which has to be calculated according to the Fees Regulations.[25] Where a fee is required, the 20 working days is extended by up to three months until the fee is paid. The Freedom of Information (Time for Compliance with Request) Regulations 2004: SI 2004/3364 allow certain schools and operations of the armed forces of the Crown a longer maximum period of time than the 20 working day limit provided that this longer period expires on a date not later than the 60th working day following the receipt of the request for information and subject to the obligation on the public authority to comply promptly. (For further information on the time limit for responding to requests see the Information Commissioner Freedom of Information Awareness Guidance number 11 – *Time for Compliance.*)

In the case of the Environmental Information Regulations 2004, Regulation 7 says:

Where a request is made under regulation 5, the public authority may extend the period of 20 working days . . . to 40 working days if it reasonably believes that the complexity and volume of the information requested means that it is impracticable either to comply with the request within the earlier period or to make a decision to refuse to do so.

4.8   Exemptions and appeals

While the FOIA creates a general right of access to information held by public bodies, it also sets out 23 exemptions where that right is either disapplied
or qualified (see Figures 4.6 and 4.7). The exemptions relate to information
held for functions such as national security, law enforcement, commercial
interests and personal data.

---

s22   Information intended for future publication
s24   National security (other than information supplied by or relating to named security
      organizations, where the duty to consider disclosure in the public interest does not
      arise – see Section 23)
s26   Defence
s27   International relations
s28   Relations between administrations in the United Kingdom
s29   The economy
s30   Investigations and proceedings conducted by public authorities
s31   Law enforcement
s33   Audit functions
s35   Formulation of government policy
s36   Prejudice to effective conduct of public affairs (except information held by the
      House of Commons or the House of Lords)
s37   Communications with Her Majesty, etc. and honours
s38   Health and safety
s39   Environmental information (Regulations covering environmental information may be
      made under Section 74)
s42   Legal professional privilege
s43   Commercial interests

Figure 4.6   Exemptions where the public interest test applies

---

These are the exemptions where, if the exemption applies, there is no duty to consider
where the public interest lies:

s21   Information accessible to the applicant by other means
s23   Information supplied by or relating to bodies dealing with security matters
s32   Court records
s34   Parliamentary privilege
s36   Prejudice to effective conduct of public affairs (applies only to information held by
      House of Commons or House of Lords)
s40   Personal information (access is given in accordance with the rules in the DPA)
s41   Information provided in confidence
s44   Prohibition on disclosure where a disclosure is prohibited by an enactment or
      would constitute contempt of court

Figure 4.7   Absolute exemptions

Most of the exemptions require a public authority to consider a test of prejudice and a public interest test:

1 There is a *test of prejudice*. For example, in the case of the s31 exemption, where
   a public authority considers the information to be exempt because it is held
   in connection with law enforcement, it can only withhold that information
   if its release would prejudice the prevention or detection of a crime.
2 In the case of the *public interest test*, a public authority must consider
   whether the public interest in withholding the exempt information out-
   weighs the public interest in releasing it; the balance lies in favour of
   disclosure, in that information may only be withheld if the public interest in withholding it is greater than the public interest in releasing it.

Public authorities do need to take care when applying the exemptions.
Where a requested document contains some exempt information, only those
specific pieces of exempt information can be withheld and the remainder of
the document must be released.

Usually the public authority will give you a special notice explaining why
it is not providing the information you have asked for. A public authority is
not required to give you a full explanation if this would involve giving you
information that is itself exempt. So in some circumstances you will only be
given a partial explanation. However, the notice will:

- explain how you can complain to the authority about the way your request
  has been handled, or explain that the authority has no complaints procedure
- explain your right to ask the Information Commissioner to decide whether
  your request has been properly dealt with.

Cases that 'would, or would be likely to prejudice' the specified interest mean
that the exemptions could be used even where the likely prejudice is actually quite small.

4.9   Enforcement

A person who has made a request for information and is unhappy with the
response received should first go through the public authority's own
complaints procedure. However, if still unhappy, he/she may apply to the

Information Commissioner for a decision as to whether the request has been dealt with according to the FOIA. In response the Information Commissioner may serve a decision notice on the public authority and applicant setting out any steps which are required in order to comply.

The Information Commissioner has the power to serve information notices and enforcement notices on public authorities. In certain circumstances the Information Commissioner may issue a decision or enforcement notice requiring disclosure of information in the public interest. However, this may be subject to an 'executive override'. In such a case the public authority has 20 days from receipt of the notice to obtain a signed certificate from a cabinet minister overriding the Information Commissioner's notice. There is no right of appeal against the ministerial certificate. All notices may be appealed to the independent Information Tribunal.[26] The Information Commissioner may issue a practice recommendation in respect of non-conformity with the codes of practice.

The Information Commissioner has made it clear that the ministerial override should only be used in exceptional circumstances; if it is ever used, this will be reported to parliament.

4.10   The Environmental Information Regulations

The Environmental Information Regulations 2004 came into force on 1 January 2005, coinciding with the implementation of the right of access to information under the Freedom of Information Act 2000. The Regulations clarify and extend previous rights of access to environmental information held by public authorities. The rights in the EIR stem from Council directive 2003/4/EC of 28 January 2003 on public access to environmental information and repealing council directive 90/313/EEC.

On 25 June 1998 the European Community signed the United Nations Economic Commission for Europe (UN/ECE) Convention on Access to Information, Public Participation in Decision-making and Access to Justice in Environmental Matters (the Aarhus Convention), and provisions of Community law must be consistent with the Convention.

The FOIA extends these rights to allow access to all the types of information held by public authorities, whether it is personal or non-personal, so long as it is not exempt. Section 74 of the FOIA contains an order-making power to allow environmental information regulations to be made.

The Information Tribunal considers appeals from notices issued by the Information Commissioner under the Environmental Information Regulations.

The Environmental Information (Scotland) Regulations 2004 (SSI 2004/520) provide for the making available of environmental information held by Scottish authorities. There is also a code of practice on the discharge of functions by public authorities under the EI(S)R 2004, and this is enforced by the Scottish Information Commissioner.

Destroying information with the intention of preventing disclosure is an offence under the FOIA (Section 77); the DPA and the Environmental Information Regulations 2004 (Regulation 19).

4.11   Freedom of Information in Scotland

The Scottish Executive's objectives in passing the FOI(S)A 2002 were:

• to establish a legal right of access to information held by a broad range of Scottish public authorities
• to balance this right with provisions protecting sensitive information
• to establish a fully independent Scottish Information Commissioner to promote and enforce the freedom of information regime
• to encourage the proactive disclosure of information by Scottish public authorities through a requirement to maintain a publication scheme
• to make provision for the application of the freedom of information regime to historical records.

The FOI(S)A came into force in January 2005, in line with the rest of the UK. A detailed list of the public authorities covered by the Act is contained in Schedule 1. It includes:

• the Scottish Executive and its agencies
• local authorities
• NHS Scotland
• schools, colleges, and universities
• the police
• the Scottish Parliament.

The Act provides for other authorities to be added later, and for organizations to be designated as public authorities if they exercise functions of a public nature or provide a service under contract which is a function of a public authority. This provision would enable private companies to be brought within the scope of the Act should they be involved in significant work of a public nature such as major PFI contracts. In such cases, only the company's involvement in work of a public nature would come within the freedom of information remit.

As part of the devolution settlement, UK government departments operating in Scotland and cross-border public authorities such as the Ministry of Defence are not covered by Scottish freedom of information legislation, but instead by the UK FOIA.

Scottish public authorities are required to respond to requests within 20 working days, as is the case for the UK. But in certain circumstances the Keeper of the Records of Scotland has 30 working days to respond to requests.

Most requests under the FOI(S)A should be dealt with free of charge and where a fee is charged it is likely to be small. If someone has a disability and because of that wants the information in a particular format, an authority cannot pass on to them any extra costs it has to pay in order to provide it in that format.

If the cost to the authority is more than £100 but less than £600, the authority can charge you 10% of the cost of providing the information, but the first £100 is always free. So the maximum it can charge you in most situations is £50 (this would be where the cost to the authority is £600). For example, if the cost to the authority is £200, it can only charge you £10 – 10% × (£200 – £100). Or if the cost to the authority is £600, it can charge you £50 – 10% × (£600 – £100).

If the total cost to the authority is more than £600 the authority can refuse your request. If, however, it decides to deal with your request, the authority can charge you the full costs (i.e. up to £15 an hour for staff time plus reasonable photocopying costs) over and above this £600 limit. The authority may be able to advise you how to reduce the costs by making changes to your request.

As far as the exemptions are concerned (see Figure 4.8), a key difference is that the test is whether the information would prejudice substantially the purpose to which the exemption relates. In other words, the exemptions are harder to justify in Scotland than in England and Wales.

FOI(S)A Part 2 – Exempt information (ss25–41)

Exemptions to which the public interest test does not apply:
25   Information otherwise accessible
26   Prohibitions on disclosure
36(2)   Confidentiality
37   Court records, etc.
38   Personal information

Exemptions to which the public interest test does apply:
27   Information intended for future publication
28   Relations within the United Kingdom
29   Formulation of Scottish Administration policy etc.
30   Prejudice to effective conduct of public affairs
31   National security and defence
32   International relations
33   Commercial interests and the economy
34   Investigations by Scottish public authorities and proceedings arising out of such investigations
35   Law enforcement
36(1)   Confidentiality
39   Health, safety and the environment
40   Audit functions
41   Communications with Her Majesty etc. and honours

Figure 4.8   Exemptions under the Freedom of Information (Scotland) Act 2002

The Scottish Executive's website contains useful advice on the application of freedom of information in Scotland, such as:

- Freedom of Information (Scotland) Act 2002 overview[27]
- code of practice on the discharge of functions by public authorities under the FOI(S)A[28]
- code of practice on records management[29]
- frequently asked questions about freedom of information.[30]

4.12   Freedom of information and data protection

The Data Protection Act 1998 (DPA) gave individuals the right to find out what structured information was held about them by organizations in both the public and the private sectors, and to obtain a copy of that information. In the case of public authorities, Section 69 of the FOIA extended this to give individuals a right of access to all the personal data held about them. Manual records only fall within the remit of the DPA where they are structured, but the FOIA says that for public authorities individuals have a right of access to all personal data, whether structured or unstructured (see Section 3.2).

Under the FOIA and the FOI(S)A, citizens are entitled to make a request for information from a public body without specifying whether or not they are doing so under freedom of information legislation. Below are outlined some of the discrepancies between the freedom of information and the data protection legislation.

4.12.1 Fees and charges

4.12.1.1 Data protection fees

Organizations can charge people who make subject access requests under the data protection legislation. Many organizations do not make a charge, but where they do, this can be up to a maximum of £10. In the case of credit records the fee would be £2, and in the case of medical and educational records the maximum fee is £50.

4.12.1.2 Freedom of information fees

In the case of freedom of information requests, many are free of charge. Calculation of fees is undertaken in accordance with the Freedom of Information and Data Protection (Appropriate Limit and Fees) Regulations 2004: SI 2004/3244. The Regulations state that where the prescribed costs are over £600 in the case of government departments and £450 in the case of other public bodies they are not required to provide the information, but, with the agreement of the enquirer, they can charge the full prescribed costs for any costs above that threshold. In addition, the full costs for disbursements such as photocopying and postage and packing can be charged back to the enquirer.

With the freedom of information regime it is important to make a clear distinction between costs associated with answering freedom of information requests and costs for items within the publication scheme. The publication scheme should set out what is free and what is chargeable, but the prices charged should not be listed within the publication scheme itself. Otherwise, every time you wanted to change the price of an item, you would need the authorization of the Information Commissioner because any amendment to the scheme has to be authorized by the Commissioner. The best solution, therefore, is to have a separate schedule of charges to which the publication scheme can make reference. A public authority might make some information in their publication scheme available free of charge on their website, but they might levy a charge to cover the costs of printing information from their website for those without web access.

4.12.2 The time limit for responding to requests

Under data protection legislation, data controllers have 40 days to respond to requests, and this means 40 calendar days rather than 40 working days. There are different periods for copies of credit files (seven working days) and school pupil records (15 school days).

Under the Freedom of Information legislation, public bodies have 20 working days following receipt of the request within which to provide the information to the enquirer.

4.12.3 The exemptions

The third key area where the two legislative regimes differ is in the list of exemptions. Even if the government wanted to harmonize the two systems, it wouldn't have a completely free hand because in the case of data protection it is obliged to follow EC directive 95/46/EC. The exemptions under the FOIA are set out in Figures 4.6 (exemptions where the public interest applies) and 4.7 (absolute exemptions), and the exemptions under the FOI(S)A are set out in Figure 4.8. Figure 4.9 lists subject access exemptions under the Data Protection Act 1998. Figure 4.10 lists some helpful sources of advice about freedom of information.

4.13   European Union documents

The Amsterdam Treaty introduced a new Article 255, which gives citizens a right of access to European Parliament, Council and Commission documents. It was under this article on 30 May 2001 that European Union regulation 1049/2001[31] was passed on access to European Parliament, Council and Commission documents.

People can request access to any unpublished documents (subject to exemptions) as per Figure 4.11. This covers documents which have not been finalized or which are not intended for publication. It also includes documents from third parties, received and kept by the Commission.

Section 28:	Provides an exemption to protect national security.
Section 29*:	Covers personal data processed for:
	• the prevention or detection of crime
	• the apprehension or prosecution of offenders
	• the assessment or collection of any tax or duty or of any imposition of a similar nature.
Section 30*:	Provides powers for the Lord Chancellor to make orders providing exemptions in relation to health, education and social work records. Orders relating to all three categories of record have been made.
Section 31*:	Covers personal data processed for the purposes of discharging a wide range of regulatory functions.
Section 32:	Covers personal data processed for journalistic, literary or artistic purposes.
Section 33:	Covers personal data processed only for research, statistical or historical purposes, subject to certain conditions.
Section 34:	Covers personal data which are statutorily made available to the public.
Section 38:	Provides a power for the Lord Chancellor to make orders providing exemptions where disclosure of information is statutorily prohibited or restricted, subject to certain conditions.
Schedule 7	
Paragraph 1:	Covers confidential references given by data controllers in relation to education, employment or the provision of services.
Paragraph 2*:	Provides an exemption to protect the combat effectiveness of the armed forces.
Paragraph 3:	Covers personal data processed for the purposes of making appointments of judges and QCs, and the conferring of honours.
Paragraph 4:	Provides a power for the Lord Chancellor to make orders providing exemptions in relation to Crown appointments. An order designating a limited number of appointments has been made.
Paragraph 5*:	Covers personal data processed for the purposes of management forecasting or management planning.
Paragraph 6*:	Provides an exemption for personal data processed for corporate finance services.
Paragraph 7*:	Covers personal data consisting of records of the data controller's intentions in relation to negotiations with the data subject.
Paragraph 8:	Modifies the 40 day maximum period for dealing with subject access requests in relation to examination marks.
Paragraph 9:	Covers examination scripts.
Paragraph 10:	Covers personal data in respect of which legal professional privilege could be claimed. Legal advice is that this exemption covers legal advice given by departments' in-house lawyers.
Paragraph 11:	Provides an exemption for circumstances in which by granting access a person would incriminate himself in respect of an offence other than one under the 1998 Act.

* Exemptions including 'case by case' restriction

Figure 4.9   Data Protection Act 1998: subject access exemptions

Office of the Information Commissioner	www.ico.gov.uk/eventual.aspx?id=33
Department for Constitutional Affairs Information Rights Division	www.dca.gov.uk/foi/index.htm
National Archives	www.nationalarchives.gov.uk/foi/
JISC Legal Information Service	www.jisclegal.ac.uk
Campaign for Freedom of Information	www.cfoi.org.uk

Figure 4.10   Where to go to seek freedom of information advice

1	Make the request in writing and send it by post, fax or e-mail.
2	Check to see if the document you want is listed in the document register on the Europa server http://europa.eu.int.
3	If it is there, quote the reference number of the document you require.
4	If it is not, make your request as detailed as possible to help the Commission to identify the document you want.
5	The request can be made in any one of the official EU languages.
6	Send the request to the Commission's Secretariat General or directly to the department responsible.
7	Receipt of applications will be acknowledged.
8	Within 15 working days from registration of your application, you will either be sent the document you requested or you will be given the reasons for its total or partial refusal.

Europe Direct was set up to answer questions of a general nature from the public:

The Secretariat-General, European Commission, Unit SG/B/2, B-1049, Brussels
Freephone number: 00800 6789 1011
Website: http://europa.eu.int/europedirect/index_en.html

Figure 4.11   How to access European Union information

4.14   Summary

In this chapter we looked at the general principles of freedom of information (4.2), and in particular at how this applies in the UK through the FOIA and the FOI(S)A. We considered how publication schemes are being used as guides to what public authorities publish or intend to publish as a matter of routine (4.4). The chapter also outlined the right of access to information, and the appeals process that exists when individuals are not satisfied that their request for information has been handled properly. The role of the information professional in freedom of information was examined (4.6). The chapter concluded by highlighting the discrepancies between the data protection and freedom of information legislation (4.12).

In the next chapter the role of the Information Commissioner is considered, and the chapter seeks to clarify the data protection and freedom of information responsibilities of the Information Commissioner in the light of the creation of the post of Scottish Information Commissioner under the Freedom of Information (Scotland) Act 2002.

4.15   Further information and keeping up to date

4.15.1 Organizations

The Campaign for Freedom of Information
Suite 102, 16 Baldwins Gardens, London EC1N 7RJ
Tel: 020 7831 7477; Fax: 020 7831 7461
E-mail: admin@cfoi.demon.co.uk
Website: www.cfoi.org.uk

Department for Constitutional Affairs
Information Rights Division, 6th Floor, Selborne House, 54 Victoria Street, London SW1H 6QW
Tel: 020 7210 8034; Fax: 020 7210 8388

Office of the Information Commissioner
Wycliffe House, Water Lane, Wilmslow, Cheshire SK9 5AP
Tel: 01625 545745; Fax: 01625 524510
E-mail: mail@ico.gsi.gov.uk
Website: www.ico.gov.uk

Scottish Executive Freedom of Information Unit
G-A North, Victoria Quay, Edinburgh EH6 6QQ
Tel: 0131 244 2410
E-mail: foi@scotland.gsi.gov.uk
Website: www.scotland.gov.uk/topics/government/foi

Scottish Information Commissioner
Kinburn Castle, Doubledykes Road, St Andrews, Fife KY16 9DS
Tel: 01334 464 610; Fax: 01334 464 611
E-mail: enquiries@itspublicknowledge.info
Website: www.itspublicknowledge.info

4.15.2 Journals

Freedom of information (ISSN 1745-1825), www.foij.com
Information Rights Journal – Department for Constitutional Affairs,
   www.dca.gov.uk/foi/irj.htm
Open Government: a journal on freedom of information (ISSN 1745–8293)
   www.opengovjournal.org

4.15.3 Weblogs and news feeds

Freedom of Information Act Blog (Stephen Wood)
   http://foia.blogspot.com
Out-law.com RSS feed on freedom of information,
   www.out-law.com/feeds/out-law_foi.aspx
Your Right to Know (Heather Brooke)
   www.yrtk.org

4.15.4 Other

Banisar, D. (2005) *Effective Open Government: improving public access to government information*, OECD
CILIP, freedom of information web resources,
   www.cilip.org.uk/professionalguidance/foi/webresources

freedominfo.org

Suite 701, Gelman Library, The George Washington University,
2130 H. Street NW, Washington DC 20037
E-mail: email@freedominfo.org
Website: www.freedominfo.org/

The Guardian

Special report on freedom of information
www.guardian.co.uk/freedom

Notes and references

1   Freedom of Information Act 2000, Chapter 36, www.legislation.opsi.gov.uk/
   acts/acts2000/20000036.htm; and explanatory notes, available at www.legislation.
   opsi.gov.uk/acts/en/2000/2000en36.htm.

2   In Section 84 of the Freedom of Information Act 2000, the interpretation of the word 'information' is explained as meaning 'information recorded in any form'.

3   The annotated list of public bodies covered by the Act can be found at www.dca.gov.uk/foi/coverage.htm.

4   Freedom of Information (Scotland) Act 2002 asp 13. Available at www.opsi.gov.uk/legislation/scotland/acts2002/20020013.htm.

5   Department for Constitutional Affairs, *Code of practice on the discharge of the functions of public authorities under part I of the Freedom of Information Act 2000*. Available at www.dca.gov.uk/foi/ codepafunc.htm.

6   Lord Chancellor's Department (2002), *Code of Practice on the Management of Records*, www.dca.gov.uk/foi/codemanrec.htm.

7   See Section 69 of the Freedom of Information Act.

8   Code of Practice of the Discharge of the Obligations of Public Authorities under the Environmental Information Regulations 2004 (SI 2004/3391): issued under Regulation 16 of the Regulations, February 2005, www.defra.gov.uk/corporate/opengov/eir/pdf/cop-eir.pdf.

9   Public Record Office, *Records Management News* (PRO), November 2002.

10 Office of the Information Commissioner (2003, February), *Freedom of Information Act 2000. Preparing for implementation – publication schemes guidance and methodology.*

11 Steve Wood maintains a disclosure log index at http://foia.blogspot.com/log.htm.

12 Office of the Information Commissioner (2002, February) *Freedom of Information Act 2000: preparing for implementation – publication schemes methodology: p4, v1.0.*

13 See www.dca.gov.uk/foi/codepafunc.htm.

14 See Freedom of Information Publication Schemes (OPSI guidance note 19) at www.opsi.gov.uk/advice/crown-copyright/copyright-guidance/freedom-of-information-publication-schemes.htm.

15 See www.dca.gov.uk/foi/guidance/proguide/chap08.htm.

16 See www.opsi.gov.uk/si/si2004/20043089.htm.

17 CILIP (2005) *Intellectual Freedom, Access to Information and Censorship* (CILIP position statement), www.cilip.org.uk/professionalguidance/foi/intellfreedom.htm.

18 CILIP (2005) Ethical Principles and Code of Professional Practice for Library and Information Professionals, www.cilip.org.uk/professionalguidance/professionalethics/code.

19 See www.cilip.org.uk/professionalguidance/foi.

20 See www.cilip.org.uk/professionalguidance/foi/intellfreedom.htm.

21   Source: CILIP Scotland (2002) *Freedom of Information (Scotland) Act 2002: a guide for the information professional*. Reproduced with the kind permission of CILIP Scotland.

22   See www.itspublicknowledge.info/yourrights/faqs/librariesfaqs.htm.

23   The Panel reported to the CILIP Council, 10 December 2003: see www.cilip.org.uk/professionalguidance/foi/foireport.htm.

24   Library Association (2002) *National Information Policy: report of the policy advisory group*.

25   The Freedom of Information and Data Protection (Appropriate Limit and Fees) Regulations 2004: SI 2004/3244.

26   See www.informationtribunal.gov.uk.

27   Available at www.scotland.gov.uk/government/foi/foioverview.pdf.

28   Available at www.scotland.gov.uk/library5/government/sedfpa-00.asp.

29   Available at www.scotland.gov.uk/Topics/Government/FOI/18022/13383.

30   Available at www.scotland.gov.uk/Resource/Doc/1066/0003705.pdf.

31   Regulation (EC) No 1049/2001 of the European Parliament and of the Council of 30 May 2001 Regarding Public Access to European Parliament, Council and Commission Documents, *Official Journal* L145/43 (31 May 2001).

5 The Information Commissioner

5.1   Introduction

This chapter considers the role and functions of the Information Commissioner in relation to data protection, freedom of information and environmental information (5.2). It examines the implications of devolved government (5.3), and considers the functions of the Scottish Information Commissioner (5.4). Finally the chapter looks at how both the Information Commissioner and the Scottish Information Commissioner can charge for certain services (5.5).

5.2   The role of the Information Commissioner

The ICO (Information Commissioner's Office) is not a typical non-departmental public body. Such bodies usually have a relationship with ministers based on the delegation of ministerial powers. However, the ICO is a UK independent supervisory authority reporting directly to the UK parliament and has an international role as well as a national one.

The Information Commissioner enforces and oversees the Data Protection Act 1998 (DPA) and the Freedom of Information Act 2000 (FOIA) using only the powers which these pieces of legislation set out. Decisions of the Information Commissioner are subject to the supervision of the courts and the Information Tribunal.

The Commissioner was previously known as the Data Protection Commissioner and became the Information Commissioner on 30 January 2001,[1] when responsibility for freedom of information was added to the Commissioner's remit. This dual role enables the Commissioner to provide an integrated and coherent approach.

The mission statement of the Information Commissioner's Office[2] says:

We shall develop respect for the private lives of individuals and encourage the openness and accountability of public authorities: by promoting good information handling practice and enforcing data protection and freedom of information legislation; and by seeking to influence national and international thinking on privacy and information access issues.

The Information Commissioner's Office annual report 2004–2005 states:

Our overall objective is to achieve, cost-effectively and with minimum burden, the outcomes for which we exist:

- Getting official information into the open unless there are good reasons for non-disclosure; and
- Ensuring that personal information is properly protected.

The ICO does this by providing guidance to individuals and organizations, solving problems where possible and taking appropriate action when the law is broken.

The Information Commissioner's Corporate Plan 2004–2007 identifies three key objectives:

We will be seen as a successful and well-respected organisation if we stay focused on three over-riding imperatives between now and 2007:

1. Top priority for our Freedom of Information responsibilities – deciding cases in ways which command public and organisational confidence and getting well down the road towards a genuine 'open government' culture;
2. Taking a practical, down-to-earth approach to our data protection activities – simplifying and making it easier for the majority of organisations who seek to handle personal information well, and tougher for the minority who do not;
3. Aiming to be a 'top-of-the class' office, with clear values, of which we are all proud – influential, well-run, outward-looking and delivering real service to society.

A strategic review by the Office of the Information Commissioner – under the banner of a 'Home Improvement Project' – identified the organization it wants to be as consisting of the following features:

- educator – proactive, promoting rights, influencer
- remedy provider – using its powers to solve real problems
- enforcer – firm but fair, prepared to take risks
- customer focused – responsive, approachable, helpful
- high profile – respected by organizations and individuals across public and private sectors
- well managed – cohesive, co-operative, motivated and rewarded
- efficient – focused, organized and using its resources well.

The ICO produces guidance for data protection and freedom of information practitioners in order to promote compliance with the law and the following of good practice. The ICO helpline gives guidance and advice to organizations and members of the public. It investigates complaints from people who believe that they have been affected by those breaking the law and, if necessary, takes legal action in order to ensure that the law does not continue to be broken.

The Information Commissioner participates in, and contributes to, European and international developments in the fields of data protection and freedom of information.

5.2.1   Data protection

The Information Commissioner's role in relation to data protection is set out in Sections 51–4 of the DPA. Key elements of the role are:

- to promote good practice
- to make assessments
- to serve information notices
- to serve enforcement notices
- to use its powers of entry and inspection
- to commence proceedings for offences under the DPA
- to prepare and disseminate codes of practice for guidance on good practice.

The ICO maintains a public register of organizations that hold information about people, known as the register of data controllers.[3]

The aim of the Information Commissioner's Office is to take a practical, down-to-earth approach, to make data protection easier for the majority of organizations who seek to handle information well and to be tough on the minority who don't.

The Information Commissioner has obligations to assess alleged breaches of the DPA. The Office may serve information notices requiring data controllers to supply the information needed to assess compliance. Where there has been a breach, it can also serve an enforcement notice requiring data controllers to take specified steps (or to stop taking steps) in order to comply with the law. Such notices can be, and usually are, appealed to the Information Tribunal (formerly known as the Data Protection Tribunal), and while they are subject to appeal their application is suspended. Therefore, when a notice has been appealed it has no application until either the appeal is withdrawn or the Information Tribunal has adjudicated on the matter. Once a notice is in force, further contravention will, subject to a defence of reasonable diligence, be an offence. The whole enforcement process is time-consuming and makes significant demands upon the resources of the Information Commissioner's Office. This means that, where a business chooses to ignore the requirements of the law, it can be many months before the Information Commissioner's Office is in a position to seek a criminal prosecution by the courts. In England, Wales and Northern Ireland, the Commissioner or the Director of Public Prosecutions may institute proceedings. In the case of Scotland all prosecutions must be brought by the Procurator Fiscal.

In recent years the Information Commissioner has taken enforcement action against a number of fax marketing companies following breaches of the Regulations in which unsolicited marketing faxes were sent to subscribers listed on the fax preference service register. Where an enforcement notice is in force, those who fail to comply with it will have commited a criminal offence punishable by a fine.

If an individual believes that one of the data protection principles has been breached (or any other requirement of the DPA), and is unable or unwilling to sort the problem out, he/she can ask the Information Commissioner to assess whether the requirements of the DPA have been met. The Commissioner will always try to deal with matters informally. However, if the

Commissioner's assessment is that the requirements of the DPA have not been met and the matter cannot be settled informally, then his office may decide to take enforcement action against the data controller in question.

If the Commissioner takes enforcement action against a data controller, the controller can appeal to the independent Information Tribunal. However, if the Tribunal agrees with the Commissioner's enforcement action and the data controller continues to break the principles, a criminal offence can result for which the data controller can be prosecuted.

During 2004–2005 the ICO's compliance teams dealt with over 20,000 data protection complaints, while the notification department dealt with 225,257 renewals and processed 40,932 new applications. The total number of entries on the register of data controllers (after removals and clearance of fees) was 259,296 on 31 March 2005.

Figure 5.1 gives a couple of examples of proceedings instigated by the ICO as a result of people infringing the Data Protection Act 1998.

A private detective was fined a total of £6,250 for Data Protection Act offences and ordered to pay a further £600 costs by Brent Magistrates Court. Ray Pearson, a director of Pearmac Ltd., based in North London, was prosecuted by the Information Commissioner's Office for four offences under Section 55 of the Data Protection Act together with three further charges of attempting to obtain information unlawfully. In addition, he pleaded guilty to an offence under Section 17 of the Act relating to the non-notification of Pearmac Ltd. His fellow director, Alan McInerney, also pleaded guilty to an offence under Section 17 of the DPA, as did Pearmac Ltd. Mr McInerney was fined £500, and ordered to pay £150 costs and Pearmac Ltd. was fined £750 and ordered to pay £150 costs.[4]

The Information Commissioner's Office successfully prosecuted solicitor Ralph Harold Donner after his firm, Feld Mackay and Donner, failed to notify under the Data Protection Act 1998. Following a guilty plea at Bolton Magistrates Court, Ralph Donner was fined £3150 and ordered to pay £3500 towards prosecution costs. Mr Donner, a senior partner at the Rochdale-based firm, was contacted more than five times by the Information Commissioner over a period of two years and yet still failed to notify. Under the 1998 Act organizations that process personal information may be required to notify with the Information Commissioner at a nominal cost of £35 per year.[5]

Figure 5.1   Examples of proceedings instigated by the Information Commissioner's Office

5.2.2   Freedom of information

The Information Commissioner is also responsible for freedom of information in England, Wales and Northern Ireland, and the general functions of the

Commissioner are set out in Section 47 of the Freedom of Information Act 2000 (FOIA). With respect to freedom of information, the Commissioner's duties are:

- to approve or revoke publication schemes, including model schemes
- to promote the following of good practice by public authorities
- to promote public authorities' compliance with the FOIA and the provisions of the codes of practice made under Sections 45 and 46, which relate respectively to dealing with requests for information and desirable practice in connection with the keeping, management and destruction of records
- to disseminate information to the public about the operation of the FOIA and give advice about it
- to assess whether a public authority is following good practice
- to arrange for the dissemination of information about any other matters within the scope of the Commissioner's functions under the FOIA (he may give advice to any person about any of those matters)
- to consider complaints about any alleged failure to comply with the Act
- to issue decision notices and exercise enforcement powers to ensure compliance
- to report annually to Parliament.

As independent referee, the Information Commissioner ensures information is released where it is required under the law. The approach is to be reasonable, responsible and robust, recognizing that greater openness should strengthen, not undermine, effective government.

The ICO has a range of tools it can use in the decision-making process when dealing with complaints: decision notices (the ICO decision on a case), information notices (requiring more information on the issue) and enforcement notices (directing an organization to amend its practices). Preliminary notices are used in appropriate cases to inform the parties in dispute of the ICO's likely decision.

Freedom of Information decision notices are published on the website of the Office of the Information Commissioner.[6] A decision notice outlines the Information Commissioner's final assessment as to whether or not a public authority has complied with the Freedom of Information Act 2000, or the

Environmental Information Regulations 2004, with regard to specific complaints.

At the same time as issuing a decision notice the ICO informs both parties of their right to appeal to the Information Tribunal.

The Information Commissioner is responsible for setting priorities for his Office and deciding how they should be achieved.

5.2.3 Environmental Information Regulations

The Information Commissioner has been given powers to promote and enforce the Environmental Information Regulations 2004. As with the Freedom of Information Act, the role of the Commissioner is to ensure that information is released where it is required under the law.

Regulation 16 of the Environmental Information Regulations 2004, which covers the issuing of a code of practice on the EIR and the functions of the Commissioner, states:

16. – (1) The Secretary of State may issue, and may from time to time revise, a code of practice providing guidance to public authorities as to the practice which it would, in the Secretary of State's opinion, be desirable for them to follow in connection with the discharge of their functions under these Regulations.

(2) The code may make different provision for different public authorities.

(3) Before issuing or revising any code under this regulation, the Secretary of State shall consult the Commissioner.

(4) The Secretary of State shall lay before each House of Parliament any code issued or revised under this regulation.

(5) The general functions of the Commissioner under section 47 of the Act and the power of the Commissioner to give a practice recommendation under section 48 of the Act shall apply for the purposes of these Regulations as they apply for the purposes of the Act but with the modifications specified in paragraph (6).

(6) For the purposes of the application of sections 47 and 48 of the Act to these Regulations, any reference to –

(a) a public authority is a reference to a public authority within the meaning of these Regulations;

(b) the requirements or operation of the Act, or functions under the Act, includes a reference to the requirements or operation of these Regulations, or functions under these Regulations; and

(c) a code of practice made under section 45 of the Act includes a reference to a code of practice made under this regulation.

5.3   The Information Commissioner and devolved government

Data protection is a reserved matter. This means that the UK Parliament is responsible for data protection throughout the UK, and the legislation applies in England, Scotland, Northern Ireland and Wales. Freedom of information is not similarly reserved, and it can therefore be devolved to national legislatures. Consequently, the Information Commissioner is responsible for both data protection and freedom of information in England, Wales and Northern Ireland, but in Scotland is only responsible for data protection.

The Office of the Information Commissioner decided that, in view of the new constitutional arrangements for devolved government, it would establish an office presence in Scotland, Wales and Northern Ireland. Assistant Commissioners for Scotland, Wales and Northern Ireland were appointed, and this is a recognition that local issues and sensitivities need to be fully understood and integrated into the promotion of good information handling across the UK.

The Assistant Commissioners all report directly to the Information Commissioner. They are responsible for taking forward the Commissioner's work in promoting and enforcing both the DPA and the FOIA. In Scotland, Scottish public authorities are subject to the Freedom of Information (Scotland) Act (FOI(S)A), enforced by the Scottish Information Commissioner.[7] The Assistant Commissioner (Scotland) liaises closely with the Scottish Commissioner's office to uphold access to information rights under UK and Scottish legislation.

In England and Wales, proceedings for a criminal offence under the FOIA can be commenced by the Information Commissioner, or by or with the consent of the Director of Public Prosecutions; in Scotland, criminal proceedings will normally be brought by the Procurator Fiscal; in Northern Ireland, proceedings for an offence under the FOIA can be begun by the Information Commissioner, or by or with the consent of the Director of Public Prosecutions for Northern Ireland.

5.4   Scottish Information Commissioner

The Freedom of Information (Scotland) Act 2002 (FOI(S)A)[8] was passed by the Scottish Parliament on 24 April 2002 and received Royal Assent on 28 May 2002. It established the freedom of information regime for devolved Scotland. The FOI(S)A created the post of Scottish Information Commissioner. The Commissioner is appointed by the Queen on the nomination of the Scottish Parliament. Section 43 of the FOI(S)A sets out the Scottish Information Commissioner's general functions. It places a duty on the Commissioner to promote good practice and Scottish public authorities' compliance with the FOI(S)A, their publication schemes and codes of practice. The Scottish Information Commissioner is also obliged, where he considers it expedient, to disseminate information to the public about the operation of the freedom of information regime. The Commissioner can also make 'practice recommendations' specifying what a Scottish public authority should do to comply with the codes of practice, and is required to lay annual reports before the Scottish Parliament.

The key functions of the Scottish Information Commissioner are:

- to promote good practice by Scottish public authorities in relation to the Scottish freedom of information regime
- to raise public awareness of the Scottish freedom of information regime
- to consider appeals from people seeking the disclosure of information.

Statutory rights under the FOI(S)A and the Scottish Information Commissioner's regulatory powers extend to information contained in historical public records, such as those held by the National Archives of Scotland.

The main role of the Commissioner is to promote observance by public authorities of the Act, under which a person who requests information from a Scottish public authority is entitled to be given it by the authority.

The main task for the Scottish Information Commissioner is to enforce the right to access public information created by the Freedom of Information (Scotland) Act. The Act came into force on 1 January 2005, giving anyone, anywhere in the world, the right to access information held by more than 10,000 public authorities in Scotland.

If one of these authorities refuses a request for information, members of the public have the right to appeal against the decision to the Commissioner.

He will then investigate whether the information should or should not be released. The Commissioner has powers to force an authority to release information if he decides that it has acted wrongly in refusing a request.

Before the Act came into force, the Commissioner approved publication schemes from all the relevant public authorities.

Alongside the job of enforcing freedom of information the Commissioner is responsible for ensuring that as many people as possible are aware of their new right to access information. He and his staff have been organizing and speaking at events around Scotland to promote the Act and raise public awareness.

The Scottish Information Commissioner's Office has a promotion strategy which sets out the Commissioner's proposals to deliver a clear and effective public promotion campaign to raise awareness of the new right to information held by public authorities and how to use it. In addition to a widespread public campaign, the strategy aims to ensure the message is received as widely as possible, particularly by target groups, through:

- working with other organizations to communicate the new right to traditionally hard-to-reach groups
- directly promoting the Act to groups most likely to use it.

5.5   Charging for services

The Information Commissioner can charge for certain services, with regard to both data protection and freedom of information responsibilities. This is set out in the legislation as follows: 'The Commissioner may charge such sums as he may with the consent of the Secretary of State determine for any services provided by the Commissioner' [DPA, Section 51(8)] and a similar form of words is used in the FOIA.

This is also true of the Scottish Information Commissioner, who also has the right to charge for services, as outlined in the FOI(S)A Section 43(5), which states that 'the Commissioner may determine and charge sums for services provided under this section.'

5.6   Summary

This chapter has looked at both the role and the functions of the Information Commissioner in relation to data protection, freedom of information and the Environmental Information Regulations (5.2). It has examined the implications of devolved government for the remit of the Information Commissioner (5.3), and the functions of the Scottish Information Commissioner have been outlined (5.4). The chapter finished off by outlining how both the Information Commissioner and the Scottish Information Commissioner are able to charge for certain services (5.5).

In the next chapter the re-use of public sector information is considered, as opposed to obtaining access to such information.

5.7 Further information

Department for Constitutional Affairs

Freedom of Information and Data Protection Division, Room 151, Selborne House, London SW1E 6QW
Tel: 020 7210 8755; Fax: 020 7210 1415
Website: www.dca.gov.uk/

Information Commissioner

Wycliffe House, Water Lane, Wilmslow, Cheshire SK9 5AF
Tel: 01625 545745; Fax: 01625 524510
E-mail: mail@ico.gsi.gov.uk
Publication order line: 08453 091 091
Website: www.ico.gov.uk

JISC Legal Information Service

Learning Services, Level 3, Alexander Turnbull Building, 155 George Street, Glasgow G1 1RD
Tel: 0141 548 4939; Fax: 0141 548 4216
Website: www.jisclegal.ac.uk

Scottish Executive Freedom of Information Unit

St Andrew's House, Regent Road, Edinburgh EH1 3DG
Tel: 0131 244 4615; Fax: 0131 244 2582
E-mail: foi@scotland.gsi.gov.uk
Website: www.scotland.gov.uk/government/foi

Scottish Information Commissioner

Kinburn Castle, Doubledykes Road, St Andrews, Fife KY16 9DS

Tel: 01334 464610; Fax: 01334 464611

E-mail: enquiries@itspublicknowledge.info

Website: www.itspublicknowledge.info

Notes and references

1   By virtue of Sections 18(1) and 87(2)(a) of the Freedom of Information Act 2000.

2   As set out on page 5 of the *Information Commissioner Annual Report and Accounts for the Year Ending 31 March 2002*, HC 913, The Stationery Office, June 2002.

3   This can be accessed through the website of the Information Commissioner at www.ico.gov.uk.

4   Source: Office of the Information Commissioner (2005) Private Detective Convicted for Data Protection Offences, press notice (19 October).

5   Source: Information Commissioner (2005) Solicitor Fined for Flouting Data Protection Act, press notice (1 March).

6   See www.ico.gov.uk/eventual.aspx?id=8617.

7   (2002 asp 13), available at www.scotland-legislation.opsi.gov.uk/legislation/scotland/acts2002/20020013.htm.

8   Ibid.

6 The re-use of public sector information

6.1 Introduction

The European information industry has been estimated as being worth €68 billion.[1] By contrast, the United States information industry is approximately five times that size.

The European Commission and other commentators attribute this to the fact that in the United States, federal government information is not subject to copyright, and therefore most information, certainly at federal government level, can be re-used with virtually no restrictions. The European Commission judged, therefore, that there is enormous scope for growth in this area, especially in terms of developing pan-European products and services. This led to the European Directive on the Re-use of Public Sector Information (2003/98/EC) which was implemented in the United Kingdom through the Re-use of Public Sector Information Regulations 2005: SI 2005/1515.

6.2 General principles

The Re-use of Public Sector Information Regulations came into force on 1 July 2005. They established a framework for making re-use easier and more transparent. The main obligations under the Re-Use of Public Sector Information Regulations 2005 are:

- public sector documents that are available for re-use should be readily identifiable
- documents should generally be available for re-use at marginal cost
- public sector bodies should deal with applications to re-use information in a timely, open and transparent manner
- the process should be fair, consistent and non-discriminatory
- the sharing of best practice should be encouraged across the public sector.

The scheme to help make the re-use of public sector information both easy and transparent is overseen by the Office for Public Sector Information (formerly HMSO). The key elements of the scheme are shown in Figure 6.1.

1	Licence terms: public sector bodies have an obligation to publish licence terms whether in the form of a standard licence or a copyright notice on the material.
2	Details of charges: where applicable these must be published and must be fair and consistent.
3	Responses to be within set time limits: the time limit is 20 working days in line with freedom of information.
4	Asset lists: there is an obligation on public sector bodies to produce a list of material, both published and unpublished, which is available for re-use.
5	Robust complaints procedures: public sector bodies are required to publish details of their complaints process. In addition, a dispute resolution process has been implemented.

Figure 6.1   Main elements of the scheme for re-using public sector information

The scope of the Regulations differs from the freedom of information regime. While both FOI and the Re-use of Public Sector Information relate to the public sector, nevertheless the range of public sector bodies covered by the two regimes does differ.

In the UK, the Regulations cover most of the public sector. This includes:

- central government, including government trading funds and executive agencies
- local government
- the health service
- Parliament.

There are, however, some notable exemptions. These are:

- public sector broadcasters, such as the BBC
- educational and research establishments, including universities
- cultural organizations, such as museums, libraries and archives.

FOI is all about *access* to information. The Regulations go beyond access by dealing with the *re-use* of that information, for example by publishing and making the information available to a wider audience. A key point to note is that any information that is exempt under FOI is not available for re-use.

Policy responsibility for implementing the directive is shared by the Department of Trade and Industry and the Cabinet Office.

The United Kingdom already had in place a number of practical measures to make the re-use of information easier. Much of this resulted from initiatives launched by OPSI, which is attached to the Cabinet Office. These initiatives are:

- the click-use licence (6.2.1), which is an online licensing system
- the Information Asset Register (6.2.2), which provides detailed information on what material is available for re-use
- the Information Fair Trader Scheme (6.2.3), which sets out a framework for the verification of public sector bodies' licensing and information trading activities.

6.2.1 Click-use licence

'Click-use' is the term used to describe OPSI's online licences for the re-use of Crown and Parliamentary copyright material. In the case of Crown copyright material there are in fact two click-use licences – the core licence and the value added licence – and there is a click-use licence to cover Parliamentary copyright material.

Some Crown copyright material is covered by waiver conditions. This covers material where copyright is asserted, but waived. Waiver material can be re-used free of charge without requiring a formal licence provided that it is:

- acknowledged
- not used in a misleading way
- reproduced accurately and kept up to date.

The OPSI copyright guidance notes provide further information about the material that is subject to the waiver.

Applicants for a click-use licence must first register with OPSI for a user account, although registration is free of charge.

6.2.2 Information Asset Register

Inforoute[2] provides direct access to the government's Information Asset

Register (IAR). The IAR lists information resources held by the UK government, concentrating on unpublished resources. In doing so it enables users to identify, from one single source, the information held in a wide variety of government departments, agencies and other organizations. Inforoute is a key part of the government's agenda for freeing up access to official information.

The IAR aims to cover the vast quantities of information held by all government departments and agencies. This includes databases, old sets of files, recent electronic files, collections of statistics, research and so on. The IAR concentrates on information resources that have not yet been, or will not be, formally published.

Individual departments have primary responsibility for putting in place their own IARs, which they maintain on their own websites. OPSI has overall responsibility for IAR formats and standards and for maintaining the Inforoute website.

Inforoute links to other sources of official information and lists of official publications (for example Directgov, UKOP, and the Stationery Office).

Departments maintain their IARs on their own website with links and search facilities from Inforoute.

OPSI is establishing agreed indexing practices across all IAR websites to build an evolving central service.

Inforoute lists the formats in which information can be supplied, gives contact names and encourages users to investigate the most efficient methods for accessing official material.

6.2.3   Information Fair Trader Scheme

The Information Fair Trader Scheme (IFTS) sets and assesses standards for public sector bodies. It requires them to encourage the re-use of information and to reach a standard of both fairness and transparency.

There are two levels to the scheme:

1 Full IFTS accreditation, which is OPSI's gold standard accreditation scheme: this involves an onsite verification and is aimed at major information traders who wish to meet a very high standard of compliance with IFTS principles and the Re-use of Public Sector Information Regulations 2005.

2 IFTS online assessment: this is an online assessment tool aimed at all public sector bodies who wish to demonstrate basic compliance with IFTS principles and the Re-use of Public Sector Information Regulations 2005.

As HMSO's information policy role has been extended to include responsibility for the public sector and not just central government, and as it also has a key role to play in the handling of disputes and complaints, it was renamed the Office of Public Sector Information.

In 2003/4 it was estimated that the turnover of the larger public sector information holders (PSIHs) was in the region of £1bn. The total value of public sector information in the UK economy is much higher than that in other European countries as the information is often re-used as inputs for other products which may be supplied by the PSIHs themselves or by private companies. Examples of PSIHs include HM Land Registry, which holds a property database with access to 20 million registered properties in England and Wales, and the UK Hydrographic Office, which holds navigational products and related information.

As well as making much information freely available some PSIHs sell on information, either in its raw data form or as 'value added' information products involving further refinement of the raw data. Some PSIHs compete with private sector companies in the sale of value added information. These competing companies have to buy the raw data on which their value added products are based from the PSIH.

At the end of July 2005 the Office of Fair Trading (OFT) launched a market study into the commercial use of information supplied by public sector information holders in order to check whether they were providing information to users fairly and reasonably. Many public bodies have a statutory obligation to collect information or do so as part of carrying out their functions. Often they may be the only body collecting and storing such information.

The study looked at whether or not the way in which PSIHs supply information works well for businesses. It examined whether PSIHs have an unfair advantage in selling on information in competition with companies who are reliant on the PSIH for that raw data in the first place. To address this question the study looked at:

- how the raw data that PSIHs collect is turned into value added information
- how pricing of raw data and access to it affects competition between PSIHs and private companies selling value added information
- what situations benefit from vertical integration in the provision of value added information
- the effectiveness of existing guidance and laws.

The study considered a number of areas relating to public bodies:

- the nature of the body
- the nature and scope of the public sector information held by the body
- the definition of the body's public task (i.e. the work that it exists as a public body to do)
- whether the body exploits its public sector information by selling it, and if so how it does so, including pricing
- the body's financial arrangements, including publicity about costs and income
- the body's own commercial activities using its public sector information, and whether and to what extent these are in competition with the private sector.

The OFT's study was not restricted to public authorities already covered by the Regulations; it also looked at a range of other public bodies holding data.

In 2002 there were challenges to Companies House and to Ordnance Survey. The Office of Fair Trading had received complaints alleging that Companies House was abusing its dominant position by subsidizing prices for its products, and thereby unfairly taking business from its competitors. In October 2002 the Office of Fair Trading published a decision of the Director General of Fair Trading about Companies House, the Registrar for Companies for England and Wales. This concluded that there was no evidence that Companies House cross-subsidized its commercial activities (Companies House Direct and WebCHeck), and that it had not infringed the prohibition imposed on it by Section 18 of the Competition Act 1998 by cross-subsidizing so as to allow it to engage in predatory pricing, or impose a margin squeeze on its competitors.

Meanwhile, in February 2002, Gettmapping, a provider of aerial digital colour imagery and the UK's largest independent aerial mapping company, commenced legal proceedings in the High Court against Ordnance Survey, the government-owned cartographic business. Gettmapping sought an injunction to restrain Ordnance Survey from breaching Section 18 of the Competition Act 1998 and from breaching its obligations under the written Resellers Agreement between the two parties which was dated September 2000.

6.3   Summary

This chapter has looked at the re-use of public sector information in the light of the European directive on the re-use of public sector information, and its implementation in the UK through the Re-Use of Public Sector Information Regulations 2005 (6.2). It has considered three practical measures for re-using information which were in place even before the implementation of the 2005 Regulations, namely the click-use licence (6.2.1), the Information Asset Registers (6.2.2) and the Information Fair Trader Scheme (6.2.3).

In the next chapter, we will look at the general principles of libel and defamation law, and in particular the pitfalls that exist when applying defamation law to the internet and to news archives.

6.4   Further information

6.4.1   Organizations

Advisory Panel on Public Sector Information

APPSI Secretariat, 1.35 Admiralty Arch, The Mall, London SW1A 2WH
Tel: 020 7276 5216
E-mail: appsi@cabinet-office.x.gsi.gov.uk
Website: www.appsi.gov.uk

Office for Public Sector Information

Admiralty Arch, North Side, The Mall, London SW1A 2WH
E-mail: opsilicensing@cabinet-office.x.gsi.gov.uk
Website: www.opsi.gov.uk

6.4.2   Legislation and guidance

Directive 2003/98/EC of the European Parliament and of the Council of

17 November 2003 on the Re-use of Public Sector Information, *Official Journal* L345/90 (31 December 2003).

OPSI (2004) *Information Fair Trader Scheme*, www.opsi.gov.uk/ifts/ifts-booklet.pdf.

OPSI (2005) *The Re-use of Public Sector Information: a guide to the regulations and best practice*.

OPSI (2005) *Procedures for Investigating Complaints Arising Under the Re-use of Public Sector Information Regulations 2005*.

Regulatory Impact Assessment: regulations implementing in England, Wales, Scotland and Northern Ireland a directive of the European Parliament and of the Council on the re-use of public sector information, December 2004, HMSO.

The Re-use of Public Sector Information Regulations 2005: SI 2005/1515.

Summary of Responses to the Consultation Document on Implementation of European Directive on the Re-use of Public Sector Information, DTI/HMSO, 2004.

Uhlir, P. F. (2004) *Policy Guidelines for the Development and Promotion of Governmental Public Domain Information*, UNESCO.

6.4.3 Other sources of information

Martin de Saulles weblog, http://rpsi.blogspot.com.

Notes and references

1   Pira International (2000, September) *Commercial Exploitation of Europe's Public Sector Information*.

2   Available at www.opsi.gov.uk/cgi-bin/searchIAR.pL?DB=iar.

7 Defamation

7.1 Introduction

Defamation law attempts to strike a balance between society's interest in freedom of speech and the individual's interest in maintaining their reputation. It is relevant to information professionals, whether they be responsible for intranets, extranets, publicly available websites or online databases; users of their organization's internet e-mail system; members of internet e-mail discussion groups; or authors of books or articles in their own right. The chapter looks at the general principles of defamation law (7.2), and what constitutes slander (7.3) or libel (7.4). It then outlines the defences that can be used in libel cases (7.5), and the remedies that the law provides (7.6). The application of defamation law to the internet is then considered (7.7), including the issues surrounding the liability of internet service providers (7.7.1), the application of the limitation period to online archives (7.7.2), the question of jurisdictions and applicable law in cases of internet defamation (7.7.3) and the risk of prosecution for contempt of court that newspaper and magazine publishers face when they operate online archives (7.7.4). Finally, the potential dangers involved in the use of internet e-mail in terms of defamation and cyberliability are outlined (7.7.5).

7.2 General principles

English law distinguishes between libel (written) and slander (spoken). An item is defamatory if one of the following tests is satisfied:

1 The matter complained of tends to lower the plaintiff in the estimation of society.
2 It tends to bring them into hatred, ridicule, contempt, dislike or disesteem in society.
3 It tends to make them shunned, avoided or cut off from society.

In Scottish law, libel and slander are virtually indistinguishable with regard to both the nature of the wrongs and their consequences. The terminology of Scottish defamation law differs from that of English law. Scots law does not recognize the offence of criminal libel. Where individual English litigants enjoy absolute privilege for what they say in court, their Scottish counterparts have only qualified privilege. 'Exemplary', or 'punitive', damages are not awarded by the Scottish courts. According to D. M. Walker,[1] 'Absolute privilege protects all statements made in judicial proceedings, whatever the rank of the court or the position of the person sued, so long as it is not a gratuitous observation.' However, the footnote confirms that in Scotland, a party only has qualified privilege in his pleadings. This also extends to tribunals if the procedures are similar in essence to a court.

7.3   Slander

Slander is oral defamation – the use of the spoken word to injure another person's reputation. To be the basis of a legal action, a publication of the words complained of must demonstrably have taken place – that is, they must have been uttered within the hearing of a third party. It should be noted that the Scottish position is different, as Scots law does not require that a defamatory statement be communicated to third parties before it is actionable. Among statements considered slanderous *per se* are:

- those that impute the commission of a felony, such as calling someone a murderer
- those that impute an individual to be suffering from a communicable disease, such as gonorrhoea
- those that are injurious to an individual in their trade or profession, such as saying that an accountant fiddles the figures.

The party charged with the slander may hold, as a defence, that the words spoken were in fact true, inasmuch as true statements result in no injury to reputation. Defining slanderous language is sometimes difficult. The disputed words themselves need not be slanderous but may hold a hidden meaning, or innuendo, that the hearer understands, and that may therefore result in damage to the reputation of the slandered party. A defendant in a slander action cannot claim as a defence that another party had made the slanderous statement and that they were merely repeating the statement, nor can the defendant claim that they gave the name of the informant and expressed no opinion as to the truth. In some cases, words that would otherwise be considered actionable, or subject to laws of slander, may be uttered as a privileged communication. Privileged communications are words uttered for a purpose or in a context which is protected by law. Words uttered with qualified privilege, for example when giving an oral reference, are protected as long as the speaker is not motivated by malice. Words uttered with absolute privilege – for example, in Parliament – can never be slander.

McManus & Ors v. Beckham [2002] EWCA Civ 939 (4 July 2002)

Background: On 26 March 2001 Victoria Beckham visited a memorabilia and autograph business (GT's Recollections) owned by the McManus family based in an outlet in a Kent shopping mall (the Bluewater Centre). On seeing a signed photograph of David Beckham in a display cabinet at the entrance, Mrs Beckham said that the signature that they were selling was not that of her husband. She did so in front of other customers, proclaiming loudly that the store was ripping off customers by selling the autograph.

The shop owners said this had damaged their reputation and sued Mrs Beckham for slander and malicious falsehood.

Outcome: Victoria Beckham paid £155,000 in damages and costs (consisting of £55,000 in damages and £100,000 in legal costs). She issued a statement apologizing for the hurt and damage her comments caused to the shop's owners; she also donated several items of merchandise which had been signed by David Beckham.[2]

7.4   Libel

Defamation published in permanent form (such as writing, printing, drawings, photographs and radio and television broadcasts) is known as libel. You libel someone if you publish a defamatory statement about them which you cannot defend. 'Published' in the legal sense means communicated to a person other than the plaintiff. So, for example, if a manuscript is sent to a publisher it would be deemed to have been published in the legal sense. A defamatory statement is one that damages a person's reputation. For example, it is defamatory to say that someone has committed a criminal offence.

The courts will evaluate matters from the perspective of the ordinary person, so a statement would not be regarded as defamatory unless it would make ordinary readers think worse of the person concerned. An ordinary person[3] in this context would be someone with the following characteristics:

- not naïve
- not unduly suspicious
- able to read between the lines
- capable of reading in an implication more readily than a lawyer
- capable of indulging in a certain amount of loose thinking
- not avid for scandal.

You can libel individuals, companies, partnerships and businesses. You cannot libel the dead and you cannot libel local authorities or other government bodies, although you can libel the individuals employed by those organizations. It is possible to libel someone even if you do not name them. Only people who are identified by the offending material can sue, but it is important to bear in mind that you might be identifying someone inadvertently. If, for example, there is only one 27-year-old male librarian living in a particular village, then describing him as such could identify him whether you name him or not. Small groups may also be identifiable and all their members may be able to sue. For example, if you were to write, 'One of the members of the ethics committee has been convicted of murder', and the ethics committee only consisted of five people, this casts suspicion on all five people as it could be referring to any of them. As such the statement would be actionable.

In an action for damages for libel, the plaintiff is required to establish that the matter they complain of:

- has been published by the defendant (publication)
- refers to the plaintiff (identification)
- is defamatory (defamatory words or gestures).

If the plaintiff does this, he/she establishes a prima facie case – that is, provides sufficient evidence for proof of the case. However, the defendant could still escape liability if he/she can show there was a good defence.

7.5   Defences to libel

The defences to a libel action are:

- justification (veritas in Scotland – see Section 7.5.1) – being able to prove that what you wrote was substantially true

- fair comment – showing it was an honest expression of opinion
- privilege – special protection to which the law determines that certain kinds of report are entitled
- offer to make amends (ss2–4 of the Defamation Act 1996).

7.5.1   Justification/veritas

The law of defamation exists to protect individuals who suffer damage to their reputation. It follows, therefore, that the law does not protect the reputation that a person does not possess. If you can prove that what you have written is true both in substance and in fact, then you have a defence against an action for damages. The key point is that you have to be able to prove that what you have written is true. Ultimately, it is not what you know or believe that matters, but rather whether your evidence will stand up in court to the satisfaction of the jury. So if you will be relying on witness evidence:

1   Make sure your witnesses are likely to be available at trial. Relying solely on written statements from overseas witnesses will have far less impact in front of a jury.
2   Do not rely on witnesses who have spoken to you only off the record.
3   Only rely on witnesses who
   - are credible
   - are independent
   - have first-hand knowledge of what they are telling you.

It is important to keep safely any supporting documentation such as a notebook, tapes or documents which might be used in evidence, because you might have to produce this material in court.

Like justification, the defence of veritas in Scotland is a complete defence. It is governed by Section 5 of the Defamation Act 1952.

7.5.2   Fair comment

The defence of fair comment provides for the right of freedom of speech for individuals. For a defence of fair comment to succeed, you must show that:

1   The comment was made honestly and in good faith, based on true facts or on privileged material, as opposed to being inspired by malice.

2 It was on a matter of public interest.

3 You were not motivated by malice, if the claimant alleges malice.

The distinction between the defences of justification and fair comment is that justification/veritas protects the publication of facts whereas fair comment protects the expression of opinion. In some cases it can be particularly difficult to distinguish whether a statement is fact or opinion. If you can prove a statement, it is a fact. If you are drawing an inference from the facts, or if there are at least two possible views on the matter, then it is an opinion.

7.5.3   Privilege

Privilege affords a defence for certain types of report whether or not they are true. Many of these are specified by statute, and include fair and accurate reports of court proceedings, parliamentary proceedings, reports in Hansard, public inquiries and international organizations, as well as a range of public meetings and the findings of governing bodies and associations.

Absolute privilege means that the statement can in no circumstances be the subject of libel proceedings. It covers contemporary, fair and accurate reports of court proceedings, communications within the government, and communications between solicitor and client about legal cases. Proceedings in Parliament are similarly protected, because the courts refuse jurisdiction over Parliamentary affairs.

Qualified privilege is available where the defendant acts without malice – that is, acts for the reasons for which the privilege exists, and not principally to harm the plaintiff. It applies generally to all communications that the defendant has a legal or moral duty to make, or makes in protecting his or her own legitimate interests. Such a defence is wide-ranging and includes reports on most public proceedings and references for employees.

7.5.3.1 Qualified privilege for general media reports

Reynolds v. Times Newspapers Limited [1999] UKHL 45[4] was a case which arose as a result of a newspaper article that implied that Albert Reynolds, the former prime minister of Eire, had lied. In its judgment (28 October 1999) the House of Lords developed the common law defence of qualified privilege to general media reports on matters of public interest. The defence applies when the circumstances are such that a 'duty to publish' and a 'right to know' test is satisfied. Lord Nicholls set out ten factors which need to be taken into account (the tests have an emphasis on responsible journalism):

1 The seriousness of the allegation: the more serious the charge, the more the public is misinformed and the individual harmed, if the allegation is not true.
2 The nature of the information, and the extent to which the subject matter is a matter of public concern.
3 The source of the information: some informants have no direct knowledge of the events. Some have their own axes to grind, or are being paid for their stories.
4 The steps taken to verify the information.
5 The status of the information: the allegation may have already been the subject of an investigation which commands respect.
6 The urgency of the matter: news is often a perishable commodity.
7 Whether comment was sought from the plaintiff: he may have information that others do not possess or have not disclosed. An approach to the plaintiff will not always be necessary.
8 Whether the article contained the gist of the plaintiff's side of the story.
9 The tone of the article: a newspaper can raise queries or call for an investigation. It need not adopt allegations as statements of fact.
10 The circumstances of the publication, including the timing.

7.5.4 Offer to make amends

The procedure for the offer to make amends is set out in Sections 2–4 of the Defamation Act 1996. The defendant must make an offer in writing to publish a suitable correction and apology and to pay damages and costs. When an offer of amends is made, a claimant must decide whether to accept or reject it. If it is accepted, no further proceedings can be taken, except to decide disputes over apologies and the amount of any compensation payable. If it is rejected, then the defendant may rely on the offer as a defence to an action of defamation where the maker neither knew nor had reason to believe that the statement complained of referred to the pursuer and was false and defamatory.

It is no defence to libel to say that you were just reporting what someone else said. Therefore you cannot avoid liability by the use of words such as 'alleged' or 'claimed'. Nor is it a defence to show that someone has published the allegations before. Newspapers and magazines are liable for the contents of whatever they publish, including material not written by them such as readers' letters and advertisements.

It isn't sufficient for newspapers and magazines to ensure that the articles they publish are libel-proof. They also have to pay careful attention to headlines and picture captions, because these can be a lucrative source of damages. In the case of picture captions, the words and the pictures should match.

7.6   Remedies

The remedies available are a civil action for damages, the awarding of costs, an injunction (known as interdict in Scotland) to prevent repetition, or a criminal prosecution to punish the wrongdoer by means of a fine or imprisonment. It is far more common for cases of libel to result in a civil action for damages or an injunction/interdict to prevent repetition.

7.6.1   Civil action for damages

Damages can be colossal, even though the Court of Appeal can now reduce libel awards. The main aim of a libel claim is to compensate the plaintiff for the injury to their reputation. A jury can give additional sums either as 'aggravated' damages, if it appears a defendant has behaved malevolently or spitefully, or as 'exemplary' or 'punitive' damages where a defendant hopes the economic advantages of publication will outweigh any sum awarded. Damages can also be nominal if the libel complained of is trivial (see Walker/Stewart on Delict[5] as awards are assessed on very different principles in Scotland and England).

Malice is irrelevant in awards for damages, although the award may be mitigated where it is shown that there was no malice involved in the defamatory statement. There is also a principle in Scots law that provocation may mitigate. Malice is not defined in the Defamation Act 1952.

However, under the European Convention on Human Rights (ECHR), damages must be necessary and there are controls on excess – as seen in Tolstoy v. UK, 1995 (English law).[6]

7.6.2   Costs

Costs go up all the time. If you were to lose a libel case, then you would have to pay the claimant's expenses as well as your own, which would be likely to add at least a six-figure sum to the bill for damages. Indeed, in many of the high-profile libel cases of the past decade, the costs have often exceeded the damages.

7.6.3 An injunction/interdict to prevent repetition

Any individual or organization can seek an injunction either to stop initial publication of an article or to prevent any further publication. Injunctions/interdicts may be granted, temporarily and for a short while, ex parte, meaning that only the claimant is represented before the judge. If both parties appear before the judge, the defendant would have to argue on grounds of public interest or, for potential libels, be ready to declare on affidavit that they could justify the story.

Injunctions/interdicts against any publication bind all other publications that are aware of the injunction. To breach an injunction is a severe contempt of court that could lead to an offender's imprisonment.

7.6.4 Criminal prosecution to punish the wrongdoer by fine or imprisonment

Where libel occurs, it can lead to a criminal prosecution against those responsible, which includes the author/artist/photographer, the publishers and the editor of the publication in which the libel appeared. To be a criminal offence the libel needs to have been calculated to provoke a breach of the peace or there needs to be some other public interest. Criminal prosecutions are rare. The main types of writing which have the potential to lead to a criminal prosecution are:

- defamatory libel
- obscene publications
- sedition
- incitement to racial hatred
- blasphemous libel.

Section 8 of the Defamation Act 1996 introduced a summary procedure under which a judge may dismiss a plaintiff's claim if it has no realistic prospect of success, or give judgment for the claimant and grant summary relief, which means ordering the defendant to publish a suitable correction and apology and pay damages.

7.7   Defamation and the internet

The Law Commission has investigated the application of libel laws to the internet.[7] In February 2002 it sent out a questionnaire to a number of interested parties, including online publishers, internet service providers, barristers and solicitors. The responses highlighted four areas of concern:

- the liability of internet service providers for other people's material (7.7.1)
- the application of the limitation period to online archives (7.7.2)
- the exposure of internet publishers to liability in other jurisdictions (7.7.3)
- the risk of prosecution for contempt of court (7.7.4).

7.7.1   The liability of internet service providers for other people's material

ISPs offer services such as website hosting and newsgroups where they do not exert editorial control over the material. Where a defamatory statement appears on a website, the ISP is considered to be a 'secondary publisher' – involved in disseminating the defamatory statement even though not the author, editor or commercial publisher. They can be held liable if they exercise discretion over how long material is stored or if they have the power to remove the material.

Under Section 1(1) of the Defamation Act 1996, an innocent disseminator such as a printer, distributor, broadcaster or ISP who is considered by the law to be a secondary publisher has a defence if:

- he was not the author, editor or publisher of the statement complained of
- he took reasonable care in relation to its publication
- he did not know, and had no reason to believe, that what he did caused or contributed to the publication of a defamatory statement.

The section builds upon the common law defence of 'innocent dissemination'. It does not apply to the author, editor or publisher of a defamatory statement but is intended for distributors. It is of particular relevance to ISPs. However, as soon as a secondary publisher such as an ISP has been told that something on a newsgroup or a web page is defamatory, it cannot use the Section 1 defence.

ISPs are seen as tactical targets and regularly receive complaints that material on websites and newsgroups is defamatory. In such instances, the safest option for them is to remove the material immediately, even if it appears to be true, and to remove not just the page in question but the entire website, although this seems at odds with freedom of speech.

In view of the number of e-mail messages, newsgroup postings or web pages that are uploaded daily, it is doubtful whether it would be practical for ISPs to pre-screen all content, and even if it were possible, whether they could do so in a cost-effective manner. It is, however, more reasonable for internet service providers to undertake post-screening. If an ISP is told that material is defamatory, it should act promptly and responsibly by:

- removing the defamatory statements once they have been notified
- posting a retraction
- making a reasonable effort to track down the originator of the defamatory remarks in order to prevent future postings.

Failure to do so would suggest that the ISP had not acted responsibly and that it should be held accountable for the consequences. ISPs are well placed to block or remove obscene, illegal, infringing or defamatory content.

In a response to the Law Commission consultation process, the industry made three criticisms of the current position:

1 Receiving and reacting to defamation complaints was 'costly and burdensome'.
2 The industry felt uncomfortable about censoring material that may not in fact be libellous.
3 It was suggested that customers might be attracted to US ISPs, which had greater protection against being held liable for defamation, and which could therefore offer customers more attractive terms.

ISPs should certainly take complaints seriously. In order to protect themselves, they should obtain warranties and indemnities from content providers, and post notices such as acceptable use policies on their services.

The Electronic Commerce (EC Directive) Regulations[8] implement the Electronic Commerce Directive 2000/31/EC.[9] The Regulations provide that intermediaries such as ISPs and telecommunications carriers are not liable for damages or criminal sanctions for unlawful material provided by third parties where the intermediary:

- is a mere conduit [10] (the intermediary does not initiate the transmission, does not select the receiver of the transmission, and does not modify the information it contains)
- simply caches the information, [11] as part of automatic, intermediate, temporary storage, without modifying it
- simply hosts the information [12] (such as a newsgroup or website) so long as the intermediary:
  — does not have actual knowledge or awareness of the unlawful activity
  — upon obtaining such knowledge or awareness acts expeditiously to remove or disable access.

Godfrey v. Demon Internet Ltd [2001] QB 201

This case concerns a posting to a newsgroup which was distributed to Usenet subscribers. An unnamed USA resident posted a contribution on another ISP purporting to come from Laurence Godfrey, which the judge described as 'squalid, obscene and defamatory'. When Dr Godfrey heard of the posting, he informed Demon Internet that the posting was a forgery and asked them to remove it from their Usenet server. They failed to do so and the posting was left on the site for a further 10 days until it was automatically removed. Demon Internet argued that they had a purely passive role similar to that of a telephone company. However, it was held that as the defendants had chosen whether to store the material and for how long they could not be said to have played only a passive role.

Following the decision in Godfrey v. Demon Internet Ltd [2001] QB 201, ISPs are often seen as tactical targets. They are regularly put on notice of defamatory material and they find themselves facing a difficult choice – whether to surrender in the face of a claim which may be without merit, or continue to publish on the basis of indemnities and assurances from primary publishers that the material is not libellous.

The defence of innocent dissemination also applies to booksellers, libraries and newsagents. The case of Weldon v. Times Book Co Ltd [13] indicates that while a library is not expected to review the contents of every book it possesses, some works may call for a more searching examination, taking account of the type of book in question, the reputation of the author and the standing of the publisher. The Law Commission report on defamation and the internet [14] quotes from a response to consultation on aspects of defamation procedure by the Booksellers Association of Great Britain and Ireland, which says that the provisions of Section 1 of the Defamation Act 1996 '. . . have encouraged plaintiffs or prospective plaintiffs with dubious claims who are unwilling to commence proceedings against the author or publisher of the allegedly defamatory publications to take or threaten action against booksellers to force them to remove such publications from their shelves. As those plaintiffs and their legal advisers clearly realize, booksellers are not in a position to put forward a substantive defence of justification because they have no direct knowledge of the subject matter of the alleged libel.'

Bookshop Libel Fund

Two independent bookshops – Housmans Bookshop and Bookmarks Bookshop – faced potentially ruinous legal proceedings for stocking the anti-fascist magazine *Searchlight*, and the Bookshop Libel Fund was originally set up in 1996 to support small shops such as these who were caught up in libel cases.

The case is not about defamation and the internet, but it is relevant here because of the innocent disseminator defence in Section 1(1) of the Defamation Act 1996.

The case was first brought in 1996 and six years later the bookshops had to relaunch their appeal for funds as the case was still continuing. British law allows anyone who claims they have been libelled to sue any shop, distributor or library handling the allegedly libellous publication, as well as or instead of suing the author, editor and publisher. Housmans and Bookmarks fought the case with a defence of innocent dissemination, in effect arguing that it is impossible for bookshops, particularly small independents, to check – and take responsibility for – the content of the thousands of publications in stock at any one time. They felt it is important to try to take a stand, otherwise there might be no end to this sort of 'legal intimidation'.

The litigant had been referred to as a plagiarist in one sentence in a 136-page pamphlet stocked in the shop. He had chosen to sue only the shop, not the author or publisher concerned.

Although he had at one stage demanded that the shop pay him £50,000 to drop the case, the jury awarded him just £14. Because he had already rejected a settlement offer higher than that, he was also ordered to pay most of the shop's legal costs; however, it was not anticipated that he has the resources to do so.

Where tactical targeting of this kind does occur, it is open to secondary publishers to protect themselves by seeking indemnities from the primary publisher. The primary publisher could also apply to be joined in the action as a defendant in order to provide the necessary evidence for a defence of justification.

According to a DTI consultation document *Electronic Commerce Directive: the liability of hyperlinkers, location tool services and content aggregators* dated June

2005, 'the Department for Constitutional Affairs is considering the wider issues raised by the Law Commission in relation to the liability of ISPs and its conclusions on online archives, with a view to a consultation in due course.'

7.7.2   The application of the limitation period to online archives

The Defamation Act 1996 reduced the limitation period for defamation actions from three years to one year, although courts have discretion to extend that period. However, the application of this limitation to online archives has proved to be extremely contentious. For while the limitation period is one year, in the case of Loutchansky v. Times Newspapers Limited,[15] the Court of Appeal held that this limitation period commenced every time someone accessed a defamatory internet page. In other words every 'hit' on an online article could be regarded as a fresh publication of that article. The judgment means that a piece put on the internet five years ago could still be the subject of legal action today so long as the relevant pages are accessible. The effect of this is that the limitation period is potentially indefinite.

Similarly, in the Scottish case of Her Majesty's Advocate v. William Frederick Ian Beggs[16] the judge ruled that information held in the internet archives of newspapers was published anew each time someone accessed it. This potentially lays newspaper publishers and editors open to charges of contempt of court unless they remove material relating to the previous convictions and other relevant background material of anyone facing criminal proceedings (see Section 7.7.4). The judge did not take the same view of the paper archives held by public libraries, and this distinction takes into account the ease with which material on the internet can be accessed.

One also has to bear in mind the way in which certain search engines and websites are automatically caching and/or archiving the content of a vast number of websites, thus making web pages available even after the site owner has removed the content from their website.

A number of people have suggested that we should adopt the US single publication rule, in which the limitation period starts running on the date of the first publication of the defamatory article, even if it continues to be sold or 'webcast' for months or years afterwards. This matter is of direct relevance to library and information professionals, who make regular use of online archives in order to carry out their research and enquiry roles; any reduction in the availability of online archives would hamper their work. The Law

Commission report [17] says that 'online archives have a social utility and it would not be desirable to hinder their development.'

7.7.3 Exposure of internet publishers to liability in other jurisdictions

England's libel laws are regarded as being 'plaintiff-friendly'. British courts, for example, do not have the First Amendment protections to consider and apply that United States courts do.[18] The nightmare scenario for online and internet publishers is for potential litigants to be able to undertake 'foreign shopping' or 'forum shopping', whereby they can launch an action in a country of their choosing, where the defamation laws are the most stringent. Foreign individuals or companies may, for that reason, be particularly interested in pursuing a British-based publication.

If pursued by overseas claimants, British publications face tricky issues in mounting a defence because subpoenaing foreign witnesses is impossible, although there is a procedure for taking written evidence abroad through foreign courts. Even if the claimant is not particularly well known here, the compensation that could be awarded for damage suffered elsewhere in the world can still be substantial.

Dow Jones v. Gutnick

In the Australian case Dow Jones and Company Inc v. Gutnick [2002] HCA 56 the High Court agreed that a person in Victoria was entitled to bring an action for defamation in Victoria in respect of the publication on the internet of an article in *Barron's* magazine in October 2000 about the tax affairs of Joseph Gutnick even thought the article was uploaded to the web by Dow Jones in America.

The court said potential litigants needed to consider practical issues, such as whether they had assets or reputations in the jurisdiction where the material was published. Otherwise, the court would rule that it was not the appropriate place to hear the case. In Australia, the tort of defamation depends on publication and therefore the fundamental question to be decided was the place of publication of the alleged damaging article. However, the High Court clearly distinguished between jurisdiction and applicable law. It was said that a court may have jurisdiction but it may equally be bound by the applicable rules of a foreign jurisdiction.

In 2004, following out-of-court mediation, lawyers acting on behalf of the publishers Dow Jones and Co issued a statement in Victoria Supreme Court and also agreed to pay Gutnick US$137,500 (AU$180,000) and a further US$306,000 (AU$400,000) to cover his legal costs.

In Dow Jones v. Gutnick, the Australian High Court justified its position, in part, by reference to the International Covenant on Civil and Political Rights,[19] which provides, among other things, that everyone shall be protected from 'unlawful attacks on his honour and reputation'. However, the covenant also provides that:

- everyone shall have the right to hold opinions without interference
- everyone shall have the right to freedom of expression; this right shall include freedom to seek, receive and impart information and ideas of all kinds, regardless of frontiers, either orally, in writing or in print, in the form of art, or through any other media of his choice.

As an article in *The Australian*[20] points out, the Gutnick decision would seem to put all of this in peril. There have been cases in the USA which have taken the opposite view to the Gutnick decision, but of course US libel law is not as plaintiff-friendly as is the case in the UK.

Traditional publishers are able to restrict sales of their publications by geography, but internet publishers do not seem to have that option. By choosing to publish on the internet they are in theory subjecting themselves to the laws of every nation from which the internet can be accessed. The court dismissed Dow Jones's contention that it would have to consider the defamation laws from 'Afghanistan to Zimbabwe' in every article published on the internet. 'In all except the most unusual of cases, identifying the person about whom material is to be published will readily identify the defamation law to which that person may resort,' the court said. Online publishers are concerned that by publishing content on the internet they have to contend with a significant burden of legal risk. What they want is greater certainty and clarity about which laws should be applied to them and their intermediaries. These publishers might feel it necessary to turn to technology for a solution. They might, for example, seek out the development of software that could let sites identify where visitors come from and then block them if they are deemed to expose the publishers to a high risk of potential lawsuits.

In an unprecedented move, the reporter who wrote the piece that Joe Gutnick objected to responded by filing a writ at the United Nations Human Rights Commission, claiming that he has been denied the right of free speech[21] and that Australia is in breach of Article 19 of the United Nations

International Covenant on Civil and Political Rights.

On 15 November 2004, Dow Jones settled the case, agreeing to pay Mr Gutnick over US$440,000 in fees and damages.

Some people argue that the UK should follow the US example and exempt ISPs from liability for material published. However, the Law Commission found that this would not prevent legal action against UK-based internet service providers in foreign courts. An international treaty is required in order to solve the problem of unlimited global risks.

7.7.4 The risk of prosecution for contempt of court

Material is held to be in contempt of court if it poses a substantial risk of serious prejudice to the administration of justice. Serious prejudice is likely to arise from publication of the following matters:

- a defendant's previous convictions
- details of a defendant's bad character
- suggestions that a witness's (particularly a defendant's) testimony is likely to be unreliable
- details of evidence that is likely to be contested at trial.

The law of contempt does not stop you writing about a case; it simply places certain limits on what you may say. For the purposes of contempt, criminal proceedings become active from the time of arrest or charge, or from the time a warrant for arrest is issued, and civil proceedings are active from the time arrangements are made for trial. The closer the case is to trial, the greater the risk of prejudice.

The rulings in Loutchansky v. Times Newspapers Limited and Her Majesty's Advocate v. William Frederick Ian Beggs (see Section 7.7.2) that a web page is published each time a user accesses that page in effect mean that the limitation period is indefinite. The UK does not have the single publication rule that applies in the USA. Consequently, online publishers are concerned over the risk of being held to be in contempt of court because their websites and online archives may well contain records of a defendant's previous convictions or acquittals which jurors could research during a trial. In order to eliminate those risks, newspapers would either have to monitor every criminal case throughout the country and to remove any offending material

from their online archive for cases that were active – which would be imprac-
tical – or they could opt for the more cost-effective option of taking down
the online archives of their publications in their entirety, which would
clearly be to the detriment of historians and researchers.

7.7.5   E-mail libel

The use of e-mail is fraught with dangers. The informal nature of the internet increases the likelihood that people will make defamatory statements in
e-mails, on discussion groups or in chat rooms. These defamatory statements
can reach the far corners of the world in a matter of seconds, whether
through e-mails being directed to a large number of recipients, or through
the forwarding or copying of e-mail correspondence that typically happens.

It is extremely easy and indeed quite common for people to send an e-mail
to unintended recipients. Some discussion groups, for example, have as a
default setting that when you reply to a message from an individual, the
response goes to all members of the group. Many is the time that I have seen
people apologizing for sending out a rather candid e-mail to an entire discussion group when they had only intended to send the message to one person.
Another common mistake is that of including the wrong file attachment in
a message. The user may have published an item which they had never
intended to publish, and thereby perpetrated an accidental defamation. Similarly, it is all too easy to forward a long e-mail without reading the whole
message. If the end of the e-mail contains a defamatory statement, the act of
forwarding the e-mail would mean that the user had unwittingly repeated
the defamatory statement and could be held liable for their actions.

The use of e-mail disclaimers is becoming more common. While the disclaimer may be of dubious legal validity in the absence of any contractual
relationship between the sender and the recipient, the sender will be in a better position if the unintended recipient has notice of the potentially confidential
nature of the e-mail and is advised what to do with it. Therefore disclaimers
may help to limit certain legal liability, but they will not of themselves be a
defence to an action for defamation.

There has been a number of legal cases dealing with defamation and cyberliability. One case which was settled out of court involved defamatory remarks
made on the internal e-mail system of Asda Supermarkets in 1995 accusing a
policeman of fraud.[22] Asda paid substantial damages to the complainant.

Western Provident Association v. Norwich Union Healthcare Ltd and The Norwich Union Life Insurance Company Ltd

In 1997 Western Provident started an action against Norwich Union, a rival private healthcare insurance provider, when it was discovered that Norwich Union was circulating messages on its internal e-mail system which contained damaging and untrue rumours about its competitor to the effect that it was in financial difficulties and being investigated by the DTI. Western Provident sued for libel and slander. Norwich Union publicly apologized to Western Provident and paid £450,000 in compensation for damages and costs.

The Norwich Union case showed that the courts are willing to step in to order employers to preserve the evidence. The High Court in an interlocutory hearing ordered Norwich Union to preserve all the offending messages and to hand over hard copies of them to its rival. The fact that e-mail creates a discoverable document means that employees should be aware that apparently deleted e-mail may be held on the system for some time or be accessible from backups.

If an employee makes a defamatory statement using his/her company's internal e-mail system, or posts a defamatory comment on the company intranet, then it is possible for a legal action to be brought against the organization as employer by way of 'vicarious liability' for acts of its employees.

It is important for employers to issue guidelines such as an e-mail and internet policy with the employee's contract of employment, prohibiting defamatory statements so as to be able to prove that employees or other categories of e-mail, intranet and extranet users have acted contrary to guidelines. It is also good practice to have employees click on an 'accept' button of the e-mail and internet policy before they are able to gain access to the computer system. You need to ensure that users are aware of such guidelines by incorporating them into the intranet home page and elsewhere, as appropriate. However, such action is not a guarantee of immunity from legal actions.

7.8   Checklist

In order to minimize the legal risk of being held liable for a defamatory statement it is worth considering the points raised in the following checklist:

1   Does your organization have a guide to acceptable use of e-mail, the intranet and the internet?
2   Does this mention anything about offensive, defamatory or derogatory material?
3   Is this covered in the staff handbook?

4 Is the policy mentioned as part of the induction process?

5 Emphasize disciplinary action for breaches of e-mail and internet policy.

6 Treat e-mails with the same care that you would show when composing a letter or a fax.

7 Educate and train employees as to the legal implications of sending messages which may be read by tens of thousands of users, and on the acceptable use of internet/e-mail.

8 Bear in mind that there is likely to be a backup of the correspondence.

9 Use a disclaimer on e-mail correspondence.

10 Consider insurance cover for liability in defamation.

7.9   Summary

In this chapter we looked at defamation law, including oral defamation (slander) (7.3) and written defamation (libel) and the law of defamation in Scotland (7.4). Defamation law is relevant to information professionals, whether they be responsible for intranets, extranets, publicly available web-sites or online databases; users of their organization's internet e-mail system; or members of internet e-mail discussion groups. The chapter then outlined the defences that can be used in libel cases (7.5) and the remedies that the law provides (7.6). The 'innocent disseminator' defence is relevant for infor-mation professionals in the hard copy world, where people can target libraries and bookshops as 'secondary publishers', just as much as in the internet arena, where publishers face a wide range of legal hazards – including the application of the limitation period to online archives (7.7.2), the question of jurisdictions and applicable law in cases of internet defamation (7.7.3) and the risk of pros-ecution for contempt of court that newspaper and magazine publishers face when they operate online archives (7.7.4). The chapter concluded with an exam-ination of the dangers of cyberliability in relation to e-mail (7.7.5).

In the next chapter we will consider the general principles of breach of con-fidence and privacy.

Notes and references

1   Walker, D. M. (1988) *Principles of Scottish Private Law*, Vol. 2, 4th edn, 637–8.

2   See 'Posh Spice' Pays £155,000 to Settle Autograph Dispute, *The Independent* (12 March, 2003); and £155,000: what Beckham's autograph will cost his wife in court, *The Mirror* (12 March, 2003).

3 See Skuse v. Granada Television Ltd [1996] EMLR 278 and Gillick v. British Broadcasting Corporation [1996] EMLR 267.

4 Available at www.parliament.the-stationery-office.co.uk/pa/ld199899/ldjudgmt/ jd991028/rey01.htm.

5 Walker, D. M. (1981) *The Law of Delict in Scotland*, 2nd rev. edn, Edinburgh, W. Green.

6 Tolstoy v. UK, unreported ECHR, 13 July 1995 (English law).

7 Law Commission (2002, December) *Defamation and the Internet : a preliminary investigation, scoping study no. 2*, www.lawcom.gov.uk/docs/defamation2.pdf.

8 The Electronic Commerce (EC Directive) Regulations 2002: SI 2002/2013.

9 EC Directive 2000/31/EC of 8 June 2000 on Certain Legal Aspects of Information Society Services, in Particular Electronic Commerce, in the Internal Market, *Official Journal* L178/1 (17 June 2000).

10 SI 2002/2013 Regulation 17.

11 SI 2002/2013 Regulation 18.

12 SI 2002/2013 Regulation 19.

13 Weldon v. Times Book Co Ltd [1911] 28 TLR 143.

14 Law Commission (2002, December) *Defamation and the Internet: a preliminary investigation, scoping study no. 2*, www.lawcom.gov.uk/docs/defamation2.pdf.

15 Loutchansky v. Times Newspapers Limited [2001] EWCA Civ 1805, available at www.bailii.org/ew/cases/EWCA/Civ/2001/1805.html.

16 Her Majesty's Advocate v. William Frederick Ian Beggs, High Court of Judiciary (2001).

17 Law Commission (2002, December) *Defamation and the Internet: a preliminary investigation, scoping study no. 2*, www.lawcom.gov.uk/docs/defamation2.pdf.

18 The First Amendment of the US constitution says that Congress shall make no law respecting an establishment of religion, or prohibiting the free exercise thereof; or abridging the freedom of speech, or of the press; or the right of the people peaceably to assemble, and to petition the government for a redress of grievances.

19 International Covenant on Civil and Political Rights, New York, 19 December 1966, ATS 1980 no. 23.

20 High Court Throws a Spanner in the Global Networks, *The Australian* (11 December 2002).

21 *Australian Laws Challenged at UN* (2003, 18 April), www.smh.com.au/ articles/2003/04/18/1050172745955.html.

22 Bright, M., Caught in the Net, *The Guardian* (25 April 1995).

8 Breach of confidence and privacy

8.1 Introduction

This chapter considers what constitutes a breach of confidence (8.2). It explores how human rights legislation has been used in privacy actions (8.3), and the differences that exist between the law on obligation of confidence and breach of privacy (8.4). The implications of the obligation of confidence on the freedom of information regime are discussed (8.5). The role of regulatory codes of practice is then considered (8.6). The chapter concludes by looking at remedies available for breach of confidence (8.7), and relevant case law (8.8) in which breach of confidence was used to protect the privacy of individuals.

8.2 General principles

The common law tort of breach of confidence deals with unauthorized use or disclosure of certain types of information and provides protection for that information to be kept secret.

This branch of the law is based upon the principle that a person who has obtained information in confidence should not take unfair advantage of it. The main means used to achieve this is the interim injunction (interdict in Scotland), which is an order of the court directing a party to refrain from disclosing the confidential information. A document may be considered confidential where there is:

- an obligation of non-disclosure within a particular document
- a duty in certain papers involving professional relationships
- a duty of confidence, which arises where a reasonable individual may determine that a document contains confidential material.

Breach of confidence is most commonly used to prevent publication of private material. The law protects confidential information from unauthorized disclosure, and an injunction may be granted unless you can show that the publication is in the public interest, usually by exposing some wrongdoing. The injunction can in extreme circumstances be against the whole world, such as the injunction granted to protect the new identities of the killers of James Bulger.

In the James Bulger case, Dame Elizabeth Butler-Sloss gave the killers of James Bulger the right to privacy throughout their life. The media were already prevented from publishing their identities as a result of information obtained from those who owed the pair a duty of confidence, such as police officers and probation service officials, but Dame Elizabeth went further and said the pair had an absolute right to privacy.

In another legal case from May 2003 the child killer Mary Bell and her daughter won a High Court injunction guaranteeing them lifelong anonymity.

There are three elements of a breach of confidence. In 1968 Mr Justice Megarry [1] said:

1 The information must have 'the necessary quality of confidence' – namely, it must not be something which is public property and public knowledge.
2 The information must have been imparted in circumstances imposing an obligation of confidence.
3 There must be an unauthorized use of that information to the detriment of the party communicating it.

If someone wishes to seek redress for disclosure of confidential information, then each of these elements must be present. Furthermore:

1 Companies use breach of confidence to protect sensitive commercial information and trade secrets.
2 Governments use breach of confidence to protect information they regard as secret.
3 Individuals use it for the same purpose and also to protect their privacy.

The duty of confidence is, as a general rule, also imposed on a third party who is in possession of information which he knows is subject to an obligation of confidence.[2] If this were not the law, the right would be of little practical value. There would, for example, be no point in imposing a duty of confidence in respect of the secrets of the marital bed if newspapers were free to publish those secrets when betrayed to them by the unfaithful partner in the marriage. Similarly, when trade secrets are betrayed by a confidant to a third party, it is usually the third party who is to exploit the information, and it is the activity of the third party that must be stopped in order to protect the owner of the trade secret.

The use of breach of confidence by individuals wishing to protect their privacy was boosted by the implementation of the European Convention on Human Rights in UK law through the Human Rights Act 1998 (HRA), because this Act gives individuals a right to privacy.

Between February and April 2003, the Culture, Media and Sport Select Committee held an inquiry into privacy and media intrusion,[3] and asked whether there was a need for legislation on privacy. The inquiry did not aim to come to the aid of public figures who have problems with the press; rather, it was concerned with ordinary people whose lives can be affected, perhaps adversely, by their relations with the media. About 11 years had elapsed since the previous inquiry on this topic by the then National Heritage Committee. The fact that the Committee undertook a new inquiry on privacy and media intrusion was a recognition that things have moved on a considerable degree since that time.

The government's response[4] to the Select Committee Report didn't accept a need for a new law in this area:

> The Government believes that people have a right to a private life, but that right is not absolute. Equally, the right to freedom of expression is not absolute. Where there is conflict between the two, they must be weighed against each other. The Government remains committed to supporting self-regulation as the best possible form of regulation for the press, and as the best possible way of balancing those sometimes conflicting demands. There is, however, room for improvement in any regulatory system, and the Committee's report has effectively opened up debate on what the improvements in this system might be. We believe that such debate is healthy and constructive, and that it should lead to a positive outcome.

8.3   Privacy and the Human Rights Act

There has never been an absolute right to privacy in English or Scots law. Yet Britain has been bound to comply with the European Convention on Human Rights (ECHR) for decades, which states that 'everyone has the right to respect for his private and family life, his home and his correspondence.' A number of the rights which are enshrined in the ECHR are in conflict with one another, and there will always be a tension between them. In particular, the right to privacy (Article 8) and the right to freedom of expression (Article 10) often conflict (see Figure 8.1). In every situation, a balance needs to be struck between those two rights; the courts need to consider the issues on a case-by-case basis. What is clear is that the right to privacy is not an absolute right.

Article 8 – Right to respect for private and family life
1   Everyone has the right to respect for his private and family life, his home and his correspondence.
2   There shall be no interference by a public authority with the exercise of this right except such as is in accordance with the law and is necessary in a democratic society in the interests of national security, public safety or the economic well being of the country, for the prevention of disorder or crime, for the protection of health or morals, or for the protection of the rights and freedoms of others.

Article 10 – Freedom of expression
1   Everyone has the right to freedom of expression. This right shall include freedom to hold opinions and to receive and impart information and ideas without interference by public authority and regardless of frontiers. This article shall not prevent states from requiring the licensing of broadcasting, television or cinema enterprises.
2   The exercise of these freedoms, since it carries with it duties and responsibilities, may be subject to such formalities, conditions, restrictions or penalties as are prescribed by law and are necessary in a democratic society, in the interests of national security, territorial integrity or public safety, for the prevention of disorder or crime, for the protection of health or morals, for the protection of the reputation or rights of others, for preventing the disclosure of information received in confidence, or for maintaining the authority and impartiality of the judiciary.

Figure 8.1   European Convention on Human Rights

Since the HRA came into force in 2000, the courts have had to interpret existing law in ways which secure this right. The existing law, however, remains piecemeal, and privacy complaints are usually found in actions for breach of confidence, harassment, trespass, malicious falsehood and data protection, or pursued under regulatory codes of practice (see Section 8.6).

In 2004 Naomi Campbell won a privacy case in the House of Lords.[5] In 2001, the *Daily Mirror* carried an article headed 'Naomi: I am a drug addict'. The article reported:

- the fact that Naomi Campbell had a drug addiction
- the fact that she was receiving treatment
- the fact that part of the treatment involved attending Narcotics Anonymous meetings
- the details of the treatment, including frequency of attendance at meetings and information of that kind.

The article was accompanied by a photograph, taken surreptitiously with a long lens, of her leaving a Narcotics Anonymous meeting in London. Prior to the publication of the article, Naomi Campbell had always maintained that she did not take drugs and had made public statements to that effect. Naomi Campbell sued the *Daily Mirror* and claimed damages for breach of confidence and for misuse of personal data under the Data Protection Act 1998. She won in the High Court and was awarded damages of £3,500 (the damages were so low in part because the judge took the view that Naomi Campbell had not been entirely frank and truthful). The *Daily Mirror* appealed to the Court of Appeal, which overturned the judgment of the High Court and found in favour of the *Daily Mirror*. Naomi Campbell then appealed to the House of Lords, and this resulted in a judgment by a three to two majority in favour of Naomi Campbell, which re-instated the judgment of the High Court.

It was decided that the publication of detailed information about the treatment she was undergoing for drug addiction was a breach of her right to keep her personal information private. In this case, the House of Lords observed that photographs of people in circumstances in which the person has a reasonable expectation of privacy can be particularly intrusive. Unless there is a compelling public interest justification for publication of such photographs, there is likely to be an invasion of privacy. The House of Lords roundly endorsed the Press Complaints Commission guidelines that state that long lens surreptitious photography is not acceptable.

The professions are subject to obligations of confidentiality. The CILIP Ethical Principles and Code of Professional Practice for Library and

Information Professionals[6] addresses the question of confidentiality from several different perspectives:

1 One of the general principles states that the conduct of information professionals should be characterized by respect for confidentiality and privacy in dealing with information users.
2 One of the specific responsibilities to information users says that information professionals should protect the confidentiality of all matters relating to information users, including their enquiries, any services to be provided and any aspects of the users' personal circumstances or business.
3 Information professionals should strive to achieve an appropriate balance within the law between demands from information users, the need to respect confidentiality, the terms of their employment, the public good and the responsibilities outlined in the Code.

Section A.3 of the EIRENE (European Information Researchers Network) Code of Professional Conduct[7] says that a broker shall:

- hold the affairs of the client in the strictest confidence, except where the law requires disclosure
- declare any conflicts of interest if they are likely to undermine confidentiality
- undertake not to re-use or misuse information gained as part of the client contract for personal or professional gain.

8.4   Obligation of confidence v. breach of privacy

An obligation of confidence, by definition, arises firstly from the circumstances in which the information is given. By contrast, a right of privacy in respect of information arises from the nature of the information itself, based on the principle that certain kinds of information are categorized as private and for that reason alone ought not to be disclosed. In many cases where privacy is infringed, this is not the result of a breach of confidence.

In the late 1980s the UK government used the law of confidence to try to silence former members of the security services (in particular Peter Wright, author of *Spycatcher*) and journalists trying to report their disclosures.

It has been established that the public has a legitimate interest, to be weighed against other interests, in knowing how it has been governed. It has, however, always been accepted that Cabinet deliberations are confidential. As a result of the publication of Richard Crossman's diaries, a case was taken by the Attorney General against the publisher for breach of confidence.[8] It was held that the public interest in disclosure outweighed the protection of information given in confidence once the material was sufficiently old. In this particular case that period was taken to be 10 years. The courts appear to retain for themselves the role of arbiter of the public interest and will consider each case on its merits.

Kaye v. Robertson [1991] FSR 62

A reporter and a photographer tricked their way into the private hospital room of the actor Gorden Kaye who was lying semi-conscious. They did so in order to 'interview' and photograph him. The court held that there was no actionable right to privacy in English law and that no breach of confidence had taken place because there wasn't a recognized relationship between Mr Kaye and the journalists (such as that between a doctor and his patient) which could be used in order to impose an obligation to keep confidential what Mr Kaye had said.

This case might be seen as the low point in the laws of privacy and breach of confidence, but since that time much has happened with the implementation of the Human Rights Act 1998 and case law which has further refined and developed the laws relating to privacy and breach of confidence. Indeed, for a breach of confidence action to succeed, there is no longer a need for there to be a confidential relationship.

8.5   Obligation of confidence and the Freedom of Information Act

Section 41 of the FOIA provides for an exemption for information provided in confidence. Under the exemption, the duty to confirm or deny does not arise if, or to the extent that, the confirmation or denial that would have to be given in order to comply would constitute an actionable breach of confidence.

There are two components to the exemption:

1 The information must have been obtained by the public authority from another person. A person may be an individual, a company, a local authority or any other 'legal entity'. The exemption does not cover information which the public authority has generated itself although another exemption may apply.

2 The exemption applies if disclosure of the information would give rise to

an actionable breach of confidence. In other words, if the public authority disclosed the information the provider or a third party could take the authority to court.

---

41. (1) Information is exempt information if –
(a) it was obtained by the public authority from any other person (including another public authority), and
(b) the disclosure of the information to the public (otherwise than under this Act) by the public authority holding it would constitute a breach of confidence actionable by that or any other person.
(2) The duty to confirm or deny does not arise if, or to the extent that, the confirmation or denial that would have to be given to comply with section 1(1)(a) would (apart from this Act) constitute an actionable breach of confidence.

Figure 8.2 Freedom of Information Act 2000 Section 41 exemption

For the precise wording of this exemption see Figure 8.2.
There is guidance available regarding the exemption for information provided in confidence from the Information Commissioner[9] and also from the Department of Constitutional Affairs.[10]

This exemption qualifies the right of access under the Act by reference to the common law action for breach of confidence. According to that action, if a person who holds information is under a duty to keep information confidential, there will be a breach of confidence if that person makes an unauthorized disclosure of that information. The concept of breach of confidence has its roots in the notion that a person who agrees to keep information confidential should be obliged to respect that confidence. However, the law has now extended beyond this: the courts recognize that a duty of confidence may also arise due to the confidential nature of the information itself or the circumstances in which it was obtained.

The concept of breach of confidence recognizes that unauthorized disclosure of confidential information may cause substantial harm. The law protects these interests by requiring the information to be kept confidential: if information is disclosed in breach of a duty of confidence, the courts may award damages (or another remedy) to the person whose interests were protected by the duty.

The s45 code of practice issued by the Secretary of State for Constitutional Affairs[11] contains guidance on freedom of information and confidentiality obligations. The guidance states that public authorities should bear clearly in mind their obligations under the Freedom of Information Act when preparing to enter into contracts which may contain terms relating to the disclosure of information by them.

When entering into contracts with non-public authority contractors, public authorities may be under pressure to accept confidentiality clauses in order that information relating to the terms of the contract, its value and performance will be exempt from disclosure. Public authorities should reject such clauses wherever possible. Where, exceptionally, it is necessary to include non-disclosure provisions in a contract, an option could be to agree with the contractor a schedule of the contract which clearly identifies information which should not be disclosed. But authorities will need to take care when drawing up any such schedule, and be aware that any restrictions on disclosure provided for could potentially be overridden by their obligations under the FOIA.

In some cases the disclosure of information pursuant to a request may affect the legal rights of a third party – for example, where information is subject to the common law duty of confidence or where it constitutes 'personal data' within the meaning of the Data Protection Act 1998 (DPA). Public authorities must always remember that, unless an exemption provided for in the DPA applies in relation to any particular information, they will be obliged to disclose that information in response to a request.

A public authority should only accept information from third parties in confidence if it is necessary to obtain that information in connection with the exercise of any of the authority's functions and it would not otherwise be provided. Acceptance of any confidentiality provisions must be for good reasons, justifiable to the Information Commissioner.

8.6   Codes of practice

A number of codes of practice govern the media, and in any cases relating to privacy or breach of confidence, the courts would have regard to any relevant privacy code. These codes include:

- the Press Complaints Commission Code of Practice,[12] applicable to newspapers and magazines
- BBC TV producers' guidelines [13]
- the Broadcasting Code [14] (Ofcom).

Ofcom has a duty to apply adequate protection to audiences against unfairness or the infringement of privacy. It issued a Broadcasting Code which came into force on 25 July 2005, and which replaced the set developed by the previous broadcasting regulators – the Independent Television Commission for commercial television, the Radio Authority for commercial radio and the Broadcasting Standards Commission on matters relating to taste, decency, fairness and privacy.

In considering whether to grant an injunction (interdict in Scotland), courts would have regard to the standards the press has itself set in voluntary codes of practice. Under the Press Complaints Commission Code, a publication will be expected to justify intrusions into any individual's private life which have been made without consent.

In March 2003, the 11th edition of the *British Code of Advertising, Sales Promotion and Direct Marketing*[15] was launched by the Committee of Advertising Practice (CAP). The code applies to non-broadcast marketing communications in the UK and is endorsed and administered independently by the Advertising Standards Authority (ASA).

The code takes account of the UK's distance selling regulations[16] and the EU's directive on privacy and electronic communications.[17] As far as the obligation of confidence is concerned, the code states that 'the ASA and CAP will on request treat in confidence any genuinely private or secret material supplied unless the courts or officials acting within their statutory powers compel its disclosure.'

8.7 Remedies

The main means of ensuring that information obtained in confidence is not unfairly taken advantage of is the use of an injunction (interdict in Scotland). A prohibitory injunction can be used in order to direct a party to refrain from disclosing information. A number of remedies are available to the courts:

- fines
- court order to reveal source
- court order that a confidential matter be 'delivered up' or destroyed
- account for the profits where a person misusing confidential information may be asked to account to the person who confided the information

- damages claim by the person whose confidences have been breached in the publication of confidential material
- contempt of court action where injunction/interdict is breached.

8.8   Case law on breach of confidence

The past few years have seen a number of high-profile cases in which well known personalities have used the law relating to breach of confidence in order to try and protect their privacy.

Even a public figure is entitled to a private life, although he or she may expect and accept that his or her circumstances will be more carefully scrutinized by the media. If the claimant has courted attention, this may lead the claimant to have fewer grounds upon which to object to the intrusion.

Naomi Campbell v. Mirror Group Newspapers [2004] UKHL 22

The Naomi Campbell case was about confidentiality, privacy, the Human Rights Act and data protection.

Naomi Campbell sued the publishers of the *Mirror* for breach of confidence and breach of the DPA in respect of articles and photographs which showed that she was attending meetings of Narcotics Anonymous.

In this case the Court of Appeal applied the practical test regarding whether information or conduct is to be considered private and confidential – the common law test of offensiveness – in order to determine whether disclosure or observation of the information would be highly offensive to a reasonable person of ordinary sensibilities. But when the case reached the House of Lords, Lord Carswell said it is not necessary in this case to ask whether disclosure of the information would be highly offensive to a reasonable person of ordinary sensibilities because it was sufficiently established by the nature of the material that it was private information which attracted the duty of observing the confidence in which it was imparted to the respondents.

Publication of the details about Naomi Campbell's attendance at therapy carried out by Narcotics Anonymous, highlighted by the photographs printed, constituted in the judgment of Lord Carswell a considerable intrusion into her private affairs, which was capable of causing substantial distress, and on her evidence did cause it to her. It is difficult to assess how much, if any, actual harm it may have done to her progress in therapy. In her evidence she said that she had not gone back to the World's End NA centre since the article was published and that she had only attended about four meetings in other centres in England, though she had gone to meetings abroad and met privately at her home with other NA attendees. Lord Carswell concluded that the publication of the article did create a risk of causing a significant setback to her recovery.

Outcome: By a three to two majority, the House of Lords upheld Naomi Campbell's appeal in her claim against the *Daily Mirror*. The Lords' decision re-instated the damages awarded in the High Court decision, and reversed the Appeals Court's award of expenses in favour of the *Daily Mirror* against Campbell.

The footballer's case A v. B & another [2002] EWCA Civ 337

The claimant was a premier league footballer who was granted an interim injunction restraining the first defendant B from publishing stories about his extramarital affairs with two women C and D.

The court considered the balance between Article 8 of the ECHR on the right to respect for private life and Article 10 on the right to freedom of expression. The court of appeal said that the judge had been wrong to reject any element of public interest in the publication of the proposed stories.

The Lord Chief Justice, Lord Woolf, said that the more stable the relationship, the greater would be the significance attached to it by the court. But the court should not protect brief affairs of the sort the footballer enjoyed with the two women, when the women wanted to talk about them. Banning the two women from telling their stories for publication was an interference with their freedom of expression.

Theakston v. MGN Ltd [2002] EWHC 137

Jamie Theakston sought an injunction to prevent publication of photographs and an article relating to his visit to a brothel. He relied on the grounds of breach of confidentiality and breach of his right to privacy as reflected in the Press Complaints Commission Code, and as contained in Article 8 of the ECHR. Mr Theakston claimed that he had been in a private place with friends, that the events were private and confidential and that he had never discussed the details of his private life or sex life in public.

The judge stated that he did not consider the brothel to be a private place. Mr Theakston had courted publicity regarding his private life which led to his enhanced fame and popularity.

Mr Theakston was successful in obtaining an injunction preventing publication of the photographs, but was unsuccessful in preventing publication of the article.

Douglas and others v. Hello! Ltd [2005] EWCA Civ 595, 18 May 2005

Background: Catherine Zeta Jones and Michael Douglas had signed an exclusive deal with *Hello!*'s rival, *OK!*, to publish wedding photographs. *Hello!* magazine published photographs of the wedding in breach of confidence.

Outcome: The court held that the publication of wedding photographs of Michael Douglas and Catherine Zeta Jones was a breach of commercial confidence in circumstances where photography was explicitly prohibited after their wedding. The celebrity couple succeeded in their claims for both breach of confidence and breach of privacy and the appeals against them were dismissed.

Key points from the case:

1   As a general rule (although it is not always the case), once information is in the public domain it will no longer be protected by the law of confidence; this also applies to private information of a personal nature. Once intimate information about a celebrity's private life has been widely published, it is not likely to serve any useful purpose to prevent further publication. It is important to distinguish between textual articles and photographs, because this is not necessarily true with respect to photographs. A photograph enables the viewer to focus on intimate personal detail

Continued on next page

Douglas and others v. Hello! Ltd (*continued*)

---

and, as such, there may be a fresh invasion of privacy every time the photograph is seen by someone. This is true even if precisely the same photograph has been published before, and it is also true even if it is the same person or people who had seen the picture before.

2   In addition to their right to keep private information about their wedding private, Michael Douglas and Catherine Zeta-Jones also had a right to protect their opportunity to profit from confidential information about themselves. This is similar to the right of a company to protect its potential to profit from information amounting to a trade secret.

3   With regard to the right to privacy, photographs are in a different category to verbal information and special considerations apply to them. In short, the courts will apply stricter standards to photographs than to their verbal equivalent. This is because a photograph is a particularly intrusive means of invading privacy. A camera could potentially be used to gain access to scenes which those being photographed could reasonably expect would not be brought to the notice of the public. This has been recognized both by previous court decisions such as Theakston v. MGN (see page 187) and also by the various media codes of practice (see 8.6).

4   The right to privacy is something that can only be enforced by the person to whom the private information relates. It isn't akin to a property right which can be assigned to someone else.

8.9   Summary

This chapter has outlined the law relating to breach of confidence (8.2). It discussed how human rights legislation has been used in privacy actions (8.3) and the differences that exist between the law on obligation of confidence and breach of privacy (8.4). The FOIA has an absolute exemption for breach of confidence, but the code of practice issued by the Secretary of State for Constitutional Affairs makes it clear that confidentiality should not be used to prevent disclosure without there being a very good reason which can be justified to the Information Commissioner. The chapter concluded by looking at the remedies available for breach of confidence, and details of a few high-profile cases in which breach of confidence has been used by individuals to protect their privacy.

The next chapter deals with professional negligence, and while there hasn't yet been a legal case of a UK librarian being sued on the grounds that their work has caused loss or damage, information professionals must not become complacent. They do need to be aware of the risks involved and need to try and minimize those risks.

Notes and references

1   Coco v. Clark [1969] RPC 41 at 47.

2   See Prince Albert v. Strange (1840) 1 Mac & G 25 and Duchess of Argyll v. Duke of Argyll [1967] Ch 302.

3   HC 458i-iv and HC 458-I Session 2002/03, available at www.parliament. the-stationery-office.co.uk/pa/cm200203/cmselect/cmcumeds/cmcumeds.htm.

4   *The Government's Response to the Fifth Report of the Culture, Media and Sport Select Committee on 'Privacy and Media Intrusion'* (HC 458-1) Session 2002–2003 Cm 5985.

5   Naomi Campbell v. Mirror Group Newspapers Limited [2004] UKHL 22.

6   CILIP (2005) Ethical Principles and Code of Professional Practice for Library and Information Professionals, www.cilip.org.uk/professionalguidance/ professionalethics/code.

7   EUSIDIC (European Association of Information Services), EIIA (European Information Industry Association) and EIRENE (European Information Researchers Network) (1993) *Code of Practice for Information Brokers.*

8   Attorney General v. Jonathan Cape Ltd [1976] QB 752.

9   Office of the Information Commissioner, *Information Provided in Confidence: Freedom of Information Act awareness guidance no.2.*

10 Department of Constitutional Affairs, *Section 41: information provided in confidence.*

11 Lord Chancellor's Department (2004) *Secretary of State for Constitutional Affairs' Code of Practice on the Discharge of Public Authorities' Functions under Part I of the Freedom of Information Act 2000, Issued Under Section 45 of the Act,* www.dca.gov.uk/foi/codepafunc.htm.

12 Available at www.pcc.org.uk/cop/cop.asp.

13 Available at www.bbc.co.uk/guidelines/editorialguidelines

14 Ofcom (2005) *Broadcasting Code,* www.ofcom.org.uk/tv/ifi/codes/bcode

15 The Committee of Advertising Practice (2003) *British Code of Advertising, Sales Promotion and Direct Marketing,* 11th edn (came into force on 4 March 2003).

16 The Consumer Protection (Distance Selling) Regulations 2000: SI 2000/2334.

17 2002/58/EC covering the processing of personal data and the protection of privacy in the electronic communications sector (directive on privacy and electronic communications).

9 Professional liability

9.1   Introduction

This chapter considers professional liability from the perspective of library and information professionals. Although there hasn't been an instance of a UK librarian being successfully sued for negligence, that is no reason to become complacent.

The chapter looks at the general principles of professional liability (9.2), and how librarians could be held liable for their work under the law of contract (9.3) or the law of tort (delict in Scotland) (9.4). Specific types of liability are considered, including liability in relation to electronic information (9.5) and liability for copyright infringement (9.6).

Strategies for minimizing the legal liability risks that librarians face as professionals are examined (9.7), as is the role of professional indemnity insurance as part of that strategy (9.8).

9.2   General principles

Liability means having legal responsibility for one's acts, errors or omissions. It is the duty of care that one individual or organization owes to another, and it gives rise to the risk of being sued for damages if the individual or organization fails in that duty. It is certainly the case that a librarian owes the user of an information service (the client) a duty to exercise reasonable care; this duty of care basically means that he/she should do the things that a prudent person would do in the circumstances and refrain from those things a prudent person would not do.

While there is no UK legislation dealing specifically with liability for information provision, librarians do need to be aware of the potential risk of facing a professional liability claim because they could be held liable for their work under contract law or the law of tort/delict.

Any organization whose professional employees provide advice, expertise, information or a consultancy service may be legally liable for a claim of malpractice where a breach of professional duty occurs. An employer is vicariously liable for the torts/delicts of his/her employees, if they are committed in the course of the employees' employment. This only applies if the act were one of the type that the employee might have been expected to carry out in the normal course of his/her duties. The employer is likely to have insurance cover against any actions brought against the company – although it is well worth checking that this is the case. Self-employed information consultants and brokers should consider taking out professional indemnity insurance (see Section 9.8).

Even if you work for an employer, there are potential dangers involved in assuming that your firm's professional indemnity insurance will protect you if liability is established, as the case of Merrett v. Babb demonstrates.

Merrett v. Babb (Court of Appeal, 15 February 2001)

In the case of Merrett v. Babb, the Court of Appeal held that a surveyor employed by a firm of valuers who negligently prepared a mortgage valuation report for a lender owed a duty of care to the purchasers who relied on the surveyor's report when buying the property, and that the surveyor was personally liable for the purchasers' loss. Permission to appeal was refused.

In the mortgage valuation report prepared by Mr Babb on the property that Miss Merrett was about to purchase, it was noted that the property contained certain cracks, but the report failed to point out that settlement had taken place. Miss Merrett said that the property was worth £14,500 less than the valuation and she sued Babb in his personal capacity.

The surveyor was employed as branch manager of a firm of surveyors and valuers from February 1992 to January 1993. On 1 June 1992 he signed the relevant mortgage valuation report. A bankruptcy order was made against the sole principal of the firm on 30 August 1994. The principal's trustee in bankruptcy cancelled the firm's professional indemnity insurance without run-off cover in September 1994. The purchaser therefore brought an action in negligence against the surveyor personally rather than against the firm. The surveyor was not insured.

The implications of this case are that professional employees may be open to claims for negligent advice in situations where their firm has become insolvent or is otherwise under-insured. The case shows that there may be instances where individuals might need to take out personal insurance even after their employment has ended.

Taking the general principles of liability into account, it is necessary to consider how they relate to the information professional. You are expected to use reasonable skill and care when providing library and information services, and the key issue to establish is what is meant by 'reasonable'. 'Reasonable' means that which an information professional would be expected to do in the circumstances, and the judges of what is 'reasonable' are other information professionals. So 'reasonable' really constitutes good professional practice, which could be established by testimony from expert witnesses.

Only when we can say what a quality product or service consists of and how it is identified can we be clear what wouldn't be a quality service, and therefore be able to speak of liability for low-quality work. Is the service performed to the standard of an average professional? Ultimately your own reputation with colleagues and clients is the best guide.

Information professionals should seek to provide their services as well as they possibly can – that is, they should do their job with due care and attention. Did they fail to search an appropriate source and thereby miss something vital? Did they try to verify the accuracy of the information? Information professionals should also act ethically. They have a set of ethical principles to be followed. The CILIP Ethical Principles and Code of Professional Practice for Library and Information Professionals[1] sets out a number of personal responsibilities of information professionals, which among others state that they should:

- strive to attain the highest personal standard of professional knowledge and competence
- ensure they are competent in those branches of professional practice in which qualifications and/or experience entitle them to engage by keeping abreast of developments in their areas of expertise
- claim expertise in areas of library and information work or in other disciplines only where their skills and knowledge are adequate.

According to the CILIP leaflet *Working for Yourself*, 'As yet there is no record of a library or information professional being sued on the grounds that their work caused loss or damage to their client.'[2] However, this should not lure people into a false sense of security. It begs the question: do you want to be the first information professional in the UK to be sued because your advice caused a client loss or damage?

It may seem hard to think of a situation where provision of information could lead to a client suffering loss or damage, but information professionals need to think about the nature of the information they are dealing with and the levels of risk attached to different types of information. For example, if an enquirer were to ask you to find a set of instructions on how to make your own parachute, you would need to make it absolutely clear that you had not tested the validity of the instructions and give the enquirer a disclaimer, along the lines that you could not take any responsibility for any damage caused to the enquirer if they were to follow the instructions that you had given them. This probably sounds rather a frivolous example, but when dealing with legal, financial, patent or medical information, you need to be particularly careful. If you obtained a credit rating on a company for a user, it is quite feasible that, if the credit rating was out of date or was inaccurate, the user could end up experiencing financial loss if they were to do business with the company based largely on a seemingly healthy credit rating that turned out to be inaccurate.

9.3 Contract

Contract law can also be relevant to the liability of information professionals. If, for example, an enquirer contacts an information centre and asks a researcher to find some information for him, the researcher provides the requested information and the user accepts it in exchange for a fee, this whole transaction will be subject to contract law. This is the case even if there is nothing written down. It has to be said that where money does change hands, clients have a higher expectation of the quality of service that is being provided; that is, they have higher customer expectations of the duty of care that is applied in delivering the service. In any question of liability, the courts too may well expect a higher level of duty of care for a priced service than is required for a free service.

A contract is a legally binding agreement between two or more parties which is enforceable in a court of law. One party offers to do something for the other party and the other party accepts this offer. The essential elements of a contract are:

1 Offer – this is the proposal to make a deal. This offer must be communicated clearly to the other party and remain open until it is either accepted, rejected, withdrawn or has expired.
2 Acceptance – this is the acknowledgement by the other party that the offer has been accepted, except where a qualified acceptance is made, as this amounts to a rejection of the offer and is instead regarded as a counter-offer, which also requires acceptance.

3 Consideration – this is what supports the promises made. It is the legal benefit
   that one person receives and the legal detriment on the other person. This
   could, for example, take the form of money, property or services.

Consideration is not necessary for a contract in Scots law. Contracts arise where
the parties reach agreement as to the fundamental features of the transaction;
this is often referred to as *consensus in idem* ('meeting of the minds'). To
determine whether agreement has been reached, contracts in Scotland are
analysed in terms of offer and acceptance.

The contract doesn't have to be a signed document. It could be entered
into orally, although this does make it more difficult to establish whether or
not there is a contract. A written contract contains the terms and conditions
of the agreement and can be used in any dispute, although the very fact that
someone has a carefully worded written contract can help prevent a dispute
occurring because a written contract sets out clearly the rights and obligations
of the parties.

The increasing trend for librarians to work for themselves as freelance consultants, who charge for their expertise, is accompanied by the ever-increasing
risk that they could be held liable for their expertise and advice. Many consultants and information brokers will have a set of terms and conditions which
they will send to the client before they start working on an assignment. It is
in their interests to do so, because the terms and conditions will set out what
the client can expect from the information broker, and there will be a number of disclaimers and exclusion clauses limiting the broker's liability.

Any contracts entered into with users should include a formal disclaimer
of liability. However, this needs to be carefully worded, because if an exclusion clause is too general it could be deemed to be invalid. The exclusion clause
should, therefore, be specific. It could put a limit on the extent of any potential liabilities, such as: putting a maximum figure of £5,000 on any damages
to be paid; stating that the liability is capped at the monetary value of the contract between the broker and the client; or in the case of an online service,
allowing the subscriber to terminate the contract if he or she finds errors.

A number of information brokers use the Code of Practice for Information Brokers which was produced by the now defunct EIRENE[3] – the
European Information Researchers Network -- in order to demonstrate
competence in performing the services that they provide.

9.4 Tort (delict in Scotland)

Library and information services which provide their services free of charge cannot ignore professional liability issues, because they could become the subject of an action under the law of tort. Tort/delict refers to behaviour causing loss or harm to other people where no contract exists. It covers the concept of negligence or carelessness, such as where a librarian carelessly provides inaccurate information to a user who suffers loss as a result. The legal basis for the law of tort/delict is the assumption that citizens owe each other a duty of care. If you cause your fellow citizens loss by your negligence, you lay yourself open to claims for compensation.

Tort/delict does not require any contractual relationship between the parties involved, and it therefore follows that third parties who suffer loss because of your actions can sue for compensation. For such an action to succeed, the injured party would need to establish the following:

- that the other party owed him a duty of care
- that this duty had been breached
- that there had been damage
- that the damage had been a direct result of the breach
- that the damage could have been reasonably foreseen.

The English law of tort and the Scots law of delict are similar but have considerable differences. For example, the law of defamation, nuisance, trespass and property, and the award of exemplary or penal damages, does not exist in Scotland. However, the law of negligence is now the same in both jurisdictions.

A number of key legal cases set important precedents in the law of tort.

Donoghue v. Stevenson [1932] AC 562

The case of Donoghue v. Stevenson is important because it established the 'neighbourhood principle' which defines classes of persons to whom a duty of care is owed. In his judgment, Lord Atkin said that 'one owes a duty of care to one's neighbour' and he explained that 'neighbour' refers to 'such persons as are so closely affected by my acts or omissions that I ought reasonably to have them in my contemplation when directing my mind to the acts or omissions called into question'. This duty of care extends to financial loss where an expert is consulted, as illustrated by Hedley Byrne v. Heller.

Hedley Byrne and Co v. Heller and Partners [1964] AC 465

A bank advised that a certain business would be a good investment. It was not and the investor lost a lot of money. The case dealt with the question of whether someone who provides advice to another person without a contract being in place could be held liable for negligence. The House of Lords found that if the advice was being sought in circumstances in which a reasonable man would know that he was being trusted or that his skill or judgement was being relied upon, then if he doesn't clearly qualify the answer so as to show that he does not accept responsibility, then he accepts a legal duty to accept such care as the circumstances require. The case established that a duty of care could arise to give careful advice and that a failure to do so could give rise to liability for economic loss caused by negligent advice. Liability arose because the individual consulted had claimed expertise in business investments, his advice would be relied upon and was intended to be definitive. Financial harm can be compensated only in such cases where specific expertise is consulted.

Anns v. London Borough of Merton [1978] AC 728

The case of Anns v. London Borough of Merton developed the 'neighbourhood principle' further. In this case Lord Wilberforce said that first the court should establish proximity, using the 'neighbourhood test'; then, if proximity is established, the court must take account of any 'consideration which ought to negate, reduce or limit the scope of the duty or the class of persons to whom it is owed or the damages to which breach of it may give rise'. For example, in the case of a public library providing a free enquiry service, a court might decide in any claim for liability that it would not be in the public interest to set a precedent which allows users to sue public libraries providing their services free of charge.

Caparo Industries plc v. Dickman [1990] 2 AC 605

This was an important case in defining the duty of care in the field of information provision. The case dealt with the liability of auditors to potential investors. It established that the concept of 'duty of care' existed when a number of factors were present:

- the information is for a specific purpose
- the purpose is made known at the time that the advice is given or that the advice is sought
- the advisor knows that his or her advice will be communicated to the advisee or recipient.

9.5   Liability and electronic information

In the late 1980s and early 1990s there was a lot of interest in the question of information quality and liability in relation to electronic information, as evidenced by the number of articles written on the topic at that time. Unlike the situation with hard-copy material, it isn't always possible with electronic information to browse the data or examine the indexes in detail, and there are added restrictions on time and cost. Users of online databases may find errors when they search for information, ranging from simple spelling errors and inconsistent use of controlled vocabulary through to factual errors. In the case of incorrect spellings, these can mean the difference between retrieving a record and not being able to retrieve that record.

To address such concerns, the Centre for Information Quality Management (CIQM) was established in 1993 under the auspices of the Library Association and the UK Online User Group (UKOLUG) with the aim of providing a clearing house through which database users could report quality problems. In a 1995 CIQM survey on the effects of poor data on workflow, a surprisingly high figure (31.11%) was returned for retrieval of unusable records (either missing data, badly formatted tables or erroneous data). The questionnaire was addressed to professional intermediaries and it was noted that end-user searchers might be affected more seriously.

If information professionals obtain data from an online service, the information provider's contract is likely to have a liability exclusion clause, making it more difficult to take action against it. Library and information professionals need to take steps which protect themselves from potential claims for liability. CILIP's Ethical principles and Code of Professional Practice for Library and Information Professionals [1] sets out a number of responsibilities of information professionals, and as far as responsibilities to their users are concerned the first two listed in the code are particularly relevant:

1 Ensure that information users are aware of the scope and remit of the service being provided.
2 Indicate to information users the reliability of the information being provided.

Information professionals need to warn their users that output from an online service doesn't necessarily carry a guarantee of accuracy. You are not in a position to promise that all of the information retrieved from an online database is correct, complete and accurate because the database provider is responsible for that, and it is outside your control.

Librarians should watch out for signs of how reliable an online database is:

- How frequently is the database updated?
- Does it contains typographical errors?

- Are there any gaps in coverage?
- Are there any inconsistencies or errors in the indexing?

Where information workers have reservations about the accuracy, reliability or trustworthiness of an information source, they should convey these to the user and make the user aware that there is no guarantee of accuracy. Where the service is chargeable, your terms and conditions of service should make clear that you cannot accept responsibility for errors or omissions in the databases or other sources that you use in your search. Whenever possible the information professional should seek to double-check and verify the accuracy of data. Information staff should maintain good records of the sources used to answer an enquiry. This is particularly important in cases where a fee is charged. The record that is kept can be used as a checklist to ensure that the key sources have all been consulted, and can also be referred back to in the event that a user of the service challenges you about not doing a thorough job.

9.6   Liability for copyright infringement

There are a number of situations where an information professional could potentially be held liable for copyright infringement. For example, with the implementation of the copyright directive,[5] copying for a commercial purpose is no longer permitted under the fair dealing provisions or the library regulations (SI 1989/1212). In the case of the library regulations, librarians working in 'prescribed libraries' (and these are limited to libraries in not-for-profit organizations) are given an indemnity to make copies on behalf of their users that users would themselves be entitled to make under s29 of the Copyright, Designs and Patents Act 1988 (CDPA). (For further information on the library provisions in the CDPA 1988 see Section 2.5.2.) The copyright declaration is the librarian's indemnity and if this is false the onus is on the signatory and not the librarian. However, if a user is unsure as to whether or not a particular instance of copying is permitted, he/she may understandably turn to the librarian for advice before signing the declaration form. The librarian should be careful not to decide for people whether or not a commercial purpose applies, because he/she could subsequently be held jointly liable for a false declaration.

Library staff also need to be particularly careful to ensure that in answering a user enquiry they are not infringing someone's copyright. As the CILIP Ethical Principles and Code of Professional Practice for Library and

Information Professionals[6] says, 'Information professionals should defend the legitimate needs and interests of information users, while respecting the moral and legal rights of the creators and distributors of intellectual property.'

9.7   Risk management

It is important for librarians to be aware of how liability arises, in order to be aware of the risks involved and to be able to take steps to minimize the possibility of legal action. Jonathan Tryon says: 'In a litigious society every library administrator must take care to institute procedures which will minimise the likelihood of law suits based on harm caused by the library's negligence.'[7] However, while effective risk management can help reduce exposure to allegations of neglect, error or omission, it can never completely eradicate that risk. A simple error, omission or mis-statement could potentially trigger a claim. The best defence against such claims is to:

- pay attention to your own professional development
- keep yourself up to date
- be aware of the range and content of the available sources
- be aware of the accuracy, timeliness and reliability of the sources.

Indeed, the CILIP Ethical Principles and Code of Professional Practice for Library and Information Professionals[8] says that information professionals should 'ensure they are competent in those branches of professional practice in which qualifications and/or experience entitle them to engage', and also that they should 'undertake continuing professional development to ensure that they keep abreast of developments in their areas of expertise'.

In any promotional material about your information service, you might wish to note that you follow the code of ethics of the professional organization to which you belong, such as the Chartered Institute of Library and Information Professionals (CILIP) or the Society of Competitive Intelligence Professionals (SCIP).

The professional guidelines of the American Society for Information Science and Technology (ASIST)[9] state that as part of their responsibility to the profession, members are required truthfully to represent themselves and the information which they utilize or which they represent. ASIST sets out a number of key ways in which this is achieved. These include:

- not knowingly making false statements or providing erroneous or misleading information
- undertaking research conscientiously: in gathering, tabulating or interpreting data; in following proper approval procedures for subjects; and in producing or disseminating research results
- pursuing ongoing professional development and encouraging and assisting colleagues and others to do the same.

The Business Reference and Services Section of the Reference and User Services Association (RUSA) has produced a set of guidelines for medical, legal and business responses,[10] which states:

> Libraries should develop written disclaimers stating a policy on providing specialized information service denoting variations in types and levels of service. The level of assistance and interpretation provided to users should reflect differing degrees of subject expertise between specialists and non-specialists. When asked legal, medical, or business questions, information services staff should make clear their roles as stated in their library's specialized information services policies.[11]

In a case of professional liability, the courts would take into account a number of key factors:

1 The nature of the information service being provided. Was the information service, for example, a general service providing information about a wide range of subjects and thus it would be unreasonable to expect an information professional to be an expert in all of the areas covered by the information service? Or was it a specialist information service covering a narrowly defined subject area, where the information service had built up an international reputation and in which the information staff had specialist knowledge, and which had made claims of having expertise in that field?
2 The level of knowledge of the user of the information service. If the topic that enquirers are asking about is one in which they themselves have considerable expertise, then they can be expected to use their own judgement regarding the validity of the information received. Or was it a

member of the general public who could not be expected to use professional judgement on the quality of information?

The EIRENE code of practice for information brokers [12] has a section relating to liability, in which it says that a broker shall:

- clearly state the accuracy limits of the information provided, within the bounds of their professional competence and available sources
- state clearly their liability and not use total disclaimers
- abide by the existing local laws regarding liability, arbitration procedures or professional negligence, when providing information services
- accept limited liability up to the value of the contract between broker and client
- indicate their arbitration procedures in their terms of business.

9.8 Indemnity and insurance

Indemnity is protection or insurance against future loss or damage. Professional indemnity insurance is an insurance against a claim from a client or any other independent third party who suffers financial loss as a result of alleged neglect, error or omission.

Any organization whose employees provide advice, information or a consultancy service may be legally liable at law for a claim of malpractice where a breach of professional duty occurs. If you give professional advice, your clients will regard you as an expert. These days clients are often well aware of their legal rights and are ready to assert those rights, so you could find yourself facing a claim from a client who feels that he/she has received substandard advice.

CILIP recommends professional indemnity insurance for self-employed information consultants and brokers, particularly if they are giving advice that could result in financial loss to their clients. This is because someone working as a sole practitioner would be personally liable for negligence, if proven, whatever the legal form of their company. The insurance provides financial protection. CILIP says that 'clear and reasonable disclaimers are also helpful, for example stating that you have no liability for errors in published sources. Pay attention to deadlines and keep records – ideally for six years.' [13] Professional indemnity insurance is not compulsory for the library and information profession. Some information professionals may not be keen on taking out professional indemnity insurance because of a perception that the premiums are quite high and that they don't always provide the desired protection. In the case of freelance workers it makes sound business sense and should not be regarded as an expensive or unnecessary business overhead. Furthermore, for freelance workers the premiums are tax-deductible.

In June 2005, CILIP announced a partnership with insurance intermediary Endsleigh, who will provide insurance and personal financial services for CILIP members, including independent financial advice. The range of insurance products includes professional indemnity insurance cover.[14]

9.9   Summary

This chapter has considered the question of professional liability and the general principles of this branch of the law (9.2), including how it relates to the law of contract (9.3) and the law of tort (9.4). Information professionals need to be careful to avoid making any claims to have expertise in areas of library and information work or in other disciplines where their skills and knowledge are inadequate. It is important that they are honest with their users about what can be expected from the service provided. Although there hasn't been an instance of a UK librarian being successfully sued for negligence, that is not a reason to be complacent. Specific types of liability were considered such as liability for inaccurate information or liability for copyright infringement (9.6). The chapter concluded by outlining some strategies for minimizing the legal liability risks that librarians face as professionals (9.7), as well as the importance of professional indemnity insurance (9.8).

With a greater and greater reliance on electronic information, information professionals are regularly having to negotiate licences or contracts in order to use electronic journals, online databases or other fee-based information services. The next chapter will look at some of the key issues involved with licences and contracts, as well as highlighting a number of pitfalls and things to watch out for.

Notes and references

1   CILIP (2005) Ethical Principles and Code of Professional Practice for Library and Information Professionals, www.cilip.org.uk/professionalguidance/ professionalethics/code.

2 CILIP (2002) *Working for Yourself* (pamphlet).
3 EUSIDIC (European Association of Information Services), EIIA (European Information Industry Association) and EIRENE (European Information Researchers Network) (1993) *Code of Practice for Information Brokers*.
4 CILIP (2005) Ethical Principles and Code of Professional Practice for Library and Information Professionals, www.cilip.org.uk/professionalguidance/professionalethics/code.
5 Directive 2001/29/EC of the European Parliament and of the Council of 22 May 2001 on the Harmonization of Certain Aspects of Copyright and Related Rights in the Information Society, *Official Journal* L167/10, 22 June 2001.
6 CILIP (2005) Ethical Principles and Code of Professional Practice for Library and Information Professionals, www.cilip.org.uk/professionalguidance/professionalethics/code.
7 Tryon, J. S. (1990) Premises Liability for Librarians, *Library and Archival Security*, **10** (2).
8 CILIP (2005) Ethical Principles and Code of Professional Practice for Library and Information Professionals, www.cilip.org.uk/professionalguidance/professionalethics/code.
9 ASIST professional guidelines, available at www.asis.org/AboutASIS/professional-guidelines.html.
10 American Library Association (2001) *Guidelines for Medical, Legal and Business Responses*, www.ala.org/ala/rusa/rusaprotocols/referenceguide/guidelinesmedical.htm.
11 American Library Association (1992) *Guidelines for Medical, Legal and Business Responses at General Reference Desks*.
12 EUSIDIC (European Association of Information Services), EIIA (European Information Industry Association) and EIRENE (European Information Researchers Network) (1993) *Code of Practice for Information Brokers*.
13 CILIP (2002) *Working for Yourself* (pamphlet).
14 CILIP (2005) *CILIP Acts to Meet Demands for Professional Indemnity Insurance and Agrees New Insurance Package for Members*, press release (22 June).

10 Contracts and licensing agreements

10.1 Introduction

Information professionals need to be able to negotiate licence agreements with information providers, because licences are often the means by which access to information products is controlled. This chapter sets the scene for licensing in a library setting (10.2), and then examines the issues that information professionals need to take account of when negotiating licence agreements (10.3). The key elements of a licence are outlined (Figure 10.1). The chapter then looks at a number of consortia and other initiatives which have led to model licence agreements being produced (10.4). There is a brief mention of how technology is increasingly being used to ensure compliance with licence agreements (10.5). Finally, a list of sources of further information on licensing is provided (10.7).

10.2 General principles

Information professionals are in the business of providing access to information. They also have an obligation to respect the moral and legal rights of the creators and distributors of intellectual property.

Some would argue that copyright exceptions and limitations have been rendered practically meaningless in the digital arena. How, for example, are the limitations and exceptions to be applied in the digital environment in view of the widespread deployment of technological protection measures?

The exceptions available under the CDPA are extremely limited in their application to electronic information sources. Consider, for example, matters such as multiple copying, converting from one format to another or storage in a central repository. With the implementation of EC directive 2001/29/EC through the Copyright and Related Rights Regulations 2003: SI 2003/2498 the exceptions are even less generous.

To get around these limitations, information professionals are increasingly turning to licences as the means of providing access to works. Licences are binding on both parties. They are governed by the law of contract, and enable information professionals to reach agreement with rights holders to permit their users to access electronic information services such as online databases, e-journals, websites or CD-ROMs in ways that meet users' needs.

It is important to point out that a licence does not confer ownership rights. It merely specifies the conditions upon which databases and other copyright works can be used and exploited, and by whom. There needs to be a mindshift from ownership to leasing. Licences merely provide access to content for a limited period of time. Typically, the licences that information professionals negotiate are non-exclusive, granting the same rights to many different users.

An effective licence can be granted orally or by implication from particular circumstances, but it is always better to have a written agreement in order that the terms and conditions of your relationship with the licensor are clear.

A few terms have been set as non-negotiable, and cannot therefore be overridden by a contract. For example, Regulation 19 of the Copyright and Rights in Databases Regulations 1997[1] says:

Avoidance of certain terms affecting lawful users

19. – (1) A lawful user of a database which has been made available to the public in any manner shall be entitled to extract or re-utilize insubstantial parts of the contents of the database for any purpose.

(2) Where under an agreement a person has a right to use a database, or part of a database, which has been made available to the public in any manner, any term or condition in the agreement shall be void in so far as it purports to prevent that person from extracting or re-utilizing insubstantial parts of the contents of the database, or of that part of the database, for any purpose.

10.3   Negotiating licences

It may sound trite, but it is important to read the licence terms thoroughly. When you get a licence to sign, this should be viewed as the starting point of a negotiation process. Every licence should be subject to discussion of its terms, rather than being signed immediately. There are some instances, though, where there is no scope for negotiation – such as 'click through' licences or 'shrink wrap' licences.

Information professionals do need to be extremely careful when signing licence agreements. You might think that, if an agreement contains unfair terms, the courts will overturn it. It is certainly the case that under the Unfair Contract Terms Act 1977 agreements should satisfy a test of reasonableness, but there are very limited circumstances in which the courts would overturn an unfair contract term.

In a Court of Appeal ruling in 2001,[2] Lord Justice Chadwick said that the courts should be reluctant to interfere in contractual relationships where each party has freely entered into a contract and where each party enjoys reasonably equal bargaining power:

> Where experienced businessmen representing substantial companies of equal bargaining power negotiate an agreement, they may be taken to have had regard to the matters known to them. They should, in my view, be taken to be the best judge of the commercial fairness of the agreement which they have made; including the fairness of each of the terms in that agreement. They should be taken to be the best judge on the question whether the terms of the agreement are reasonable. The court should not assume that either is likely to commit his company to an agreement which he thinks is unfair, or which he thinks includes unreasonable terms. Unless satisfied that one party has, in effect, taken unfair advantage of the other – or that a term is so unreasonable that it cannot properly have been understood or considered – the court should not interfere.

It is essential that you read and understand the whole agreement. You cannot get out of contractual terms on the basis that you didn't read that particular term. For example, the licence agreement might be 13 pages long, but unless you spend time reading it in detail you won't spot that page 8 makes it clear that the agreement automatically renews unless you give three months' notice. In these instances you might want to consider handing in the signed agreement and the cancellation notice at the same time, in order to have maximum flexibility at the time when the licence agreement is due for renewal.

You also need to be careful about signing a licence agreement if there is anything that you don't fully understand (see Figure 10.1 for a typical structure found in licence agreements, as well as some of the key legal terms used). It is no defence to say that the agreement is invalid because you didn't understand a particular clause. If there is something that you don't understand, ask the supplier for clarification or refer it to your in-house legal team (if you have one).

Parties: the full contractual names of the parties to the licence.

Key definitions: essential terms are defined (e.g. Authorized Users, Licensed Materials, Library Premises, Secure Network, Term, Permitted Purpose, Licence Fee, Intellectual Property etc.).

Services: description of the material to be licensed. This is likely to explain also how the form and content may change during the contract period, particularly if the provider is an information aggregator who is reliant on data from a range of publishers. However, you should check carefully how you will be told about any changes, and whether you are happy with those arrangements.

Usage rights and prohibited uses: sets out precisely what authorized users are entitled to do with the licensed materials such as access, use, display, download and print, and any restrictions on their use such as removing copyright notices or altering, adapting or modifying the licensed materials.

Warranties and indemnities: it is essential that the licence contains a warranty which confirms that the licensor has the legal right to license use of the copyright material, and that this does not infringe any third party intellectual property rights; the warranty should also be backed up by an indemnity to this effect.

Term and termination: sets out the subscription period and the conditions under which the licence can be terminated by either party.

Force majeure: this 'Acts of God' clause excuses the supplier for circumstances beyond its reasonable control (such as riots, war, floods etc.).

Legal jurisdiction and dispute resolution: this clause makes clear which law governs interpretation of the licence, and any arrangements for the resolution of disputes.

Fees and payment: the subscription price, payment arrangements and details of any other charges such as taxes.

Assignment: whether or not the licence is transferable, either by the licensor or by yourself to another third party.

Schedules: there may be one or more schedules appended to the main licence agreement setting out a number of additional terms and conditions.

Figure 10.1   Contract clauses

Information professionals are increasingly having to sign licences with information providers in order to sort out access to electronic information products. The negotiation process can sometimes be quite lengthy and involve discussion over very specific points. Where this is the case, there is likely to be a certain amount of correspondence in the form of letters, faxes and e-mails that relate to the licence, and these should be kept on file. You might, for example, have asked for clarification on access restrictions, service content or acceptable download limits. You might have sought clarification on whether the definition of authorized users enables you to send information from the online service to your clients, or to staff in your overseas offices. You might even have managed to negotiate a special deal with your account manager which will give you the option of renewing the service at the same rate as for the current subscription period. It is essential to retain all this documentation – not just the licence, but all the accompanying e-mails, faxes and letters as well. Even where the clarification was given orally, you should keep a written record. You shouldn't rely on staff working for the information provider being aware of what has been agreed; having everything carefully documented will come in extremely useful if your account manager moves on to another job, or if a dispute arises.

Librarians need to develop their negotiation skills. There are several documents on licensing matters which information professionals will find particularly helpful when negotiating licences. In May 2001, the International Federation of Library Associations (IFLA) announced that it had approved a set of licensing principles [3] which should prevail in the contractual relationship and written contracts between libraries and information providers. These principles touch upon aspects such as the applicable law, access, usage and users, and pricing. A helpful guide to the licensing of electronic information [4] and the pitfalls to watch out for has been produced by EBLIDA, the European Bureau of Library, Information and Documentation Associations, and is full of practical tips and advice. Finally, it is worth mentioning Lesley Ellen Harris's book *Licensing Digital Content*. [5]

A number of key issues need to be considered when you negotiate a licence for an information product. These include:

1 Applicable law – this should preferably be the national law of where your organization is located. If you are based in the UK, for example, you would not want the applicable law to be that of a state in the USA; otherwise, if there is a problem relating to the interpretation of your licence, you could end up having to travel to a US court in order to plead your case.

2 Ensure that statutory rights are recognized – to avoid any doubt, the licence should contain a term which explicitly acknowledges that nothing in the licence prevents the licensee from dealing with the licensed materials in ways which are expressly permitted by statute: 'This agreement is without prejudice to any acts which the licensee is permitted to carry out by the terms of the Copyright, Designs and Patents Act 1988 and nothing herein shall be construed as affecting or diminishing such permitted acts in any way whatsoever.' This is particularly important in preserving the right to copy materials under the fair dealing provisions of the CDPA.

3 Perpetual access to the licensed material – when libraries subscribe to a journal in hard copy, then even if they cancel their subscription, they still have the back issues available for future reference. This is not automatically the case with electronic products. Are there any arrangements outlined in the licence agreement for perpetual access? Does it, for example, have a clause along the lines that 'on termination of this licence, the publisher shall provide continuing access for authorized users to that part of the licensed materials which was published and paid for within the subscription period or by supplying a CD-ROM to the licensee'?

Both publishers and the users of their services have turned their attention to the question of perpetual access, and have tried to come up with solutions to this issue. For example, Nature Publishing amended its site licence policy to provide customers with post-cancellation rights to content associated with their licensed publications, subject to payment of an annual access fee. Meanwhile the LOCKSS system, devised at Stanford University, has been deployed in selected UK libraries since January 2006. LOCKSS [6] – 'Lot of copies keep stuff safe' – is a low cost system that preserves access to a library's online journals in a local 'LOCKSS box' in a manner acceptable to publishers.

4 Warranties and indemnities – the licence should contain a clear warranty that the publisher/licensor is the owner of the intellectual property rights in the licensed material and/or that they have the authority to grant the licence. This helps to protect the library against an author who subsequently claims to be the real owner of the intellectual property rights, or against claims from a new owner that you have to buy a fresh licence from him/her. It is also common to have a clause that the licence will not be assigned to a third party without the agreement of the other. Indemnities

back up a warranty with a promise to insure or compensate the other party against losses and expenses arising from a breach of the warranty. The licence should indemnify the library against any action by a third party over the intellectual property rights that are being licensed. This indemnity should cover all of the losses, damages, costs and expenses that are incurred, including legal expenses, on a full indemnity basis.

5 End users – the library should not incur legal liability for each and every infringement by an authorized user. It is perfectly reasonable to ask the library to notify the publisher/licensor of any infringement that comes to the library's notice and for them to co-operate with the publisher/licensor to prevent further abuse. Of course, if the library condoned or encouraged a breach to continue after being notified of the breach by the publisher/licensor, then it would be held liable.

6 Non-cancellation clauses – for example, there should be no penalty for cancelling the print version in order to sign up to the electronic version of an information source.

7 Non-disclosure clauses – if the licence contains a non-disclosure clause, it needs to be clear what information is subject to the obligation of confidence, and you need to decide whether this is reasonable. There are obviously some things – most notably the price – which it is in the supplier's interests to keep confidential, especially if you have negotiated a preferential rate. Public authorities should bear in mind their obligations under the Freedom of Information Act 2000, and vendors should recognize that public authorities can't simply 'contract out' of their FOIA obligations.

8 Termination clause – licences should always contain a clause which sets out the mechanism or circumstances in which the licence terminates.

9 'Reasonable effort' and 'best effort' clauses – the phrases 'reasonable effort' or 'best effort' are ambiguous and should, wherever possible, be avoided. It is important that the terms in a contract provide both parties with legal certainty, especially terms dealing with prices, quantities, time, obligations and performance of the contract.

Both sides will usually have some things which are non-negotiable, and which could therefore be potential deal-breakers. It is important for both sides to be clear about what they are trying to achieve with the licence agreement, and to be up-front about what is non-negotiable. If an issue is a deal-breaker, then the party which feels so strongly about that issue needs to recognize it, and to know when negotiation isn't going to resolve the issue and that it's therefore time to walk away from the negotiations.

Factors which can make or break a deal:

- governing law and venue
- indemnifications
- remote access
- price
- access by walk-in users
- interlibrary loan
- fair use
- archival access/perpetual rights
- adequate definition of authorized user
- IP access
- definition of university/campus as single site
- 'escape clause' for multi-year licence agreements.

10.4 Consortia and standard licences

Negotiating licences can be extremely time-consuming. If you have to negotiate separate licences with each information provider, this is not only going to take up a lot of time but it also creates practical issues relating to compliance. Can you really be expected to know each of the licences you have signed up to inside out, especially if you have to take account of the terms and conditions in the licences for a large number of products? (See also Section 2.7.3 on licensing electronic resources.)

Consortia purchasing and/or the use of standard licences is a recognition of the amount of time and effort involved in negotiating licence terms, as well as the expertise required. A number of initiatives have produced a standard form of licence. These include:

1 Licensingmodels.com from John Cox Associates [7] is an initative led by a number of subscription agents. Model standard licences for use by publishers, librarians and subscription agents for electronic resources have been created. There are four different types of licence covering the whole

range of library types: single academic institutions, academic consortia, public libraries, and corporate and other special libraries.

2 In the academic sector, the Joint Information Systems Committee (JISC) often negotiates access to digital materials on behalf of interested universities. There is also a model licence that was negotiated by JISC with the Publishers Association. The Standard Licensing Arrangements Working Party was asked by the JISC and the Publishers Association to explore options for developing 'umbrella' licence models which individual publishers could employ. These generic tools were intended to cover different products and different types of use and would set out the more routine conditions of use, but leave a limited number of commercial issues – such as price per access or territory – to be added by different suppliers. There are a number of standard licences available.

3 The European Copyright Users Platform (ECUP)[8] has produced four model licences: for public libraries, national libraries, university libraries and company libraries. These contain clauses favourable to libraries.

4 The International Coalition of Library Consortia (ICOLC)[9] produced a statement of current perspective and preferred practices for the selection and purchase of electronic information back in 1998. This was primarily aimed at the higher education community. The original statement has since been updated.[10]

5 The Model NESLi2 Licence for Journals[11] is based on the National Electronic Site Licence Initiative (NESLI) site licence. It is the model licence used by JISC staff or its agents in negotiations with publishers for JISC journal agreements.

The corporate sector has generally not created consortia in order to negotiate agreements with information providers. There are a number of reasons for this. The sector is quite disparate, consisting of a wide range of organizational types: media, law, property, professional services, engineering, pharmaceutical, etc. There is also the competitive nature of the corporate sector to bear in mind. Many commercial organizations will not want their competitors to know of any specially negotiated contractual terms, especially not the price agreed, and may even be cagey about what services they subscribe to. One exception is the sample licence for electronic journals produced by the Pharma Documentation Ring.[12]

Some large companies have produced a standard licence agreement for the supply of online information services, and have used their buying power to persuade information providers to let them access their products using the standard licence agreement that they, the customers, have drafted.

10.5   Technology solutions

Compliance with the terms and conditions of licences for electronic products is certainly going to be a major concern for both publishers and librarians in the future, and suppliers will increasingly look to technology in order to control access to electronic information products.

SI 2003/2498, which implements EU directive 2001/29/EC, recognizes electronic copyright management systems and promotes their adoption, protection and use. It also provides legal protection against circumvention of technological measures designed to restrict infringement of copyright.

When a library purchases a journal article or book in electronic format, the supplier might require them to accept a set of terms and conditions restricting access to, and use of, the item being purchased. But the supplier may not rely solely on a set of terms and conditions to protect its intellectual property. Rather, it may use the technology to build in a number of security settings. Examples of how this could be applied in practice might include building in settings such as:

* any use of the file is limited to the machine on which it is downloaded
* printing is set to one copy only
* saving and viewing of the article is permitted, but for a limited period of time
* forwarding and copying functions are disabled
* annotations and conversion to speech are permitted
* data encryption ensures that the material can only be read by one person who has been given access to the software that unencrypts the data.

10.6   Summary

This chapter has looked at the use of licence agreements by information providers as a means of controlling access to electronic information products (10.2). It outlined the key elements that are likely to form part of a licence agreement (Figure 10.1). A number of essential points to watch out for when negotiating licences, such as the applicable law under which any dispute would be resolved, or the warranties and indemnities that need to be present in a licence agreement, were outlined (10.3). There have been a number of instances where people have come together to prepare a model licence and examples of these were discussed (10.4). Information providers and users are both concerned about compliance issues, and the final part of the chapter looked at how technology is increasingly being used to ensure compliance with the licence terms (10.5).

The next chapter deals with computer misuse such as hacking, viruses, fraud and other areas of cybercrime. It deals specifically with how the Computer Misuse Act 1990 is used to combat computer misuse crimes and considers how well it is suited to that task, as well as considering the Cybercrime Treaty which the United Kingdom will need to implement in due course.

10.7   Further information

ALPSP www.alpsp.org/htp_licens.htm on licensing and related issues.

Bebbington, L. (2001) Managing Content: licensing, copyright and privacy issues in managing electronic resources, *Legal Information Management*, **1** (2), 4–13, www.biall.org.uk/docs/pulimv1n2bebb.doc.

EBLIDA (2001) *Licensing Digital Resources*, 2nd edn, www.eblida.org/ecup/docs/licensing.pdf.

ECUP: Copyright licensing issues, www.eblida.org/ecup/licensing/.

Durrant, F. (2006) *Negotiating Licences for Digital Resources*, Facet Publishing.

Giavarra, E. (2001) *Guidelines for Negotiations by Libraries with Rightsholders* (TECUP project report D6.5), http://gdz.sub.uni-goettingen.de/tecup/d6-5_4fv.pdf.

Harris, L. E. (2002) *Licensing Digital Content: a practical guide for librarians*, ALA Editions.

International Coalition of Library Consortia (ICOLC) *Statement of Current Perspective and Preferential Practices for the Selection and Purchase of Electronic Information*, www.library.yale.edu/consortia/statement.html.

JISC/Publishers Association Working Party Papers and Reports, www.ukoln.ac.uk/services/elib/papers/pa/.

LIBLICENSE: Licensing digital information, www.library.yale.edu/~llicense/index.shtml.

Licensing models as drawn up by John Cox Associates, www.
licensingmodels.com.
SURF: Copyright Management for Scholarship, www.surf.nl/copyright
Tilburg University, *Tilburg University Licensing Principles*, http://webdoc.sub.
gwdg.de/ebook/aw/prinzliz/1_lizp-e.htm.
UK Serials Group, www.uksg.org.
US principles for licensing electronic resources, www.arl.org/scomm/
licensing/principles.html.

Notes and references

1 Copyright and Rights in Databases Regulations 1997: SI 1997/3032.
2 Watford Electronics v. Sanderson 2001 EWCA Civ 317 para 55.
3 Available at www.ifla.org/V/ebpb/copy.htm.
4 Giavara, E. (2001) *Licensing Digital Resources: how to avoid the legal pitfalls*, 2nd edn,
   EBLIDA.
5 Harris, L. E. (2002) *Licensing Digital Content: a practical guide for libraries*, American Library Association.
6 See http://lockss.stanford.edu.
7 Available at www.licensingmodels.com.
8 See www.eblida.org/ecup/licensing/ for details of ECUP, and for the four models see: www.eblida.org/ecup/docs/heads/publib.htm; www.eblida.org/ecup/docs/
   heads/natlib.htm; www.eblida.org/ecup/docs/heads/unilib.htm; www.eblida.org/
   ecup/docs/heads/company.htm.
9 See www.library.yale.edu/consortia/statement.html.
10 ICOLC (2001, December) *Update No. 1: new developments in e-journal licensing*,
   www.library.yale.edu/consortia/2001currentpractices.htm; ICOLC (2004, October) *Update No. 2, Pricing and Economics*, www.library.yale.edu/consortia/
   2004icolcpr.htm.
11 See www.nesli2.ac.uk/model.html.
12 See www.p-d-r.com.

11 Cybercrime and computer misuse

11.1 Introduction

Cybercrime and computer misuse covers activities such as hacking, viruses, fraud, theft and copyright abuse. This chapter looks at the Council of Europe Convention on Cybercrime (11.3), the Computer Misuse Act 1990 (CMA) (11.4), the three offences created by that statute, and at proposals for the revision of the Act (11.5). It then looks at hacking (11.6) and viruses, worms and trojans (11.7). Other forms of cybercrime are also examined including intellectual property infringement (11.8), pornography (11.9) and various types of computer fraud (11.10) such as phishing (11.10.1). In the case of denial of service attacks (11.11), there are those who feel that the CMA as presently constituted is inadequate. In due course there are likely to be a number of changes to the CMA in order for the UK to be fully compliant with the Council of Europe's Cybercrime Convention and Council of Europe decision 2005/222/JHA on attacks against information systems, which has to be implemented in the UK by 16 March 2007. Finally, there is a brief look at the role of the Telecommunications Act 1984 in relation to computer misuse (11.13).

11.2 Background

Cybercrime is defined by the British police as the use of any computer network for crime; in the Council of Europe's Convention on Cybercrime it is defined as 'criminal offences committed against or with the help of computer networks'.

The phrase 'computer misuse' could be used to refer to a wide range of activities including: accessing inappropriate material on the internet such as pornographic material; inappropriate use of e-mail; hacking; spreading viruses; fraud; theft; copyright abuse; or the use of a computer to harass others, whether that be sexual harassment, racial harassment or some other form of harassment.

Cyberspace has provided new opportunities for criminals. They are attracted by the anonymity factor and the ability to communicate simultaneously with an unlimited number of users around the world. Hackers find a thrill in penetrating networks and destroying data, while terrorists could purposely disrupt the critical infrastructures that are dependent upon networked computers. Meanwhile, consumers hesitate to disclose personal and credit card data on the internet, with security and privacy being their number one concern, and businesses face the potential loss of proprietary data, intellectual property and online access to customers and suppliers through breaches of security and intentional service disruptions.

In 2001, the CBI's Cybercrime Survey[1] ranked the main threats from cybercrime as being:

- viruses
- hacking
- illegal access to databases
- adverse comments on the internet
- intellectual property infringements.

The survey found that most attacks on corporate computer networks are from outside, contrary to the conventional view that most computer security problems are due to insiders. It also found that technological crimes such as viruses and hacking dominate, rather than financial crimes such as credit card fraud, and that loss of reputation, through adverse publicity and loss of trust, is a greater fear than financial loss for most organizations.

The Department of Trade and Industry undertakes an information security breaches survey every two years. The 2004 survey[2] found that:

- 74% of all UK businesses had a security incident in the previous year (whether through accidental system failure and data corruption or malicious incidents)
- the average UK business now receives roughly 20 viruses a year, and has its website scanned or probed many times
- large businesses are attacked more frequently, receiving on average a virus a week

- 63% of all UK businesses had a malicious incident in the previous year (viruses, unauthorized access, misuse of systems, fraud and theft).

With regard to cybercrime, the computer can play a number of different roles:

- the computer can be the target of crime, for example when someone is intent on stealing information from, or causing damage to, a computer or computer network
- a computer can be the tool that is used in order to commit an offence such as fraud, or the distribution of child pornography
- a computer stores evidence, and can be of great value to criminal investigators.

11.3   Council of Europe Convention on Cybercrime[3]

The Convention was adopted by the Council of Europe in 2001. Cybercrime is a major global challenge which requires a co-ordinated international response, and the Convention tries to achieve its aims by having legislation at an international level and by fostering international co-operation.

The Convention places the onus on internet service providers as regards encryption and provides for the use of 'coercive powers' such as electronic surveillance, interception, search and seizure in dealing with offences.

The Convention covers three key sets of issues:

- substantive computer crimes
- government access to communications and computer data
- trans-border co-operation.

The offences covered by the Cybercrime Convention are listed in Figure 11.1. The offences covered by the Convention are not all 'pure' cybercrimes in the sense that some of the crimes can exist whether or not a computer is involved – such as copyright infringement.

Each of the offences uses a form of words along the lines 'when committed intentionally and without right'. In other words, to qualify as an offence the action must have been committed intentionally, and in circumstances where the person committing the offence did not have the right to do what they did.

Illegal access	Article 2
Illegal interception	Article 3
Data interference	Article 4
System interference	Article 5
Misuse of devices	Article 6
Computer-related forgery	Article 7
Computer-related fraud	Article 8
Offences related to child pornography	Article 9
Offences related to infringement of copyright and related rights	Article 10

Figure 11.1   Offences covered by the Cybercrime Convention

The Convention is the first international treaty on crimes committed via the internet and other computer networks, dealing particularly with infringements of copyright, computer-related fraud, child pornography and violations of network security. It also contains a series of powers and procedures such as the search of computer networks and interception.

Its main objective, set out in the preamble, is to pursue a common criminal policy aimed at the protection of society against cybercrime, especially by adopting appropriate legislation and fostering international co-operation.

The Convention is the product of four years of work by Council of Europe experts, but also by the United States, Canada, Japan and other countries which are not members of the organization. An additional protocol makes any publication of racist and xenophobic propaganda via computer networks a criminal offence from 28 January 2003.[4]

11.4   General principles of the Computer Misuse Act 1990

The CMA was published in the wake of a Law Commission report[5] in order to create specific offences to secure computers against unauthorized access or modification. It pre-dates the dramatic growth of the internet, and some people consider it to be not very well suited to certain types of computer misuse, most notably denial of service attacks (see Section 11.11). While the Act was originally intended mainly to address the problems caused by computer hacking, it is also being used effectively to deal with the deliberate release of computer viruses.

The CMA created three offences:

- unauthorized access to computer material (s1)
- unauthorized access with intent to commit or facilitate commission of further offences (s2)
- unauthorized modification of computer material (s3).

Under Section 1 of the CMA, it is an offence to cause a computer to perform any function with intent to gain unauthorized access to any program or data held in any computer, knowing at the time that it is unauthorized. The section specifically provides that the intent of the person need not be directed at any particular program or data, a program or data of any particular kind, or a program or data held in any particular computer. This means that the Act is suitable for use against activities carried out across networks.

A 17-year-old clerk was sacked from an insurance company. He decided to get his own back on his former employer. He downloaded a 'useful' piece of software from the internet – which is often referred to as a 'bomber' – and proceeded to use the software in order to send five million e-mails to his former employer over a period of three days. This resulted in the ex-employer's website becoming overloaded, and the site having to be taken down for a period of time, with a consequent loss of revenue.

Actions of this kind are likely to cause an unauthorized modification of the contents of the computer to which the e-mails are directed and as such this would be a potential breach of the Computer Misuse Act 1990. If the perpetrator's actions were intended to impair the operation of, or hinder access to, the computer or any program held on it, this would constitute a criminal offence under Section 3 of the Computer Misuse Act 1990. If the consequences of these actions could be said to be reasonably foreseeable, then the perpetrator would be likely to be treated as having such intent.

As a result of his actions, the ex-clerk was interviewed by the Metropolitan Police.

Figure 11.2   Case study: sacked employee wreaks revenge on former employer

Under Section 17(5) a person's access is unauthorized if the person is not himself entitled to control access of the kind in question to the program or data, and he does not have consent to access by him of the kind in question to the program or data from any person who is so entitled.

Under Section 2 of the CMA, it is an offence to commit an offence under s1 with intent to commit or facilitate a further offence, whether or not both offences occur on the same occasion.

Under Section 3 of the CMA, it is an offence to do anything intentionally and knowingly to cause an unauthorized modification of the contents of any computer which will impair its operation, prevent or hinder access to any program or data, or which will impair the operation of the program or the reliability of the data (see Figure 11.3 for an example).

The requisite knowledge is knowledge that any modification he intends to cause is unauthorized. The section provides that intent need not be directed to any particular computer, any particular program or data, a program or data of any particular kind, or any particular modification or modification of any particular kind.

The penalty for the first offence could be up to six months in prison or a fine (up to Level 5 on the standard scale) or both. The second and third offences are considered to be much more serious and carry a maximum penalty of up to five years in prison or an unlimited fine or both.

According to Section 17 of the Act, a person secures access to any computer program or data held in a computer if by causing a computer to perform any function he:

- alters or erases the program or data
- copies or moves it to any storage medium other than that in which it is held or to a different location in the storage medium in which it is held
- uses it
- has it output from the computer in which it is held (whether by having it displayed or in any other manner).

Deliberately obtaining unauthorized access to a computer system is not the only way in which a computer system can be damaged. Many disputes arise where software has been written with a time lock or a similar device built into it so that it disables itself after a certain period of time or unless new passwords are regularly put into it. Where people develop or supply software to clients for their use and the use of such devices has not been agreed upon, when the device activates and damages or disables the software, it is possible that the supplier will be committing an offence under the CMA.

Computer crime can raise a number of issues relating to jurisdiction, since it is obviously possible for someone anywhere in the world to access a computer located in the UK. Sections 4–9 of the Act deal with the whole question of jurisdiction and, in short, ensure that, so long as either the accused or the computer was within the jurisdiction at the time of the offence, then a prosecution is permitted.

In a legal case from 2002 a manufacturing business decided to update its computer system. It employed an IT contractor to do the work. Unfortunately, the business felt that he had not done a very good job and went to a second contractor to get the job completed. When it came to payment, it clearly had to pay for the services of the new contractor and decided not to pay the original contractor.

Access to the IT system had been set up for the original contractor to work from home, and this access was still available at the time of the dispute. When the company refused to pay the original contractor he was upset about this and decided to take matters into his own hands. He accessed the system and deleted all of the files on it. These files included three years' worth of fairly complicated design drawings. The company assessed the amount of damage it had suffered as a result at around £50,000.

It is a criminal offence under Section 3 of the Computer Misuse Act 1990 to carry out an unauthorized modification of material held on computer, when your intention is to prevent or hinder access to the data or impair its operational reliability. The contractor was prosecuted and convicted and was jailed for 18 months.

A number of lessons may be drawn from this case, even if some of them may seem rather obvious:

- take regular backups
- keep the backups in a separate place
- be careful about who can access the computer system
- be prompt at disabling access for employees and contractors as soon as they cease working for you
- be very careful about who you give remote access to
- for contractors – don't damage or disable a computer system, no matter what the provocation might be, as it is surely not worth a prison sentence.

Figure 11.3   Computer Misuse Act 1990 – Section 3 offence

11. 5 Revision of the Computer Misuse Act

The All Party Internet Group (APIG)[6] published its report *Revision of the Computer Misuse Act: report of an inquiry by the All Party Internet Group* at the end of June 2004. In the report they made six main recommendations in relation to the CMA and the wider cybercrime debate:

1 Sentences for hacking should be increased from six months to two years (see example in Figure 11.4, page 224) – the current sentence (under Section 1) was considered too low given the serious consequences that can result from hacking. Additionally, increasing this sentence to two years would make the offence extraditable and therefore meet the requirements of the Treaty on Cybercrime.

2 The Director of Public Prosecutions should set out a permissive policy for private prosecutions under the CMA – although the right to bring a private prosecution is well established under English law, the Director of

Public Prosecutions (DPP) has the power to assume conduct of such proceedings and to discontinue them in the public interest. The APIG recommended that the DPP adopt a policy of intervening to discontinue cases only where they are 'totally inappropriate or clearly vexatious'. This move would allow private companies or private individuals to tackle cases that the police/CPS do not presently consider a priority.

3 Educational material about the CMA should appear on the Home Office website – there is an obvious need for accurate, updated material that provides clear English explanations of legislation to the general public. The Home Office should therefore provide educational material which explains the scope of the Computer Misuse Act and the effect of the now substantial case law. Evidence to the inquiry showed a remarkable lack of understanding of what the CMA already criminalized. Other laws are well described on the Home Office website – and the APIG said that priority should be given to the CMA to ensure it is covered in similar detail.

4 Statistical information on cybercrime should be improved – it is difficult to formulate policy on cybercrime issues because there are no figures (and not even very many anecdotes) to base that policy upon. Full-scale data collection remains a long way off. There is a role here for statistical sampling to estimate overall totals.

5 A new fraud bill should be introduced – the APIG received a number of responses that are best dealt with by reforming the law on fraud rather than the CMA. The Law Commission proposed a fraud bill back in July 2002. The APIG said there should be no further delay and a new fraud bill should come before Parliament as soon as possible. The Theft Act 1978 as amended by the Theft Amendment Act 1996 doesn't apply to 'deceiving a machine' (according to case law in the field). One aim of having a new fraud bill is to ensure that phishing (see 11.10.1) and fraud against computer systems, which is currently not an offence, are explicitly made illegal.

6 A denial of service (DoS) offence should be added to the CMA – the CMA already makes many DoS attacks illegal but there is significant value in adding an explicit offence to the legislation. In particular, this would send a clear signal to the police, the CPS and the courts that these attacks should be taken seriously. Also, publicity about the new offence will reach DoS attackers and some will be deterred by knowing that their actions are clearly criminal.

On 7 July 2005 Derek Wyatt submitted a written parliamentary question which asked what plans the Secretary of State for the Home Department had to reform the Computer Misuse Act 1990. Paul Goggins responded by saying that changes to the Computer Misuse Act 1990 will be required in order to implement the requirements of the European Union Framework Decision on Attacks Against Information Systems and the related provisions contained in the Council of Europe Cybercrime Convention. These measures will be brought forward when parliamentary time allows.

Simon Vallor, a web designer, created viruses on his home computer in Llandudno which he then distributed over the internet in September and October 2001. The viruses were designed to e-mail themselves to everyone in each recipient's address book. One virus was designed to delete all the data on the recipients' hard drives on 11 November. At least 29,000 computers were infected in 42 countries, while another 300,000 copies of the virus were stopped by anti-virus software. The cost of the episode ran to millions of pounds for businesses and computer users. Mr Vallor was sentenced to two years' imprisonment for offences under the Computer Misuse Act 1990. This was the harshest sentence to date for this type of offence.

Figure 11.4 Prison sentence for offences under the Act

11.6   Hacking

Hacking is the act of deliberately gaining unauthorized access to an information system. Many instances of hacking might be classed as nuisance attacks, but far more serious are instances where the hacker has malicious intent.

Section 1 of the CMA 1990 makes hacking per se a criminal offence, regardless of whether or not any harm is intended. If, for example, a hacker broke into a computer simply out of curiosity, he or she would have committed an offence so long as he or she was aware that his/her access was unauthorized.

Hackers can be deterred through well configured firewall protection, intrusion detection software and filtering software.

11.7   Viruses, worms and trojans

Computer viruses, in the same way as biological viruses, make copies of themselves and cannot exist without a host. They may infect program files, programs in disk sectors, or files that use a macro. There are also computer worms and trojans. Worms are similar to viruses. Like viruses, they make copies of themselves, but do so without the need to modify a host. By repeatedly making copies of itself, a worm tries to drain system resources.

Trojans are named after the Trojan Horse – a giant wooden horse that concealed Greek soldiers who used it in order to invade the ancient city of Troy – because trojan horse programs conceal hidden programming which can cause significant damage to your computer.

It is no longer the case that a computer user has to click on a file attachment in order to trigger a virus infection. It may be sufficient merely for the user to read an infected e-mail in order for the virus to be launched.

The CMA clearly applies to those who release damaging viruses into the wild, even if the person doing so does not have an intent to damage a particular computer. Some e-mails may not be specifically intended to destroy data or prevent programs from operating, but might simply use e-mail directories to propagate themselves around e-mail systems. Nevertheless, there could still be the possibility of a criminal conviction. The use of a recipient's e-mail program to cause the incoming e-mail virus to propagate onwards by means of the e-mail system could be said to be access of an unauthorized nature and would therefore be liable to prosecution under Section 1.

Section 3 of the CMA can be used to prosecute people who introduce viruses, worms or trojans to computer systems. Under s3(6), an offence under the Criminal Damage Act 1971 occurs if damage to a computer impairs its physical condition, but it specifically excludes damage which is non-tangible. The wording of s3(6) states that 'a modification of the contents of a computer shall not be regarded as damaging any computer or computer storage medium unless its effect on that computer or computer storage medium impairs its physical condition.'

11.8 Intellectual property infringement

There are a number of cybercrimes which represent various different aspects of intellectual property infringement. These include cybersquatting, plagiarism, software piracy, making illegal downloads of music files and other examples of copyright abuse.

Cybersquatting is the deliberate registration of a domain name knowing that it is a name used by an existing party. In 2004, there were 1,179 cases filed at WIPO – the World Intellectual Property Organization – based on the Uniform Domain Name Dispute Resolution Policy (UDRP). Since the UDRP went into effect in December 1999, WIPO has handled over 7000 disputes about the abusive registration of trademarks as domain names.

Plagiarism is to use or to pass off as one's own the ideas or writings of someone else. In the academic community, JISC has a Plagiarism Advisory Service which has published a number of items on the topic.[7] Electronic detection tools such as Turnitin software are increasingly being used to detect student plagiarism electronically.

Software piracy is the copying of software without permission. This is a crime which can potentially be punished by imprisonment and a fine. Ongoing auditing and tracking of software use is essential to ensure compliance with software licensing agreements.

In 2004, 35% of the software installed on personal computers worldwide was pirated. Losses due to piracy increased from $29 billion to $33 billion. These are among the key findings of a global software piracy study[8] conducted by the Business Software Alliance (BSA), the international association of the world's leading software developers. The study was conducted by IDC (International Data Corporation) for the BSA, and the BSA claims that it indicates that software piracy continues to be a major challenge worldwide.

In 2004, the world spent more than $59 billion on commercial packaged PC software, up from $51 billion in 2003. But according to the BSA over $90 billion of software was actually installed, up from $80 billion the year before. The increase in losses was, in part, the result of the fact that the PC software market grew over 6% and the US dollar fell against many of the world's currencies.

Among the key findings:

1 Although piracy rates (percentage of the total packaged software base that is pirated) decreased in 37 countries, they increased in 34 countries. They remained consistent in 16 countries.
2 In more than half of the 87 countries studied, the piracy rate exceeded 60%. In 24 countries, the piracy rate exceeded 75%.
3 The countries with the highest piracy rates were Vietnam (92%), Ukraine (91%), China (90%), Zimbabwe (90%) and Indonesia (87%).
4 The countries with the lowest piracy rates were the United States (21%), New Zealand (23%), Austria (25%), Sweden (26%) and the United Kingdom (27%).
5 The emerging markets in the Asia Pacific, Latin America, Eastern Europe and the Middle East and Africa account for over one-third of PC shipments today, but only one-tenth of spending on PC software.

A primary factor in determining losses due to piracy in a specific country is the size of that country's software market. For instance, at 21%, the United States had the lowest piracy rate of all countries studied, but it also had the greatest losses at $6.6 billion. That is almost double the amount lost in the country with the second highest losses, China, at $3.5 billion. In very large software markets, comparatively low piracy rates still amount to huge losses.[9]

A number of peer-to-peer filesharing networks have been used by internet users in order to make illegal music downloads. Organizations representing the music industry such as the International Federation of the Phonographic Industry (IFPI) and the British Phonogram Industry (BPI) have taken out legal actions in order to protect the interests of their members. Indeed, they have taken court action, to force internet service providers to disclose the details of people alleged to have used peer-to-peer file sharing services, in order to copy or to share unlawfully copied files.

According to a story which appeared in *Out-law News*[10] a Hong Kong man has received what is reported to be the world's first jail sentence for making movies available online on a filesharing website. The 38-year-old man was given a three-month custodial sentence. The Motion Picture Association of America (MPAA) said that the man faced a maximum of four years in prison and a possible $6,400 fine for every copy distributed without permission. The MPAA has filed a considerable number of lawsuits. These have been targeted both at users themselves and at website operators, who stand accused of helping online pirates to make millions of illegal copies of movies and television programmes.

11.9 Pornography

Computers have made it much easier for people to store and disseminate offensive material than was the case in the paper-based world. Indeed, the availability of hard-core pornography has helped to give the internet a bad name. There have been instances where employees have used company servers as a repository for pornographic material. From the point of view of an employer, the key issue is that such material may already be stored on their company's systems without their knowledge. Pornography can be split up into two main types, according to whether it is legal or not. First, there is pornography directed at adults which it is illegal for adults to read or view according to the rules of a particular legal system. The material most universally accepted as falling into this category would be child pornography. Second, there is pornography or other sexual material which is not illegal for adults to access, but which may nevertheless be considered to be harmful or upsetting for others, including children, to see. The traditional approach of UK legislation has been that it is acceptable to possess obscene material in private as long as there is no attempt to publish, distribute or show it to others – particularly for gain. With regard to child pornography – which by its very nature features the sexual abuse of children – the UK Parliament has taken the view that posses-sion as well as circulation of such material should be criminalized. In 2005, the UK government also sought views on tightening the law with regard to extreme pornography – that is pornography which contains actual scenes or realistic depictions of serious violence, bestiality or necrophilia.

R v. Perrin [2002] All ER 359

In R v. Perrin a Frenchman was convicted under the Obscene Publications Act 1959 in relation to a website hosted in France. The only occurrence of downloading in the UK from the website that the prosecution relied upon was undertaken by a police officer at New Scotland Yard who accessed the site and downloaded material from it. When the defendant happened to be passing through the United Kingdom, the opportunity was taken to arrest, charge and convict him on the basis of that download by the police officer. Mr Perrin was given a 30-month prison sentence.

This case would seem to suggest that issues such as where the website was devel-oped and hosted, where the website owner lives or which countries the site is aimed at are all irrelevant.

Storage and transmission of material which is obscene is a criminal offence under the Obscene Publications Acts 1959 and 1964. It is also an offence under the Obscene Publications Act 1959 to publish an obscene article whether for gain or not, and this is further extended in the Criminal Justice and Public Order Act 1994 which deals specifically with 'obscene publications and indecent photographs of children'.

Other relevant legislation includes the Protection of Children Act 1978. There is also the Criminal Justice Act of 1988 which makes it an offence for a person to have any indecent photograph of a child in his possession. (A 'child' in this context is defined as a person under the age of 16. The test for 'obscenity' is set out in the Obscene Publications Acts 1959 and 1964 as being material which tends to 'deprave and corrupt' those who are likely, having regard to all relevant circumstances, to read, see or hear it.)

R v. Schofield

This case involved a trojan virus which, as its name suggests, is something that looks innocuous and does not do anything until it has installed itself on your computer. Once there, it can do all sorts of nasty things. In particular, someone else can use it to obtain remote access to, and control of, your computer.

Background:

1   Mr Schofield was charged in relation to the making of indecent images of children, based on 14 'depraved images' that were found on his PC.

2   Mr Schofield claimed that he didn't know how these images had got onto his computer.

3   Vigilantes drove him out of his home and he had to spend a month in hiding.

4   When an expert examined Mr Schofield's PC, a trojan virus was discovered; this had been installed on the machine a day before the offending images had been downloaded. The expert concluded that the trojan could have downloaded the images from the internet without the knowledge of Mr Schofield, and the prosecution accepted that they were not able to show that Mr Schofield was the only person who could have downloaded these images onto the PC. He was consequently acquitted.

This case is interesting for a number of reasons:

1   It is extremely worrying that trojans might be used to download illegal material to an individual's PC without the individual knowing.

2   There is a real risk of an innocent person being convicted (and subsequently having their life ruined, as nearly happened to Mr Schofield).

3   There have been a number of reports of trojans that, once installed on an individual's computer, allow that computer to be used as a sort of mini server to enable the downloading of pornography. The person actually responsible for the pornography can, in effect, conceal himself behind a number of other people's computers whose owners will be unaware of it.

4   This is possibly the first time a defence has been used based on the suggestion that 'the computer did it'.

5   It makes investigation of genuine offenders more difficult. Not only may law enforcement agencies have to be more cautious when they find images on a PC, but genuine offenders may also seek to use the 'trojan' defence themselves. In the end, if this happens with any frequency it may reduce the chances of achieving successful prosecution of genuine offenders.

6   Unless there is clear evidence that there has been no third party interference with a computer, using an argument about a computer virus may be enough to introduce a reasonable doubt into the minds of a judge or jury. The defence may well be a genuine one in some cases, but it may also prevent successful prosections being brought against genuine offenders and thus reduce the effectiveness of laws against hacking or the dissemination of offensive or pornographic material.

The European Commission has called for increased efforts to protect minors in the context of new media services. The Community's Safer Internet Action Plan also encourages initiatives such as the development of rating and filtering systems and the establishment of 'walled gardens' (portals where the operators guarantee the quality of sites which can be accessed through them).[11]

In August 2005 the Home Office issued a consultation paper on the possession of extreme pornographic material[12] which sought views on a proposal to make illegal the possession of a limited range of extreme pornographic material featuring adults. The aim was to mirror the arrangements already in place in respect of indecent photographs of children, possession of which is already an offence. It set out options for creating a new offence of simple possession of extreme pornographic material which is graphic and sexually explicit and which contains actual scenes or realistic depictions of serious violence, bestiality or necrophilia. It would be illegal to publish, sell or import the material in question under the Obscene Publications Acts 1959 and 1964, and in Scotland the Civic Government (Scotland) Act 1982, but it is not currently an offence to possess it other than for gain in England and Wales or, in Scotland, with a view to sale or distribution.

11.10   Fraud

Computers can be used as a tool to commit fraud. A wide range of different types of fraud can be classed as cybercrimes. This includes securities and financial fraud, credit card fraud and other types of computer-related fraud such as phishing or identity theft (see also section 3.7). Identity theft is said to be Britain's fastest growing fraud, whereby a thief steals someone's identity which could then potentially be used in order to open a bank account or set up a number of credit cards. As mentioned above (11.5), the APIG has called for a new fraud bill to be introduced without delay.

11.10.1 Phishing

Phishing is the fraudulent acquisition, through deception, of sensitive personal information such as passwords and credit card details, by masquerading as someone trustworthy with a genuine need for that information. The term was coined back in the 1990s by crackers attempting to steal AOL accounts. A fraudster would pose as an AOL staff member and send an instant message to a potential victim. The message would ask the victim to reveal his or her password, for instance to 'verify your account' or to 'confirm billing information'. Once the victim gave over the password, the fraudster could access the victim's account and use it for criminal purposes, such as spamming.

This has become very common in relation to websites of financial services companies, auction websites or internet payment services. Companies are trying to educate their customers not to give out personal data in response to an e-mail.

In the struggle against phishing there are tools available such as 'Spoof-stick', which makes spoofed websites easier to spot by prominently displaying only the most relevant domain information. Spoofed websites are ones which are deliberately designed in order to look like a legitimate website. In order to verify whether a website is genuine or not, it is best to verify the security certificate of the site. To do this, users should click on the yellow lock icon on the status bar. This symbol signifies that the website uses encryption to help protect any sensitive personal information. The activities of the Anti-Phishing Working Group are also worth noting.[13]

11.10.2 Pharming

Pharming occurs when someone connects to your PC or laptop with the purpose of retrieving sensitive information and even your keystrokes (these can be used to trap your login names and passwords). You do not necessarily even know this is happening; generally these attacks happen wirelessly.

A rogue dialler is an application which affects people with a dial-up internet connection. Rogue diallers work by sending internet users a pop-up window, quite often one which offers access to pornography. They often display a large button which says something along the lines of 'click here to close this window'. However, clicking on the button results in the rogue dialler software being installed onto the PC. The software routes the computer's internet connection away from the default connection settings to a premium-rate number which costs up to £1.50 per minute.

Tips for those who get stung by this scam:

- Install a firewall to block diallers
- Use pop-up blocker software
- If you do get a suspicious pop-up window, close this by holding the Alt key while pressing F4
- Don't click anywhere within the pop-up window
- Call your telephone company
- Contact ICSTIS, which regulates premium-rate numbers.

Figure 11.5 Rogue diallers

In order to minimize the risks posed by pharming, it is advisable to make sure you have up-to-date antivirus protection – which means not only installing anti-virus software, but also making sure that you run weekly updates – and that you instal Spyware scanning software on your equipment and run regular scans.

The APIG report on the Computer Misuse Act 1990 concluded that there is plenty of current legislation other than the CMA covering this type of conduct. The group encouraged the Independent Committee for the Supervision of Standards of Telephone Information Services, which regulates premium rate phone services, to take immediate steps to prosecute the operators of fraudulent auto-dialler systems under that existing legislation.

11.11 Denial of service attacks

There might be occasions where accessing a website could be said to be an offence under the CMA. Accessing a publicly available website is not an offence in itself, as there is an implied authorizatison for people to access the website. Where it gets more tricky is in those instances when that access is abused. Is, for instance, a denial of service attack an offence? Such an attack consists of sending massive quantities of otherwise normal messages or page requests to an internet host, with the result that the server is overloaded, is unable to deal with legitimate requests and in effect becomes unavailable.

The perpetrator of a denial of service attack might use the space on your hard drive and your CPU, combined with the computer power of many thousands of other machines, in order to direct traffic on the web to one well known internet site. This then overloads the site's server, making the site unavailable.

If the access could be regarded as unauthorized, then there is potentially a Section 1 offence and possibly a Section 3 offence. However, denial of service attacks are difficult to regulate because they do not necessarily require a breach of security. This means that in some instances it would be difficult to initiate a prosecution for a denial of service attack under the current CMA. For this reason, the Earl of Northesk introduced a Computer Misuse (Amendment) Bill,[14] which sought to extend the powers of the CMA to denial of service attacks. The bill reached its second reading on 20 June 2002, but did not progress any further.

The European Commission issued a consultation document in April

2002 on attacks against information systems.[15] This has in part been prompted by the Council of Europe's cybercrime convention.

More recently there was a Council framework decision 2005/222/JHA on 24 February 2005 on attacks against information systems in *Official Journal* L69/67, 16 March 2005. The decision has to be implemented in member states by 16 March 2007. The objective of the framework decision is to improve co-operation between judicial and other competent authorities responsible for law enforcement in the member states, by approximating rules on criminal law in the member states in the area of attacks against information systems and ensuring that such attacks are punishable by effective, proportional and dissuasive criminal penalties in all member states.

The specific crimes covered by the directive are:

* unauthorized access to information systems (hacking)
* disruption of information systems (denial of service)
* execution of malicious software that modifies or destroys data
* interception of communication
* malicious misrepresentation.

Member states are required to take the necessary measures to ensure that illegal access to an information system and interference with the integrity of an information system or of its data are punishable as criminal offences. Given that information systems are the subject of attacks, particularly from organized crime, and the increasing potential for terrorist attacks against information systems which form part of the critical infrastructure of the member states, a response at the level of the member states is required to avoid compromising the achievement of a safer information society and an area of freedom, security and justice.

The government recognizes that while existing UK legislation already covers many of the requirements of these texts as they relate to offences against computer and information systems, nevertheless there must be some amendments to UK legislation in order to be fully compliant, and on a number of occasions it has indicated that this will happen when parliamentary time allows (see 11.5).

11.12 Acceptable use policies

Companies should set policies for employees to abide by, so that they know what is expected of them. This can be in the form of a written policy statement on reasonable use of the internet, e-mail and the company intranet. All employees should be given a copy, including new members of staff when they join. It could, for example, be covered as part of the induction process. Well drafted policy statements are of no use if they are not sent to all employees, or some employees are unaware that the policy exists.

It is also important that the principles enshrined in these policies are policed adequately and any breaches are dealt with in a consistent manner through the company's disciplinary policy. If companies fail to enforce these policies adequately, they cannot seek to rely on them indiscriminately when dealing with breaches, as employees would be able to challenge the enforceability of the policy if it were not adequately policed and implemented. There has to be a consistency in approach.

Examples of unacceptable content should be outlined. For example, in the case of publishing content to the company's intranet, you might want the list of unacceptable content to cover:

- offensive material (such as pornographic, abusive, indecent or profane items)
- items which insult or intimidate someone
- lewd comments, jokes or banter
- swearwords and offensive language
- chain letters
- disclosing personal data without consent of the data controller, contrary to the Data Protection Act 1998
- any purpose which is illegal or contrary to the employer's interest.

11.13 Telecommunications Act 1984

It is also necessary to take account of Section 43 of the Telecommunications Act 1984 in relation to computer misuse, and not merely the CMA. Section 43 makes it a criminal offence to use a public telecommunications network to send grossly offensive, threatening or obscene material, and a public telecommunications network is defined widely enough to cover internet traffic which goes through telephone lines or other cables.

11.14 Summary

This chapter has considered cybercrime and computer misuse, and how the CMA and the Telecommunications Act 1984 are used to deal with various aspects of computer misuse. The forms of computer misuse considered include viruses, worms and trojans, computer hacking and denial of service attacks, intellectual property infringement, pornography and various forms of computer fraud such as phishing. The chapter has also looked ahead to changes likely to take place to ensure that the UK is fully compliant with the Council of Europe's Cybercrime Convention, and the Council of the European Union's framework decision on attacks against information systems.

The next chapter looks at the legal implications of discrimination on the grounds of disability, including visual impairment.

Notes and references

1   CBI (2001), *Cybercrime Survey 2001: making the information superhighway safe for business* (for the full list of main threats from cybercrime see exhibit 12 in the survey).

2   See www.security-survey.gov.uk.

3   Council of Europe (2001) *Convention on Cybercrime*, http://conventions.coe.int/treaty/en/treaties/html/185.htm.

4   See http://conventions.coe.int/treaty/en/treaties/html/189.htm.

5   Law Commission (1989, October) *Criminal Law: computer misuse*, Law Commission Working Paper no. 186, Cm 819.

6   See www.apig.org.uk.

7   The Plagiarism Advisory Service's website is at www.jiscpas.ac.uk. See also JISC (2005) *Deterring, Detecting and Dealing with Student Plagiarism* (briefing paper); Carroll, J. (2004) *Institutional Issues in Deterring, Detecting and Dealing with Student Plagiarism*, JISC.

8   See www.bsa.org/usa/press/newsreleases/global-piracy-study-05-18-2005.cfm.

9   Ibid.

10 First Jail Sentence for Movie File Sharing, *Out-law News* (7 November 2005), www.out-law.com/page-6310.

11 See the Europa Safer Internet Programme web pages at http://europa.eu.int/information_society/activities/sip/index_en.htm.

12 See www.homeoffice.gov.uk/documents/cons-extreme-porn-300805?version=1

13 See www.antiphishing.org.

14 The Stationery Office (2002) HL Bill 79 session 2001/2.

15   European Commission (2002) *Proposal for a Council Framework Decision on Attacks Against Information Systems*, COM (2002) 0173, http://europa.eu.int/eur-lex/en/com/pdf/2002/com2002_0173en01.pdf.

12 Disability discrimination

12.1 Introduction

This chapter looks at the legal implications of discrimination on the grounds of disability. It considers the general principles involved (12.2) and how these apply to information services. A number of checklists are provided. In addition to the Disability Discrimination Acts of 1995 and 2005 (DDA 1995 and DDA 2005) and the Special Educational Needs and Disability Act 2001 (SENDA), another key piece of legislation relating to disability is the Copyright (Visually Impaired Persons) Act 2002 (12.3), which came into force in October 2003; this is considered along with the joint industry guidelines which were produced by the Publishers Licensing Society. The availability of accessible publications for those with sight problems is considered (12.4), as is the issue of website accessibility for those who are blind, partially sighted or dyslexic (12.5). The chapter rounds off with a listing of sources of information on disability (12.7) and how it applies in the context of library and information services.

12.2 General principles

Disabled people are among the most excluded in society. They encounter many barriers to accessing the services of archives and libraries, including physical, sensory, attitudinal, cultural and intellectual barriers. Library and information services need to ensure that they do not discriminate against those who are disabled. This is not solely a moral issue – it is also a legal obligation. The DDA 1995 makes it illegal to discriminate against disabled people in employment, provision of goods, facilities and services, and access to buildings and premises. It was extended to education from September 2002 following amendments introduced by SENDA.

Discrimination against disabled people can take place in either of two ways:

- by treating them less favourably than other people (DDA 1995 s20)
- by failing to make a 'reasonable' adjustment (DDA 1995 s21) when they are placed at a 'substantial disadvantage' compared to other people for a reason relating to their disability.

A reasonable adjustment might be any action that helps to alleviate a substantial disadvantage. This could involve changing the organization's standard procedures, providing materials in Braille as an additional service, providing appropriate adjustments to the physical environment or training staff to work with disabled people. The DDA 1995 requires institutions to anticipate the needs of people with disabilities and make reasonable adjustments to ensure an appropriate, non-discriminatory environment.

People with disability can include those with physical or mobility impairments, hearing impairments, dyslexia, medical conditions, mental health difficulties, visual impairment or learning difficulties. In Section 19(3)(c) of the DDA 1995, 'access to and use of information services' is given as an example of the type of service to which the DDA applies. So it is quite clear that the DDA 1995 applies to those who provide library and information services to the public. In order to ensure that they do not discriminate on the grounds of disability, library services therefore need to take account of disability issues when considering matters of service planning, delivery and quality; they need to be able to provide equality of physical access to their services; and they also need to assess, deliver and evaluate disability training.

Managers of library and information services can make use of a number of toolkits, checklists and best practice standards (see the list of resources in Section 12.7) to help them identify and assess whether or not their existing policies and procedures result in disabled people receiving a level of service which is inferior to that available to everyone else. They should think about the accessibility of their service to people with disabilities, both in terms of physical access and in terms of intellectual access.

Libraries can invest in a number of adaptations for people with disabilities. Adjustments made to the physical access can include:

- ramps
- colour-contrasting handrails
- swing-resistant automatic doors

- ensuring the appropriate widths needed for wheelchairs
- checking the rise of steps and the height of lift-call buttons
- signage and guiding, including international access symbols
- appropriate shelf heights
- access to catalogues and terminals
- access to library publications and websites
- fully adjustable tables and chairs.

If the library is planning a refurbishment, staff should take account of best practice guidance and any relevant British Standards. For example, there is a British Standard covering the slip resistance of different floor surfaces. Access requirements are often equated with wheelchair access when only around 5% of disabled people are wheelchair users. This lack of awareness can be a barrier to serving the majority of people with disabilities.

There are many adaptations to technology which can greatly assist people with disabilities. These include:

- different-sized keyboards
- mouse alternatives
- lap trays
- wrist rests
- screen magnifiers
- dyslexia and literacy software
- document readers
- voice-recognition technology.

It is also important to ensure that staff are equipped with the knowledge they need in order to serve disabled users effectively – for example, by being able to adjust a computer to an individual user's needs. Library and information services need to have appropriate policies, procedures and plans in place to serve the needs of their disabled users effectively, and staff training is a key part of ensuring that this isn't just a theoretical aim, but that the policies and procedures are put into practice.

Library and information services need to be mindful of the needs of their disabled users when they prepare promotional literature about their services, and the material must be accessible to those users (see Figure 12.1).

1	Is the information about library facilities accessible to disabled people?
2	Is promotional literature available in alternative formats such as Braille, audio tape or large print?
3	Is web-based material accessible to those using assistive technology, such as screen-reading software, or those not using a mouse?
4	Does information about services and facilities make clear the adjustments that are already in place? And does it also point out that additional adjustments can be made on an individual basis?

Figure 12.1   Promotional material

Institutions are expected to make 'anticipatory' adjustments, and not simply to wait until a disabled person requires a particular adaptation. In considering what anticipatory adjustments should be made, it is important to ask a number of key questions. For example:

1 Are the library buildings accessible?
2 Do they have accessible toilets?
3 Are the fire and emergency procedures appropriate for the library's disabled users?
4 Are the catalogue and instructions on its use available in accessible formats?
5 Are aisles wide enough for wheelchairs?
6 Are there sufficient staff to fetch books for those who cannot reach or see them?
7 Does the library provide materials in large print or online in order to cater for those who cannot use standard print?
8 Are longer loan periods available for those who need them?
9 Have staff been given the appropriate training? For example, could they support someone having an epileptic seizure?

It will ultimately be for the courts to decide what anticipatory adjustments it is reasonable to expect organizations to make. Library and information centres need to be ready to make adjustments on behalf of individuals as necessary. Such adjustments could include:

• allowing extended loan periods to dyslexic or other users
• setting aside books in advance for those who find it difficult to get into the library because of their disability

- assisting disabled people in using the catalogue, finding resources or using equipment
- fetching books from high or inaccessible shelves.

Libraries need to take reasonable steps to find out if a person is disabled in order for adjustments to be made, and this information needs to be kept confidential. Ignorance of someone's disability is not an adequate defence, if an adjustment could have been anticipated.

It is essential to review services periodically in order to take into account any changes in good practice or advances in technology. Figure 12.2 provides a checklist of areas to address in order to ensure compliance with current disability discrimination legislation.

1	Do you have an equal opportunities policy that makes specific reference to disabled people?
2	Has your organization carried out a disability access audit?
3	Does your organization carry out staff training to increase awareness of disability access?
4	How does your organization consult with its disabled users and non-users?
5	In what ways are your services accessible to disabled people?
6	How is technology used in order to improve access for disabled people?
7	How is publicity and promotion targeted towards disabled people?
8	How does your organization keep abreast of the growing body of best practice on access issues for disabled people?

Figure 12.2 Compliance checklist

The Disability Discrimination Act 2005 extended the scope of the DDA 1995. Some of its duties came into force on 5 December 2005. These include:

- extending the DDA 1995 to protect, effectively from the point of diagnosis, people with HIV infection, cancer or multiple sclerosis. Around 250,000 more people with multiple sclerosis, cancer and HIV are estimated to be covered by the change in definition effectively from the point of diagnosis.
- ending the requirement that a mental illness must be clinically well-recognized before it can be regarded as an impairment under the DDA 1995.

- making it unlawful for private clubs with 25 or more members, local authorities and the Greater London Authority to treat disabled members less favourably.

A key aspect of the DDA 2005 is a new duty on public bodies – from local authorities to healthcare and education providers – to promote equality of opportunity for disabled people, similar to the 'duty to promote' under the Race Relations Act 1976. Public authorities need to have 'due regard' to the need to eliminate discrimination against and harassment of disabled people, promote equality of opportunity for disabled people, promote positive attitudes to disabled people and encourage disabled people to take part in public life. This comes into force in December 2006.

The DDA 1995 generally defines disability as a physical or mental impairment which has a substantial and long-term adverse effect on the ability to carry out normal day-to-day activities.

The Office for Disability Issues[1] was launched on 1 December 2005 to provide cross-government focus on delivering the strategy for improving the life chances of disabled people.

The government plans to set up a new Commission for Equality and Human Rights (CEHR). A key aim of the CEHR is to end discrimination and harassment of people because of their disability, race, age, gender, religion, belief or sexual orientation. The new commission will merge three existing equality commissions – the Disability Rights Commission, the Commission for Racial Equality and the Equal Opportunities Commission. It is hoped that the CEHR will be up and running by 2007.

12.3   Copyright (Visually Impaired Persons) Act 2002

Visually impaired people are those who are blind or partially sighted, and people who are physically unable to hold or manipulate a book, focus or move their eyes or are otherwise physically unable to use a standard print book. However, for the purposes of the Act, it does not cover people with dyslexia.

The Copyright (Visually Impaired Persons) Act 2002 is intended to give people with sight loss easier access to alternative formats of copyright material, such as large print, Braille and audio. The Act came into force in October 2003 and it introduces two exceptions to copyright to overcome problems of access to material by people with visual impairment.

1 Part I: The 'one-for-one' exception – this entitles a visually impaired person to make a single accessible copy of a copyright work for their personal use, subject to a number of conditions. In order to be able to make an accessible copy under this exemption, you must be visually impaired, have or have access to a 'master copy' which is inaccessible because of your visual impairment and know that an accessible copy is not commercially available.

2 Part II: The 'multiple copy' exception – educational establishments [2] or not-for-profit organizations can make multiple accessible copies of a copyright work and supply them to visually impaired people for their personal use, subject to a number of conditions. For example, accessible copies cannot be supplied to anyone who can access a commercially available copy. Within a reasonable time from making accessible copies, copyright owners must be notified of activity under the exception. Where copyright owners have established a licensing scheme covering the activity that would otherwise be permitted under the exception, licences under that scheme must be taken out.

1	Only not-for-profit institutions can participate.
2	Most libraries will just be making one-to-one copies based on the user's legal access to the inaccessible copy.
3	The exception applies to non-print materials, including the internet, but it excludes databases.
4	No institution has to implement this exception if they do not wish to.
5	No institution has to be a repository if it does not wish to.
6	Institutions can charge, but only marginal costs.

Figure 12.3 The 'multiple copy' exception – salient points for libraries

The Department of Trade and Industry has been notified of several licensing schemes: the CLA operates one for books and journals, while the MPA operates one for sheet music. Therefore, the multiple copies exception does not apply to items covered by those schemes.

In 2001 the Publishers Licensing Society issued a set of joint industry guidelines on access to books, journals and magazines for people with a visual impairment. The guidelines are the result of a wide-ranging consultation among rights-holders and organizations helping visually impaired people, in an effort to strike a balance between the requirements of visually impaired people and the special problems surrounding uncontrolled copying, transcription and distribution.

There may be a number of scenarios where the Joint Industry Guidelines on Copyright and Visual Impairment will permit people to make accessible copies in more situations than those permitted by the exceptions in the Copyright (Visually Impaired Persons) Act 2002 – for example, the guidelines are not limited with regard to databases – and as long as the Joint Industry Guidelines remain in force, visually impaired people may rely on them.

12.4   The right to read

The Royal National Institute of the Blind (RNIB) has been running a 'Right to Read' campaign for some time. According to a report entitled *Written Off*, which was published in 2004 by the RNIB, three million people in the UK are being denied the right to read. They make the point that while government is pouring billions of pounds into literacy initiatives across the UK, people with sight problems or print reading disabilities are being forgotten. According to the RNIB figures, a staggering 96% of books are never published in formats that people with sight problems can read, like large print, audio or Braille.[3]

There is also a report published with the permission of the RNIB which documents the results of the 'Availability of Accessible Publications' project, undertaken for the RNIB by LISU.[4]

12.5   Website accessibility

The codes of practice produced by the Disability Rights Commission make clear that online services are subject to the anti-discrimination legislation. Indeed, the DRC is working with the British Standards Institution in order to produce guidance on website accessibility.

Blind people are the most disenfranchised, but partially sighted and dyslexic people also have problems accessing the web.

A number of tools are available to test technical aspects of accessibility. These include Bobby and W3C.[5]

> ### Maguire v. Sydney Organizing Committee for the Olympic Games
>
> The Australian case of Maguire v. Sydney Organizing Committee for the Olympic Games is useful in illustrating what adjustments might be considered reasonable in the context of web accessibility.
>
> This was an action brought in front of Australia's Human Rights and Equal Opportunities Commission (HREOC) by Maguire, who had been blind since birth. His action was in respect of the defendant's website, which he alleged was inaccessible and thus infringed the Commonwealth Disability Discrimination Act 1992.
>
> Maguire was an experienced computer user who accessed the internet using a refreshable Braille display and a web browser. Despite a number of changes made by the defendant, Maguire delivered a statement asserting that the website was still inaccessible as of 17 April 2000 and requested the HREOC to order certain changes to the website. Maguire asked the HREOC to order that the defendant ensure access from the Schedule page to the Index of Sports, among other changes.
>
> The defendant argued that access to the Index of Sports was possible by entering the URL for each sport directly into the browser. However, the Commission noted that this went against the way the internet worked – by using links to avoid having to know the correct URL for every page. The HREOC held that discrimination had taken place in that blind people were treated less favourably.
>
> The HREOC looked at the defendant's claim that unjustified hardship would be caused to it as a result of having to make changes to the website. It held that the detriment to the defendant would only be moderate, and had the issue been considered at the planning stages, detriment would have been negligible.
>
> Although this is an Australian case, the equivalent Australian legislation is very similar to the Disability Discrimination Act 1995. The case suggests that it would be a reasonable adjustment to make an inaccessible website accessible to disabled people.

12.6 Summary

This chapter has considered the requirement for library and information services to take proper account of the needs of disabled users in light of the Disability Discrimination Acts of 1995 and 2005, the Special Educational Needs Act and the Copyright (Visually Impaired Persons) Act. The word 'disability' covers a wide range of different types of impairment, and there is a legal requirement to ensure that people with disabilities are not discriminated against by being treated less favourably than other people or by reasonable adjustments not being made when they are placed at a 'substantial disadvantage' because of their disability.

The findings support the Right to Read Alliance's Campaign, which aims to increase significantly the proportion of publications available in accessible formats. In the next chapter the implications of human rights legislation are considered, especially how this relates to issues such as data protection, breach of confidence and copyright.

12.7   Further information

AbilityNet, accessible IT kits, www.abilitynet.org.uk.

Bobby, http://bobby.watchfire.com.

Burrington Partnership (2002) *Access Audit Toolkit* (available on CD-ROM).

CILIP has a set of web pages on disability, consisting of a number of equal
opportunities briefings – see www.cilip.org.uk/professionalguidance/
equalopportunities/briefings/.

Disability Policy Division, a part of the UK government's Department for
Work and Pensions (DWP), www.disability.gov.uk.

Disability Rights Commission, disability rights helpline.
DRC Helpline, Freepost MID02164, Stratford upon Avon, CV37 9BR
Telephone: 08457 622 633; Textphone: 08457 622 644; Fax: 08457 778 878
Website: www.drc-gb.org/.

Hopkins, L. (ed.) (2000) *Library Service Provision for Blind and Visually-impaired
People: a manual of best practice* (Library and Information Commission
Research Report 76), Resource.

MLA: the Museums Libraries and Archives Council (2005) *Accessibility of
Museum, Library and Archive Websites: the MLA audit.*

MLA: the Museums Libraries and Archives Council, *Disability Experts Database*, containing details of over 200 disability trainers, auditors and
consultants who have an interest or experience in working with museums,
galleries, libraries and archives, http://disabilitydatabase.mla.gov.uk.

MLA: the Museums Libraries and Archives Council, *MLA Disability Portfolio,*
www.mla.gov.uk/information/publications/00pubs.asp.
The portfolio is a collection of 12 guides on how best to meet the needs
of disabled people as users and staff in museums, archives and libraries:
1. Disability in context; 2. Meeting disabled people; 3. Training for equality; 4. Audits; 5. The Disability Discrimination Act; 6. Inclusive information;
7. Using technology; 8. Access on a shoestring; 9. Accessible environments;
10. Outreach and partnerships; 11. Consulting disabled people;
12. Employment at every level.

MLA: the Museums Libraries and Archives Council, *The Disability Directory*,
www.mla.gov.uk/documents/disdir.pdf.

My Web, My Way, BBC accessibility website (www.bbc.co.uk/accessibility)
designed to help people with disability get the most out of the web. The
site equips anyone using their computer with the tools and understanding

to enable them to make the most of the internet, whatever their ability or disability, and regardless of the operating system (Windows, Mac or Linux) they use.

National Library for the Blind (2002) *Library Services for Visually Impaired People: a manual of best practice*, http://bpm.nlb-online.org/contents.html

Owen, J. (2003) Making your Website Accessible, *Library and Information Update*, (January), 48–90.

Publishers Licensing Society (2001) *Copyright and Visual Impairment: access to books, magazines and journals by visually impaired people* (joint industry guidelines).

Publishers Licensing Society (2001) *Permission Requests for Visually Impaired Persons: guidelines for publisher rights owners*.

Raschen, B. (2004) Web Accessibility: ensuring access for all, *FreePint*, www.freepint.com/issues/141004.htm.

Resource (2002) *Access to Museums, Archives and Libraries for Disabled Users* (toolkit to help libraries measure how accessible they are to disabled users and identify areas where improvements can be made).

Resource (2002) *Resource Disability Action Plan: achieving equality of opportunity for disabled people in museums, archives and libraries*.

Revealweb, www.revealweb.org.uk.

Royal National Institute for the Blind
105 Judd Street, London WC1H 9NE
Telephone: 020 7388 1266; Fax: 020 7388 2034.

SCONUL (2003) *Access for Users with Disabilities* (SCONUL briefing on the implications of the DDA for libraries).

World Wide Web Consortium (1999) *Web Content Accessibility Guidelines*, www.w3.org/tr/wcag10/.

Notes and references

1   See www.officefordisability.gov.uk.
2   The educational establishments that are entitled to make multiple accessible copies are set out in the Copyright (Educational Establishments) Order 2005: SI 2005/223.
3   RNIB (2004) Press Release (15 November), www.rnib.org.uk/xpedio/groups/public/documents/publicwebsite/public_pr151104.hcsp; and the *Right to Read Charter*, www.rnib.org.uk.

4   Lockyer, S., Creaser, C. and Davies, J. E. (2005) *Availability of Accessible Publications*, LISU, www.lboro.ac.uk/departments/dis/lisu.
5   http://webextract.watchfire.com/bobby; and ww.w3.org/WAI/ER/existingtools.html.

13 Human rights

13.1 Introduction

The Human Rights Act 1998 requires UK legislation to be read and given effect in a way which is compatible with the European Convention on Human Rights. This chapter sets out the general principles of the Human Rights Act 1998. It then considers the implications of human rights legislation in areas such as data protection (13.3), breach of confidence (13.4), copyright (13.5) and freedom of expression (13.6).

13.2 General principles

The coming into force of the Human Rights Act 1998 in October 2000 marked the implementation of the European Convention on Human Rights in the United Kingdom. In the UK people cannot sue, or be sued by, another individual for breaking the Convention rights. But they may benefit indirectly because the Human Rights Act means that all laws have to be given a meaning and effect which is as close as possible to the Convention rights. Public authorities such as courts and tribunals need to interpret the legislation and develop case law in a way which is compatible with the rights set out in the Convention. Since the Human Rights Act 1998 came into force there have been cases in areas like copyright and data protection where the significance of human rights such as the freedom of expression and the right to privacy have been explored. UK courts have to take decisions of the European Court of Human Rights in Strasbourg into account, but are not required to follow them.

The passing of the Human Rights Act 1998 has been described as one of the biggest constitutional changes to British law for centuries. Most of the rights in the European Convention on Human Rights (ECHR) have been included in the Human Rights Act.

The ECHR was established in the aftermath of World War II by the Council of Europe. It guarantees largely civil and political rights rather than social and economic rights. The Council of Europe is quite separate from the European Union. It has its own Court of Human Rights in Strasbourg. Before the implementation of the Human Rights Act people were able to go to the Strasbourg court to claim their rights under the ECHR. The ECHR was not previously part of the UK's domestic law, so our courts were not normally able to deal with claims.

The Human Rights Act 1998 represents a unique model for implementing the ECHR. It preserves a subtle compromise between incorporating the European Convention rights and retaining parliamentary sovereignty. It does this by creating a general requirement that all legislation must be read and given effect in a way which is compatible with the Convention. It also requires all public authorities to act in compliance with the Convention unless prevented from doing so by statute.

The Act does not make the Convention directly enforceable. It does not allow the Convention to override primary legislation, even if there is incompatibility, thus retaining the sovereignty of parliament. If incompatibility occurs, then the higher courts, on appeal, may issue a 'declaration of incompatibility', which will then be fast tracked to Parliament for amendment.

Because the European Convention on Human Rights was only brought into English law relatively recently, the courts' application of the conflicting rights of individuals is somewhat unpredictable and it may be years before a firm body of case law is built up in this area.

The Human Rights Act 1998 does three key things:

1 It makes it unlawful for a public authority, like a government department, local authority or the police, to breach the Convention rights, unless an Act of Parliament means it couldn't have acted differently.
2 It means that cases can be dealt with in a UK court or tribunal. Previously, anyone who felt that their rights under the Convention had been breached had to go to the European Court of Human Rights in Strasbourg.
3 It says that all UK legislation must be given a meaning that fits with the Convention rights, if possible. If a court decides that this is not possible it will be up to Parliament to decide what to do.

Particularly relevant to library and information professionals are Articles 8 and 10 of the ECHR (see Figure 13.1). Article 8 on the right to respect for private and family life is relevant in areas such as data protection and breach of confidence, while Article 10 on the right to freedom of expression is especially relevant in areas such as copyright and freedom of information.

It is important to recognize that a number of the rights set out in the Convention are not absolute rights, and that restrictions to those rights may be necessary and can be justified in certain circumstances. For example, Article 10 on freedom of expression must always be balanced against Article 8, which protects the right to respect for private and family life.

Article 8: Right to respect for private and family life

1   Everyone has the right to respect for his private and family life, his home and his correspondence.
2   There shall be no interference by a public authority with the exercise of this right except such as is in accordance with the law and is necessary in a democratic society in the interests of national security, public safety or the economic well being of the country, for the prevention of disorder or crime, for the protection of health or morals or for the protection of the rights and freedoms of others.

Article 10: Freedom of expression

1   Everyone has the right to freedom of expression. This right shall include freedom to hold opinions and to receive and impart information and ideas without interference by public authority and regardless of frontiers…
2   The exercise of these freedoms, since it carries with it duties and responsibilities, may be subject to such formalities, conditions, restrictions or penalties as are necessary, in a democratic society, in the interests of national security, territorial integrity or public safety, for the prevention of disorder, or crime, for the protection of the reputation or rights of others, for preventing the disclosure of information received in confidence, or for maintaining the authority and impartiality of the judiciary.

Figure 13.1   Articles 8 and 10 of the European Convention on Human Rights

In May 2005, the Council of Europe's Committee of Ministers adopted a declaration which sets standards for human rights and the rule of law in the information society of mobile phones, the internet and computer communication.[1] The declaration represents the first international attempt to draw up a framework on the issue and it breaks new ground by bringing the principles set out in the European Convention on Human Rights up to date for the cyberage. It considers how stakeholders such as internet service providers, hardware and software manufacturers, governments and civil society can co-operate at both a national and also an international level. The declaration covers issues such as state and private censorship, protection of private information such as content and traffic data, education to help people evaluate and assess the quality of information, media ethics, the use of information technology for democracy and freedom of assembly in cyberspace.

13.2.1 Fundamental Rights Agency

At the end of June 2005, the European Commission adopted a proposal for a Regulation establishing a European Union Agency for Fundamental Rights. The Fundamental Rights Agency will be an independent centre of expertise on fundamental rights issues through data collection, analysis and networking, which currently does not exist at European Union level. The Agency will advise the European Union institutions and the member states on how best to prepare or implement fundamental rights-related European Union legislation. For example, when planning European Union policy or legislative measures to fight trafficking in human beings, the Agency could provide the institutions with the necessary data.

The Agency will be an effective tool in the protection of fundamental rights in the policies of the European Union. There will be no overlap but rather synergy with the work that the Council of Europe has carried out for years, which remains the major point of reference as regards human rights. Indeed, the Agency will build a close institutional relationship with the Council of Europe.[2]

13.2.2 Guiding principles for library and information professionals

All actions of library and information professionals should take place in a framework where human rights are respected. Directly relevant to the work of librarians is the right to freedom of expression, which includes the freedom to hold opinions and to receive and impart information and ideas without interference by public authorities.

CILIP's Ethical Principles and Code of Professional Practice for Library and Information Professionals states:

The conduct of information professionals should be characterized by concern for the public good in all professional matters, including respect for diversity within society, and the promoting of equal opportunities and human rights.

This commitment should be demonstrated by information professionals regardless of whether referring to hard copy or the electronic environment. The declaration of the Committee of Ministers (of the Council of Europe) on human rights and the rule of law in the information society[3] states:

> Freedom of expression, information and communication should be respected in a digital as well as in a non-digital environment, and should not be subject to restrictions other than those provided for in Article 10 of the ECHR, simply because communication is carried in digital form.

13.2.3 Human rights and the information society

Independent experts from around the world met in Geneva in early November 2003 to discuss fundamental human rights in the information society. During one of the last preparatory conferences (PrepCom 3A) for the World Summit on the Information Society (WSIS) which started in Geneva on 12 November 2003, a statement on human rights, human dignity and the information society was produced and distributed. The paper calls on governments to protect all human rights related to the information society, ranging from freedom of expression and information to privacy and intellectual property rights, and from bridging the digital divide to good governance. Paragraphs 22–27 deal with the public domain and intellectual property rights:

> Intellectual property regimes and national and international agreements on patents, copyright and trademarks should not prevail over the right to education and knowledge. This right must indeed be exercised through the concept of fair use, that is, use for non-commercial purposes, especially education, and research. (Para 26)

> The information and communication society will not contribute to human development and human rights unless and until access to information is considered a public good to be protected and promoted by the state. Information in the public domain should be easily accessible to support the information society. Intellectual property rights should not be protected as an end in itself, but rather as a means to an end that promotes a rich public domain, shared knowledge, scientific and technical advances, cultural

and linguistic diversity and the free flow of information. Public institutions such as libraries and archives, museums, cultural collections and other community-based access points should be strengthened so as to promote the preservation of documentary records and free and equitable access to information. (Para 27) [4]

13.3   Human rights and data protection

Article 8 of the ECHR says that everyone has the right to respect for his private and family life, his home and his correspondence. But the Convention makes clear that this has to be balanced against issues of national security, public safety, the prevention of disorder or crime and so on. One interesting area where human rights and data protection issues converge is in the use of thumbprints in place of library cards (as in Figure 13.2).

Over 300 schools throughout the UK have implemented technology which is used in school libraries. The system is intended to replace library cards and to save costs and time in managing the libraries. It does so by replacing the library cards with scans of the thumbprint of each individual child that uses the library. Apparently, several hundred thousand schoolchildren in the UK have now had their thumbprint scanned in order to enable them to use these systems. This appears to have been happening for some time; when it attracted the attention of the pressure group Privacy International, the group took the view that the practice breached both the Data Protection Act 1998 and the human rights of the individual children concerned.

Figure 13.2   School libraries use thumbprints in place of library cards

It is not illegal for an employer to monitor its workers. The monitoring of employees encompasses the monitoring of their use of the internet and e-mail, CCTV monitoring and so on. However, any such monitoring has to be carried out in a way that is consistent with the Data Protection Act 1998. It also has to be consistent with the right of each worker (under the European Convention on Human Rights) to respect for their private and family life and correspondence. Broadly speaking, what this means is that in deciding whether or not to carry out monitoring (and in actually carrying it out) an employer has to balance any potential adverse impact on the workers against the benefits likely to be obtained from carrying out the monitoring. The extent of the benefit has to justify any relevant adverse impact. So, the greater the potential adverse impact on workers for a particular type of monitoring, the more an employer has to do to justify carrying out that monitoring in the first place.

Another example of where both data protection and human rights issues are important is found in the introduction of identity cards (as in Figure 13.3).

The Joint Parliamentary Committee on Human Rights has expressed serious concerns over the government's plans for compulsory ID cards, warning that the recording and use of personal data envisaged under the scheme will allow for significant intrusion into private life and may breach human rights conventions.

Figure 13.3 Identity cards[5]

On 19 September 2005 *Out-law.com* published an article[6] which reported calls for a global data protection law by regulators. The article said that privacy chiefs from 40 countries had called upon the United Nations to prepare a legally binding instrument which clearly sets out the rights to data protection and privacy as enforceable human rights.

As mentioned in Chapter 8, the Culture, Media and Sport Select Committee held an inquiry into privacy and media intrusion between February and April 2003. The government response to the committee's findings made it clear that it was rejecting the Select Committee's calls for a privacy law to protect against media intrusion. It is worth noting that in outlining the rationale for the government's stance, Tessa Jowell, Culture Secretary, said that privacy was already adequately protected by the Human Rights Act and that it was for the courts, not politicians, to decide on individual cases of privacy invasion.

13.4   Human rights and breach of confidence

The Human Rights Act 1998 has had a significant impact on the English law of confidentiality (see the case law on breach of confidence in Section 8.8). When deciding whether information is confidential or not, the courts now have to take into account the right to respect for private and family life under Article 8 of the European Convention on Human Rights. However, they have to balance this with the importance of freedom of expression under Article 10 of the European Convention on Human Rights, particularly when it is the media that is trying to exercise this freedom. Freedom of the media is very important in a democratic society and this is recognized by both the European Convention on Human Rights and the Human Rights Act 1998.

13.5   Human rights and copyright

Article 27 of the Universal Declaration of Human Rights 1948 says:

1 Everyone has the right freely to participate in the cultural life of the community, to enjoy the arts and to share in scientific advancement and its benefits.
2 Everyone has the right to the protection of the moral and material interests resulting from any scientific, literary or artistic production of which he is the author.

This Article is particularly relevant within the field of copyright, because it demonstrates the difficulty of trying to balance the competing interests of the various stakeholders in copyright law. An interesting legal case which explored the boundaries between human rights legislation and copyright law was that of Ashdown v. Telegraph Group Ltd.

Ashdown v. Telegraph Group Ltd [2001] EWCA Civ 1142 (18 July 2001)

Background: Paddy (now Lord) Ashdown, the former leader of the Liberal Democrats, made a confidential record of a meeting held at 10 Downing Street on 21 October 1997, concerning plans for formal co-operation between the Labour Party and the Liberal Democrats. When Lord Ashdown was standing down from leadership of the Liberal Democrats it became known that he was considering publishing the diaries that he had been keeping of his life and political career. At this time he showed some material to representatives of various newspapers and publishers in strictest confidence. On 28 November 1999 *The Sunday Telegraph* published three separate items based on the minute of that meeting. Indeed, roughly a fifth of the minute was reproduced verbatim. *The Telegraph* revealed that Tony Blair had offered to replace two members of his Cabinet with LibDem MPs less than six months after the 1997 election. Lord Ashdown sued the newspaper for breach of confidence and copyright infringement.

Outcome: Rare circumstances could arise where the right of freedom of expression in the Human Rights Act 1998 came into conflict with the protection in the Copyright, Designs and Patents Act 1988 despite the Act's express exceptions. The court was obliged to apply the Act so as to give effect to the right of freedom of expression under Article 10 of the European Convention on Human Rights, which required the court to look closely at the facts of individual cases.

The Court of Appeal dismissed the appeal of the Telegraph Group Ltd against the decision of Sir Andrew Morrit, Vice Chancellor, that it infringed the copyright of Lord Ashdown in publishing substantial extracts from his political diaries in *The Sunday Telegraph* on 28 November 1999. Lord Phillips said that restriction of the right of freedom of expression in Article 10 of the ECHR could be justified where necessary in a democratic society in order to protect copyright. However, copyright did not normally prevent the

Continued on next page

Ashdown v. Telegraph Group Ltd (*continued*)

publication of information conveyed by a literary work. It was only the freedom to express information using the verbal formula devised by another that was prevented by copyright. That would not normally constitute a significant encroachment on the freedom of expression.

Strasbourg jurisprudence demonstrated that circumstances could arise in which freedom of expression would only be fully effective if an individual was permitted to reproduce the very words spoken by another – see Fressoz and Roire v. France (Application No 29183/95) ((1999) 31 EHRR 28).

If a newspaper considered it necessary to copy the exact words created by another, there was no reason in principle why the newspaper should not indemnify the author for any loss caused to him, or account to him for any profit made as a result of copying his work. Freedom of expression should not normally carry with it the right to make free use of another's work.

The Telegraph Group's use of Lord Ashdown's work was done to further their own commercial interests, and one could not argue that the right to freedom of expression as set out in Article 10 of the ECHR permitted them to profit from the use of Lord Ashdown's copyright without paying compensation.

13.6   Human rights and freedom of expression

The right to freedom of expression as set out in Article 10 of the ECHR has to be balanced alongside the right to privacy as set out in Article 8 of the Convention. Within a library and information context it is worth taking a look at the Council of Europe guidelines *Public Access to and Freedom of Expression in Networked Information.*[7]

The case of von Hannover v. Germany explored the issues relating to freedom of expression and the need to balance this with the right to privacy.

Von Hannover v. Germany (ECHR judgment 24 June 2004)

Background: Princess Caroline of Monaco does not hold any official position, although she does sometimes attend public events on behalf of her family. The Federal Constitutional Court in Germany refused to restrain the further publication of photographs which showed Princess Caroline in a variety of public places on the basis that there was a legitimate public interest in how a 'public figure par excellence' behaved generally in public. The Princess applied to the European Court of Human Rights on the ground that the decision of the German court infringed her right to respect for her private and family life under Article 8 of the Convention. Under German law she had protection for her privacy if she was in a 'secluded place' but the way that this was defined was too narrow to give her any assistance. Photographs that the Princess complained about showed her going about activities such as shopping, skiing, playing tennis or riding a horse.

Outcome: The ECHR considered the need to balance the competing interests of the freedom of expression guaranteed by Article 10 with the right of privacy in Article 8 of the Convention, and decided that there had been a violation of Princess Caroline's right to privacy under Article 8 of the ECHR.

13.7 Summary

This chapter has outlined the general principles of the Human Rights Act 1998. It has considered the implications of human rights legislation in areas such as data protection (13.3), breach of confidence (13.4), copyright (13.5) and freedom of expression (13.6). The next and final chapter looks at the legal deposit laws in the United Kingdom and how these have been updated in the last couple of years in order to allow for electronic content to be covered by the legislation. In practice, however, as we shall see, very little has changed as yet because there hasn't been any enabling legislation to bring new categories of material within its remit.

13.8 Further information

Department for Constitutional Affairs, *The Human Rights Act: an introduction*, www.dca.gov.uk/hract/hrintro.pdf.

de la Pena McCook, K. (2004) The Librarian and Human Rights: protecting discourse against repression, *Catholic Library World*, **75** (1), 23–8.

de Mello, R. (2001) The Right to Offend? *Library Association Record*, **103** (9), 560–1.

Oppenheim, C. and Warren, A. (2004) Integration of Roles? Implementing new information laws in UK public organizations, *Journal of Information Science*, **30** (1), 48–59.

Notes and references

1 Council of Europe (2005) Declaration of the Council of Ministers on Human Rights and the Rule of Law in the Information Society, CM(2005) 56 final (13 May).
2 IP/05/822, Brussels (2005) A European Union Agency to Protect and Promote Fundamental Rights, (30 June), an EC press release available at http://europa.eu.int/press_room/index_en.html.
3 Council of Europe (2005) Declaration of the Council of Ministers on Human Rights and the Rule of Law in the Information Society, CM(2005) 56 final (13 May).
4 Statement on Human Rights, Human Dignity and the Information Society, International Symposium on the Information Society, Human Dignity and Human Rights, www.pdhre.org/wsis/statement.doc, Palais des Nations, Geneva, 3–4 November 2003.
5 Travis, A. (2005) ID Cards May Breach Human Rights, say MPs, *The Guardian* (3 February), 7, www.guardian.co.uk/uk_news/story/0,3604,1404347,00.html.

6   Global Data Protection Law Needed, say Regulators, *Out-law News* (19 September 2005), www.out-law.com/page-6132.
7   See www.cilip.org.uk/professionalguidance/foi/intellfreedom.htm.

14 Legal deposit

14.1 Introduction

This chapter looks at the legal deposit laws and how they relate to print material (14.2.1) and non-print material (14.2.2). It also looks at the voluntary code (14.3) which is still ongoing. Copyright and the use of legal deposit material is also considered (14.6), as are other legal issues such as online defamation.

There has been a rapid growth in the publication of material in non-print forms in recent years, and unless these forms of publishing are covered by the legal deposit legislation, the danger is that we might lose an important part of the UK's national heritage. The legal deposit legislation set out in the Copyright Act 1911 was designed to ensure that the legal deposit libraries received a copy of everything published in the UK. However, it only covered material that was printed in hard copy and the existing legislation has ceased to be adequate to ensure the continuation of a comprehensive archive of the nation's published material. For that reason a number of people lobbied for the scope of the legislation to be extended and this ultimately led to the passing of the Legal Deposit Libraries Act 2003.

14.2 General principles

'Legal deposit' is the legal requirement for publishers to deposit with the British Library and the five other legal deposit libraries (see Figure 14.1) a single copy of each publication.

British Library
National Library of Scotland
National Library of Wales
Bodleian Library, Oxford
Cambridge University Library
Trinity College, Dublin

Figure 14.1 Legal deposit libraries

Legal deposit is governed by the Legal Deposit Libraries Act 2003 (see Figure 14.2 for the contents and structure of the Act). The Department for Culture, Media and Sport (DCMS) is the relevant government department and principal owner of the Act, responsible for legislation in this field. The Legal Deposit Libraries Bill progressed through Parliament as a Private Members Bill, sponsored by Chris Mole MP (Ipswich). It received Royal Assent on 31 October 2003, and the provisions for print publications commenced on 1 February 2004, with the coming into force of the Legal Deposit Libraries Act (Commencement) Order 2004: SI 2004/130.

The layout is as follows:

- duty on publishers to deposit (s1)
- voluntary arrangements for sound (British Library) and film (British Film Institute) implicitly continue (s1(5))
- new and alternative editions: deposit restricted to one edition and one medium
- printed publications: carried over with only minor amendments from 1911 Act affecting BL (s4) and five other libraries (s5)
- new consequential exceptions to the Copyright Designs and Patents Act 1988 and Copyright and Rights in Databases Regulations 1997 (s8)
- exemptions from liability for publishers in respect of breach of contract (s9)
- exemptions from liability for publishers and libraries for defamation and provision for web harvesting (s10).

Figure 14.2 Layout of the Legal Deposit Libraries Act 2003

There is a 'duty to deposit' under which anyone who publishes in the UK a work to which the Act applies must, at his own expense, deliver a copy to a deposit library.

14.2.1 Print material

In respect of works that are published in print, the Act applies to:

- books
- sheet music or letterpress
- maps, plans, charts or tables
- any part of any such work.

The previous legal deposit legislation – the Copyright Act 1911 – required a copy of everything published in the United Kingdom to be automatically deposited by publishers in the British Library, and, on request, in each of the other deposit libraries (the National Libraries of Scotland and Wales, the Bodleian Library, Oxford, Cambridge University Library and Trinity College, Dublin).

The Legal Deposit Libraries Act 2003 sets out similar obligations, but it also enables the Secretary of State to make regulations extending the system of legal deposit to non-print material. The Act re-enacted (with minor amendments) the existing obligation to deposit printed publications in the six legal deposit libraries. A copy of each book or serial or other printed publication which is published in the UK is required to be deposited, free of charge, in the British Library. The copy must be delivered to the British Library within a month of publication, and the copy must be of the same quality as the best copies published in the United Kingdom at that time. The British Library Board must provide a receipt for the deposited printed works received. In addition, the other five legal deposit libraries are each entitled to receive, on request, one free copy of any book or other printed publication published in the UK.

14.2.2 Non-print material

The Act will be implemented progressively and selectively, through enabling legislation. The 2003 Act gives the Secretary of State specific powers to make regulations which will cover the deposit (or harvesting) of publications in different formats. On 4 July 2003 the then Arts Minister, Estelle Morris, said that the legislation would be 'implemented slowly, incrementally, and above all, sensitively'. This gives the Secretary of State power to extend the system of legal deposit to cover various non-print media as they develop, including off-line publications such as CD-ROMS and microforms, online publications such as electronic journals, and other non-print materials.

If the work is published in a medium other than print, then the Act only applies if the work is of a prescribed description. These will be specified by Regulation, and the Regulations are intended to specify each new type of publication to be covered by the deposit regime and to set out in detail exactly how the regime is to work in relation to that new type of publication. Draft regulations will be consulted upon, and are subject to affirmative resolution in both Houses. At the time of writing (December 2005), no Regulations covering non-print material had yet been published.

The 2003 Act was drafted so that it would be flexible enough to cover the diverse and complex nature of the publishing industry in the 21st century. It ensures that forms of publication developed in the future can be incorporated into legal deposit, without the need to return to primary legislation. Publishers of non-print works will not be required to deposit their works until Regulations are made.

14.3   Voluntary deposit of non-print publications

At the end of 1997 the Secretary of State for Culture, Media and Sport set up a working party under the chairmanship of Sir Anthony Kenny to advise on how an effective national archive of non-print material might be achieved. The working party reported in July 1998, concluding that in the longer term only statutory deposit could secure a comprehensive national published archive. It was clear that further work was needed – consulting the publishing industry, working on the definitions of material to be covered and looking at the impact such legislation would have on business. As a result, the Secretary of State requested that a code of practice for the voluntary deposit of non-print publications should be drawn up and agreed between publishers and the deposit libraries.[1]

The code of practice covers microform and other offline electronic media (such as CD-ROM or DVD), but it does not cover online publications or dynamic databases and other continuously updated publications. The voluntary scheme for offline media is still ongoing.

14.4   Enforcement

Section 3 of the LDLA 2003 sets out the provisions regarding enforcement. If a publisher fails to deposit, the library will be able to apply to the County Court (or to the Sheriff Court in Scotland) for an order requiring deposit. In those instances where such an order would not be effective or appropriate, the Court may make an order requiring the publisher to make a payment of not more than the cost of making good the failure to comply.

14.5   Legal Deposit Advisory Panel

During the passage of the 2003 Act through Parliament, ministerial undertakings were made in relation to the creation of a Legal Deposit Advisory Panel to assist with, and advise on, the Legal Deposit Libraries Act making of secondary legislation. The DCMS has conducted a public consultation on the terms of reference and composition of the Legal Deposit Advisory Panel.[2, 3]

The Legal Deposit Advisory Panel was established on 1 September 2005 to advise the Secretary of State on the implementation of the Legal Deposit Libraries Act 2003. Chaired by Ann Limb (Group Chief Executive of the University for Industry 2001–2004), the panel has ten other members, plus four ex-officio members:

- Chair of the Intellectual Property Rights Action Group – Digital Content Forum
- Director of Scholarship and Collections – British Library
- National Librarian – National Library of Scotland
- Librarian – National Library of Wales.

The terms of reference of the Panel are to:

- advise the Secretary of State on the content of regulations for the deposit of particular classes on non-print media, making recommendations for future secondary legislation as appropriate, in line with Ministerial undertaking made in Parliament
- monitor and oversee the operation and implementation of the Legal Deposit Libraries Act 2003
- execute all these responsibilities in accordance with the letter and the spirit of the 2003 Act
- advise the DCMS as requested on the operation of the 2003 Act.

14.6   Copyright and use of legal deposit material

Section 7 of the LDLA 2003 provides that the libraries, persons acting on their behalf and readers may not do any of the following activities unless authorized by Regulations: using the material, copying it, adapting any accompanying computer program or database, lending it to a third party, transferring it to a third party or disposing of it .

These regulations may in particular make provision for the purposes for which the deposited material may be used, the time at which readers may first use the material (thereby allowing embargos to be established) and the description of readers that may use the material at any one time (which will enable cross-library limits to be imposed if there is a secure network, in addition to limiting the number of people that may access the material simultaneously in any particular library).

The Legal Deposit Libraries Act 2003 inserts section 44A into the CDPA 1988 (see Figure 14.3). It additionally inserts a new exception to database right into the Copyright and Rights in Databases Regulations 1997 (SI 1997/3032) in respect of activities permitted by regulations made under Section 7.

---

(1) Copyright is not infringed by the copying of a work from the internet by a deposit library or person acting on its behalf if –

(a) the work is of a description prescribed by regulations under section 10(5) of the 2003 Act,
(b) its publication on the internet, or a person publishing it there, is connected with the United Kingdom in a manner so prescribed, and
(c) the copying is done in accordance with any conditions so prescribed.

(2) Copyright is not infringed by the doing of anything in relation to relevant material permitted to be done under regulations under section 7 of the 2003 Act.

(3) The Secretary of State may by regulations make provision excluding, in relation to prescribed activities done in relation to relevant material, the application of such of the provisions of this Chapter as are prescribed.

(4) Regulations under subsection (3) may in particular make provision prescribing activities –

(a) done for a prescribed purpose,
(b) done by prescribed descriptions of reader,
(c) done in relation to prescribed descriptions of relevant material,
(d) done other than in accordance with prescribed conditions.

(5) Regulations under this section may make different provision for different purposes.

(6) Regulations under this section shall be made by statutory instrument which shall be subject to annulment in pursuance of a resolution of either House of Parliament.

(7) In this section–

(a) 'the 2003 Act' means the Legal Deposit Libraries Act 2003;
(b) 'deposit library', 'reader' and 'relevant material' have the same meaning as in section 7 of the 2003 Act;
(c) 'prescribed' means prescribed by regulations made by the Secretary of State.

Figure 14.3 CDPA Section 44A: legal deposit libraries

14.7   Summary

This, the final chapter, has looked at the general principles of the legal deposit legislation (14.2) and how the Legal Deposit Libraries Act 2003 will in due course enable the legal deposit libraries to collect non-print materials under Regulations which will prescribe each new type of publication to be covered by the deposit regime (14.2.2). It also considered briefly the voluntary code of practice on the deposit of non-print publications (14.3) which is still ongoing. Issues regarding enforcement (14.4), copyright and the use of legal deposit material (14.6) were also examined.

14.8   Further information

British Library legal deposit page, www.bl.uk/about/policies/legaldeposit.
UK Association of Online Publishers, www.ukaop.org.uk.

Legislation

Explanatory notes to the Legal Deposit Libraries Act 2003, www.opsi.gov.uk/acts/en2003/2003en28.htm.
Legal Deposit Libraries Act 2003.
Legal Deposit Libraries Act (Commencement order) 2004 SI 2004/130, www.opsi.gov.uk/si/si2004/20040130.htm.

Notes and references

1   See www.bl.uk/about/policies/codeprac.html.
2   DCMS (2004) *A Consultation Document on Establishing the Legal Deposit Advisory Panel*.
3   DCMS (2005) *Establishing the Legal Deposit Advisory Panel Consultation: a summary of responses*.

Bibliography

Armstrong, C. and Bebbington, L. (eds) (2003) *Staying Legal: a guide to issues and practices affecting the library, information and publishing sectors*, 2nd edn, Facet Publishing.

Birkinshaw, P. (2001) *Freedom of Information: the law, the practice and the ideal*, 3rd edn, Butterworths.

Branscomb, A. W. (1995) *Who owns Information: from privacy to public access?* Basic Books.

British Standards Institution, Data Protection Update Service. The service includes the following publications: *Guide to the Practical Implementation of the Data Protection Act 1998*; *Guide to Developing an Email Policy*; *Guide to Developing an Electronic Commerce Policy*; *Guide to Managing Your Database*; *Pre-audit Workbook*; *Guide to Data Controller and Data Processor Contracts*; *Guide to Managing Subject Access Requests*.

British Standards Institution, *Data Protection Guide*.

British Standards Institution, *Guide to Freedom of Information*.

Carey, P. (2004) *Data Protection: a practical guide to UK and EU law*, Oxford University Press.

Carey, P. (2004) *Media Law*, 3rd edn, Sweet and Maxwell.

Christie, A. and Gare, S. (2004) *Blackstone's Statutes on Intellectual Property*, 7th edn, Oxford University Press.

CILIP (2005) *A Safe Place for Children* (accessible to members only), www.cilip. org.uk/professionalguidance/youngpeople/safeplaceforchildren.htm.

CILIP (2005) *Ethical Principles and Code of Professional Practice for Library and Information Professionals*, www.cilip.org.uk/professionalguidance/ethics

Clark, C. (ed.) (1990) *Photocopying from Books and Journals: a guide for all users of copyright and literary works*, British Copyright Council.

Collins, M. (2005) *The Law of Defamation and the Internet*, 2nd edn, Oxford University Press.

Consumers International (2001) *Privacy@net: international comparative study of consumer privacy on the internet*.

Cornish, G. P. (2004) *Copyright: interpreting the law for libraries, archives and information services*, 4th edn, Facet Publishing.

Department of Trade and Industry (2005) *DTI Consultation Document on the Electronic Commerce Directive: the liability of hyperlinkers, location tool services and content aggregators*, www.dti.gov.uk/consultations/consultation-1499.html.

EIRENE (European Information Researchers Network) (1993) *Code of Practice for Information Brokers*.

European Commission (2000) *Data Protection in the European Union* (PF-39-99-008-EN-V-C).

Experian (no date) *A Simplified Guide to the Data Protection Act 1998: to assist businesses holding personal information on customers, suppliers, directors, shareholders and others*.

Law Commission (2001) *Electronic Commerce: formal requirements in commercial transactions*.

Law Commission (2002) *Defamation and the Internet: a preliminary investigation* (Scoping study no. 2).

Library Association (1995) *The Library Association Code of Professional Conduct and Guidance Notes*, 2nd edn.

Lloyd, I. (2000) *Legal Aspects of the Information Society*, Butterworths.

Lloyd, I. (2004) *Information Technology Law*, 4th edn, LexisNexis.

Lloyd, I. J. and Simpson, M. (1995) *Law on the Electronic Frontier, Hume papers on public policy Volume 2 No. 4*, www.strath.ac.uk/departments/law/dept/diglib/book/bookcon.html.

Lowenstein, J. (2002) *The Author's Due: printing and the prehistory of copyright*, University of Chicago Press.

Marett, P. (1996) *Intellectual Property Law*, 2nd edn, Sweet and Maxwell.

Marett, P. (2002) *Information Law in Practice*, Ashgate.

McLeod, T. and Cooling, P. (1990) *Law for Librarians: a handbook for librarians in England and Wales*, Library Association Publishing.

McKilligan, N. and Powell, N. (2004) Data Protection Pocket Guide: essential facts at your fingertips, British Standards Institution.

Moore, A. D (ed.) (2005) *Information Ethics: privacy, property and power*, University of Washington Press.

Norman, S. (2004) *Practical Copyright for Information Professionals*, Facet Publishing.

Office of the Information Commissioner (2000) *Using the Law to Protect Your Information*.

Oppenheim, C. (2001) *The Legal and Regulatory Environment for Electronic Information*, 4th edn, Infonortics.

Oppenheim, C. and Muir, A. (2001) *Report on Developments World-Wide on National Information Policy Prepared for Re:Source and The Library Association*, www.la-hq.org.uk/directory/prof_issues/nip/title.htm

Padfield, T. (2004) *Copyright for Archivists and Users of Archives*, 2nd edn, Facet Publishing.

Pedley, Paul (2005) *Digital Copyright*, Facet Publishing (e-book).

Pedley, Paul (ed.) (2005) *Managing Digital Rights: a practitioner's guide*, Facet Publishing.

Schulz, C. and Baumgartner, J. (2001) *Don't Panic! Do E-commerce: a beginner's guide to European law affecting e-commerce*, European Commission Electronic Commerce Team.

Sherman, B. and Bently, L. (2004) *Intellectual Property Law*, 2nd edn, Oxford University Press.

Singleton, S. (2003) *eCommerce: a practical guide to the law*, rev. edn, Gower Publishing.

Smith, G. (2002) *Internet Law and Regulation*, 3rd edn, Sweet and Maxwell.

Society of Authors (1997) *Copyright in Artistic Works, including Photographs*.

Society of Authors (1999) *Your Copyrights After Your Death*.

Society of Authors (2000) *Libel*.

Society of Authors (2002) *Copyright and Moral Rights*.

Society of Authors (2002) *Permissions*.

Tambini, D. (2002) *Ruled by Recluses? Privacy, journalism and the media after the Human Rights Act*, Institute for Public Policy Research.

Ticher, P. (2001) *Data Protection for Library and Information Services*, Aslib.

Torrans, L. A. (2004) *Law and Libraries: the public library*, Libraries Unlimited.

Welsh, T., Greenwood, W. and Banks, D. (2005) *McNae's Essential Law for Journalists*, 18th edn, Butterworths.

Wright, S. (2001) *Intellectual Property Rights*, Open University.

Index

274 ESSENTIAL LAW FOR INFORMATION PROFESSIONALS

electronic copyright 46–50
electronic copyright management systems 53, 213
electronic signatures 53–4
e-mail
  acceptable use policies 87, 165, 173, 234
  and data protection 79, 82, 84, 86–7
  disclaimers 174; libel 84, 165, 172–3;
  unsolicited commercial e-mail (spam) 92–4, 231
employee monitoring see monitoring of employees
enforcement notices
  data protection 88, 137, 138
  freedom of information 123, 140
enforcement of intellectual property rights 23, 26, 29
environmental information 107, 110, 115, 120, 121, 123–4, 126, 141–142
equal opportunities 71, 241, 252
Equal Opportunities Commission 242
ethics 54–5, 61, 94, 95, 117, 180–1, 192, 197, 198–9, 252–3
European Atomic Energy Community 13
European Community 13
European Copyright Users Platform (ECUP) 212
European Court of Human Rights 249, 250
European Court of Justice 1, 30, 34
European Economic Area 69, 72
European Economic Community see European Union
European Information Researchers Network 54–55, 181, 194, 201
European Parliament 14, 128
European Union 1, 13–14, 27, 69, 250, 252
  access to EU documents 128, 130
  legislation 14–15
  membership of 1, 69
exemptions
  data protection 80, 128, 129, 184;
    freedom of information 121–2, 125–6, 128, 182–3; legal deposit 261
Experian 67, 78

fair dealing 31–4, 39, 50, 52, 198, 209,
false attribution 23

fees
  data protection 77, 127
  freedom of information 119, 120, 127–8
filesharing 227
force majeure 207
fraud 74, 81, 172, 219, 223, 230, 232
freedom of expression 116, 117, 119, 170, 178, 179, 213, 249, 251, 252, 253, 255, 256, 257, 258
freedom of information 64, Chapter 4, 135, 136, 137, 139–41, 142, 143, 144, 148, 182–4, 210
  absolute exemptions 121
  classes of information 113
  codes of practice 109–10, 111, 114, 124, 141, 183–4
  copyright implications 113–16
  destruction of records 111, 124, 140
  disabled users needs 125
  discrepancies with the data protection legislation 126–8
  enforcement 108, 122–3, 124, 135, 140, 142, 143
  exemptions 121–2, 125–6, 128, 182–3
  fees 119, 120, 127–8
  in Scotland 107, 109, 116, 118, 124, 143–4
  obligation of confidence 182–4
  prejudice test 122, 125
  public interest test 107, 116, 121–2, 123, 128
  publication schemes 108–9, 110–13, 114, 117, 118, 124–6, 127, 138, 140, 142, 143–4
  records management 111
  right of access 64, 108, 119, 121, 123, 124
  Scottish Information Commissioner 107, 109, 118, 124, 143–4
  time limit 120, 128
Fundamental Rights Agency 252

GCHQ see Intelligence services
Goggins, Paul MP 224
Gowers review of intellectual property 30
Greater London Authority 242
Green Papers 9